Liberated From Silence

Written by Tessa Jensen

To request permissions, contact the publisher at tessa.jensen@tessajensenauthor.com

Hardcover ISBN: 979-8-9858326-1-7
Paperback ISBN:979-8-9858326-0-0
Audiobook ISBN: 979-8-9858326-3-1
eBook ISBN: 979-8-9858326-2-4

First paperback edition March 2022

Edited by Lainey Nielson

tessa-jensen.com

For all those who wonder if Jesus Christ lives,
Yes
For any who wonder if He is a God of miracles,
Unimaginable, impossible, unforgettable miracles

Contents

Introduction

Hi. I'm Tessa, the author and main character of *Liberated from Silence*. I spent years writing my memoir and almost gave up at least 107 times. I told myself that I didn't have anything worth saying.

However, when I repeatedly heard people turning from their faith, I knew the time had come for me to speak. My story, my life, is one of Jesus Christ's modern miracles. What He has done for me, He can do for you because Jesus Christ is a merciful God who has the infinite power to redeem. He cannot stop loving you, and you are never beyond His reach; it's 100% impossible.

The scope of the Lord's miracle in my life nearly burst my heart with joy when I saw the final front cover of my book; it took a few minutes to reconcile that the woman I was looking at was me.

"Is that me?" I asked myself, "When did I start looking like I know who I am? What happened to the shame-filled, scared, self-destructive woman who pleaded with God to forgive her existence? The woman who believed Jesus Christ's unconditional love must be earned with a price so high she couldn't compete in the marketplace? That her battle with years of abuse and mental illness was her fault, and if she only had more discipline, she could finally silence Tessa? And if Tessa were permanently quiet, God would finally love her like a stepdaughter instead of like, well, like a dog. A celestial dog. That woman is gone, and I don't remember the day she left."

If all you could see of my life were this moment, you would rightly conclude that I have everything I want - my faith, covenants, family, salt-of-the-earth friends, an education, a place to call home, a cozy bed to sleep in, and a few obnoxiously cute pets. I'm productive and fit. I smile willingly; start conversations with people I don't know, talk for an hour, and usually make a new friend. My husband treats me like a queen, and my kids are healthy. So, what could I know of sorrow and misery?

Well, if you saw a snapshot from 2006, the answer to that question would be self-evident. I was, at best, unstable after a life of relentless trauma and abuse. Subconsciously, I repeatedly sabotaged myself, and consciously, I couldn't look further than two or three weeks ahead. Thus, tasks and goals that required a time investment seemed impossible. I felt forever stuck in a revolving door between bursts of ambitious effort and long periods of defeat. However, in God's goodness, He gave me an inquisitive mind and a desire to find meaning, so in a way, He tethered me to Him, protecting me from total self-destruction.

Finding answers in organized religion was a repugnant thought. Tragically, though not uncommon, when I was a child, adults in my life misused the teachings of our Lord Jesus Christ to silence, control, shame, and abuse me. Their manipulations had a steep cost, a price that almost took my life and broke my soul.

Despite the anguish, I yearned to find God if for no other reason than to assert my righteous indignation and demand an answer to the question that plagued me, "Why did you betray me when you said you loved me? The devil wanted my soul, and you handed me over to him like I was no more important than a smooshed loaf of bread. Some loving father you are."

Of course, it took years until I could articulate my question because I couldn't identify what I felt. I assumed I was yet another person wearing fear and grief's great disguise called anger. Rage hung around like a chronic injury, waiting to flare at the slightest provocation, protective and self-serving.

I also assumed that I was causing my turmoil because I returned to the church of my childhood, The Church of Jesus Christ of Latter-day Saints. The decision to return was agonizing. I dragged myself into the building every Sunday, with my mind kicking, screaming, and clawing at each doorway. In protest, I caught an emotional heel to the face and claw marks down my arm without exception.

Nevertheless, I kept going because I remembered the beautiful promises taught to me by my primary teachers and the genuine love I felt in some of my friends' homes. One family, in particular, made an unforgettable impact on my heart. They were kind and generous, yes, but most importantly, the Spirit of God dwelt in their hearts. When I was in their home, I felt at peace. I could tell I was amongst people who loved the Lord and each other. I clung to those memories, convinced that they must have understood something my parents did not. I wanted the type of family they had.

However, before I could find peace and accept gospel truths with an open heart, I had to face the rampant selfishness and untreated mental illness that wreaked havoc on almost every branch of my family tree. Did Jesus teach that women should be ashamed of being women? Was that the pinnacle of femininity, an expressionless shell, quiet and acquiescing, without firmly held opinions or the right to participate as an equal partner in their homes and communities? Does the Spirit honestly tell people to do things that are insane and cause untold devastation? Learning the difference between pure and diluted doctrine was, much of the time, suffocating. Sometimes the theology I hated was the same theology I desperately wanted to be true - like eternal families and a Savior who eagerly awaits to forgive everyone, including those who caused me harm.

My struggle with mental illness compounded the inner brawl between what I studied in the scriptures and what I felt when I walked into a church building. I had a haunting suspicion that someone was holding me underwater just for the fun of watching me writhe with horror. For days and months at a time, the sickness of bipolar disorder took control until, by grace, I happened upon a period of reprieve, usually after seeking psychiatric care. Predictably, I would improve, decide I didn't need medication, stop taking it, and pretend I was fine until mounting evidence exposed my charade. Those periods of reprieve felt like a long, hot shower after hours of working in cold weather. Parts of my brain that had been numb and frozen began to work with ease and agility once more. I got to feel the freedom of life outside constant and debilitating emotional swings. Sometimes I wondered what people did with their time if they didn't spend the bulk of their waking hours devoted to mood management to remain functional.

But all that chaos did not disqualify me from joy. I met my husband, gave birth to my four children, found friends, and saw glimpses of God's promises fulfilled - a light in my wilderness.

Finally, three years ago, as of this publication, I decided to believe in Jesus Christ and stop putting limitations on His power by trying to convince Him that He had wasted His blood on me. Instead, I chose to strive to fully align my will with His, which necessitated a significant change in habits of thought and action. I had to learn to prioritize my relationship with Him above all else, including sleep and the emotional crutches of binge eating.

I once thought that to wait upon the Lord meant waiting my turn to talk to Him, like a kid who stands in line to see Santa Claus. Until my turn came, I told myself, I had to live on whatever spiritual strength fell in my direction. Happily, I was wrong. Jesus had already chosen me before I was born, as evidenced by the scars in His hands, wrists, and feet. The one who decided the quality of our relationship was me – it's still me.

In April of 2021, I pondered the question, "What would you do if you had more faith?" I wrote in my journal that I would finish writing my book. And now, here it is—another miracle.

Before you begin, I must tell you that this book is heavy and, at times, dark, very dark. It's the ugly truth of the realities of abuse and mental illness. I can't pretend or present it otherwise. But, in the end, though the battle was exacting and excruciating, Christ triumphs over darkness and evil.

I've narrated most of the book in real-time because I want you to experience each moment with me as it happened instead of telling the story with a more mature, retrospective voice. Accordingly, there are situations and people in my account that I can now examine with more understanding and compassion - but in real-time, I did not have the emotional or intellectual capacity to do anything more than what I have written.

Please remember that I am speaking from my perspective and experience alone. As soothing as it may be for me to pretend to know every variable, motivation, and intention in the minds and lives of those involved in my account, I do not; I cannot. I can only write what I know.

May you find a glimmer of Christ's light through my words,

-    Tessa

The Joy

The Love of My Family

"What blessings have I withheld from you?" The Savior asks as I push the limits of my anaerobic capacity. Struggling to maintain foot speed while experiencing self-induced oxygen deprivation usually starts a conversation with Deity. Maybe strenuous exercise has such an effect because it shows me the limits of sheer willpower. So, what has the Lord withheld from me?

Each time my heel strikes the pavement, I flip through the records in my mind, searching for the answer. I open the file labeled abusive childhood home. I see an old picture of my husband with our four kids on our favorite hike. He has a toddler on his back pulling his hair and testing the strength of her lungs, another in his arms, protesting the use of his legs, a six-year-old t-rex running from fallen tree branch to mound of dirt, roaring, and a five-year-old elaborating on the necessity of water and Eric's egregious error of leaving it in the car. My husband is smiling, laughing, and promising to remember the water next time. Behind the picture, I find a novel-sized stack of papers stained with the color of blood. None of the words is legible. When I start to separate the pages, they rapidly fall apart like ancient papyrus.

Surely the mental illness folder is intact since that's stuck with me my entire life. I anticipate the weight as if I'm about to lift a suitcase full of 50-pound dumbbells. I steady my arm before yanking the record with all my strength. The file flies in the air, nearly weightless, as I stumble backward a few steps, watching as three papers flutter to the ground. One says 'gift,' another, 'strength.' The third page is a moving antique picture of my great-great-great-grandmother on my dad's side. Her pioneer hands are clasped together as grateful tears run down her cheeks. The first verse of *Amazing Grace* plays in the background. She looks me in the eye, reminding me of what she sacrificed to the God her posterity forgot.

At least one record is set in stone. I look for the engraved details of the source of the smoke that was once my mother and sister relationships. They're gone, too. A handcrafted snow globe with rotating memories of my aunt and uncle, my brothers, and my friends sits in its place, bright and new. Happy speckles of I-love-you-with-all-my-heart swirl around the shared smiles and tears. Long talks in the morning, miles of running, hours of workouts, paint nights, playdates, and adventurous hairstyles come together and create a melody of unbreakable bonds.

"You have given me everything,' I whisper, somewhat bewildered, 'and yet, you had to take away everything first. But they're not the same everything." Sweat stings my eyes as I run towards the sun at 2:30 pm on a warm September afternoon near Seattle, reflecting on how my life changed from sorrow to joy. I don't usually run in the afternoons, but my extreme fitness partner is on vacation, and I spent the morning ignoring chores and to-do lists.

Instead, my kids cuddled on the couch like a litter of kittens while I read aloud. We recently started *The Mysterious Benedict Society,* and so far, everyone's enjoying it. The characters are young enough to get through the series before they grow up, and Bruce, my oldest, now ten years old, loses interest. We've read halfway through the *Harry Potter* and *Anne of Green Gables* series, and each time Bruce laments the moment that the main characters "grow up and get boring." We'll revisit both series in a few years, maybe. Since we started homeschooling, reading has become one of our favorite ways to spend quality time together.

About a month after the COVID school closures, Eric and I took over the kids' education because their school had zero performance or progress expectations. As such, the assignments were a mere review of what they had learned months ago. I realize the schools and teachers were grappling with an emergency, but my kids needed to advance. You may think I sound a bit intense. Still, I witnessed what the lack of a quality education, coupled with social isolation, can do to a person – their confidence, earning potential, and coping abilities. Earning an education set one of my wings free, and I refused to watch the shackles of ignorance lock around my children's wrists as they had been locked around my father's.

As I run by two parked red motorcycles, I return to the image of the disintegrating papyrus papers and imagine them riding on the wind of my dad's apologies. He loved motorcycles; he also died on one. Engines and redemption. I hope he found both when he died. His death was as harrowing as his life, one big crash with broken pieces in every direction. How can the same man have caused me so much harm and yet helped form the anchor that kept me from flying off the handle into nothingness? Working hard and fulfilling my obligations.

Significantly, all five of his kids are well-educated and work in some form of health or public service. Four of us have a penchant for extreme fitness habits; something about enduring and conquering the seemingly impossible brings us a rush of satisfaction. I used to hope that heaven kept precise and accurate records of all my dad's sins because I hated him. Now, I wish only one sentence were written in Heaven's Book of Life under his name. "Oscar Knurre left big hearts pounding in the chests of his five children."

Speaking of big hearts, mine sighs in relief at the sight of the sign for 56th Street directly ahead, signaling the end of my eight-mile run. I have one minute left, maybe fifty-seven seconds if I push myself. Between here and there stands a broken speedometer. I might be thirty-four years old, but I pretend the sign flashes 100 miles per hour as I race past. Bruce shares my affinity for imagining outstanding athletic performances. Come to think of it, his dad does, too. Bruce often pretends to be a professional football player. He conducts an entire playoff schedule in his imaginings, playing the part of all teams and players. Bruce keeps track of the scores, too. Usually, when he comes inside, all red-faced and sweaty, he tells me where each team stands. Bruce usually names his teams after a dinosaur, shark, or reptile. Occasionally, he'll choose a name that reflects his favorite foods, as 85% of our conversations center around food.

When I walk up to our half-gravel, half-paved driveway, I can see Fiona's long, curly mane of light brown hair bouncing up and down, keeping time with the rhythm of her songs. Fiona entered the world nine years ago with feelings she describes as "bigger than her body" and a fierce competitive drive. She watches everything I do and listens to everything I say, mimicking my best and worst qualities. But, unlike me, Fiona loves without reservation, whether people or animals. Currently, she's jumping on the trampoline with our black cockapoo, Snowflake. Fiona chose Snowflake's name as a four-year-old with a smirk on her face; they've been each other's bosom friends ever since. Fiona already has plans to find a replica of her faithful dog and smuggle it into her dorm room when she goes to college.

"Mom's back! Mom's back!" Fiona squeals, notifying Oliver and Vivian of my return. They are seven and five, and still my biggest fans. Oliver has a way of melting into my side when he sits next to me, and Vivian likes to hold my face between her little hands as she tries to brush her eyelashes against mine. If it weren't for her Vivian-ness, I would call the experience borderline suffocating.

I can hear the three of them racing through our kitchen to the front door. I tense as the kids fight for the position of door-opener, expecting someone to catch a doorknob in the eye.

Thankfully, I don't meet the screaming of injury, just three pairs of bright blue eyes, as round as the moon, the same as their dad's. "How was your run? Did you go fast? Can we have ice cream? Can we watch a movie? Look at this! Do you want to play a game?" I can't tell who is talking as six hands try to touch me at once, half of them holding their latest art project or newly discovered scientific fact.

"My run was great, and I went kind of fast, but not really fast."

"Why? You could have run really fast if you tried." Bruce states as he leans on his haunches at the far side of the couch and turns the page of one of his countless dinosaur encyclopedias. I can always count on Bruce to state the facts. His chronically disheveled appearance makes me smile - wild auburn hair, a smattering of freckles across his cheeks, and off-center basketball shorts. He looks a lot like me, the same expressive eyebrows, hooded eyes, high cheekbones, and a straight nose, but he has his dad's long limbs.

"You're right. I could have …."

"You're yucky stinky, Mama!" Vivian yells. "Ewwwww!" More squeals erupt, noses are plugged, and my children begin dropping to the floor in fits of laughter.

"Yes, yes, I know. I stink. Did you guys finish your homework and do your chores while I was gone?" I ask as I sit down to take off my shoes and sweaty socks. I hate wearing shoes and socks.

"Well, I finished my homework, and I tried to help Vivian, but she kept scribbling on her page and singing about her stuffed purple panda loud. I couldn't hear myself talk." Fiona explains, her hand gestures telling her story. Vivian gives me a big, crooked grin as her curly, tangled blonde hair flies in seven different directions. She knows my weakness.

"Mom, I learned about whales,' Oliver interjects, 'killer whales are my favorite whales."

"Killer whales are not whales. They are dolphins," Bruce absent-mindedly corrects Oliver as he turns another page of his encyclopedia.

"Oh. My favorite dolphin is a killer whale," Oliver says, smiling at Bruce, happy to drink from his big brother's fountain of knowledge.

"Well, you guys finish your work, and we can think about getting ice cream. It's a hot day, and Dairy Queen isn't too far away. Vivian, that includes you."

"But Mom, I don't have feet," she says as she remains in her previously collapsed state on the faux hardwood floor. Dogs and furniture scratches have long since compromised its sleek appearance. We'll replace it in a decade.

"Come on, Vivian. Get up so we can go get ice cream!" Fiona and Oliver plead in unison.

She smiles, stands in an instant, and rushes down the hall, sounding like her feet are made of tiny racquet balls. Her hands trace the walls as she runs, a habit all of my kids have. I should have corrected the practice a long time ago, but didn't. Now, there are four levels of dirt, with Bruce's being the most concentrated. One time, he walked into the house covered with so much dirt that not even the insides of his ears remained unscathed.

I asked, "What did you do, Bruce, roll in the dirt?"

He looked at me, puzzled, and responded, "Yes," then walked away like he was exhausted by my pointless questions.

Vivian's consent to comply with my ice cream requirements gives others hope that my promise will be fulfilled. "Yay! Yay! Yay!" the kids cheer as they scamper off, fully intending to finish their homework and chores. I know they'll get distracted in a few minutes with a lost dollar store toy they inevitably find between the walls and furniture, or a picture in one of their nature books. As I lean down to pick up my shoes, I notice Oliver has written his and Bruce's names underneath the light switch. I laugh. I thought we had passed the drawing on the wall phase.

Once, I suggested to Eric that we let the kids draw on their walls to see how their art skills improved as they grew. He did not think my suggestion was wise, citing the Sistine Chapel as proof that the worldwide allowance for ground-to-ceiling artistry was fulfilled hundreds of years ago.

***

"Hi, Eric. How's work going?" I ask Eric the same question whenever I walk into our 10-foot-by-12-foot bedroom. It's my polite way of getting his attention to tell him whatever's on my mind.

"It's work," he replies. Eric's been working from home since the beginning of COVID. He wakes up at 4:40 am, takes a shower, and opens his laptop. Our orange tabby cat inevitably purrs as he walks across Eric's keyboard with his feline arrogance. We are blessed to live in a cozy 923-square-foot home with three bedrooms and no space for an office. But Eric has never complained. I don't even know if he's noticed. He hardly registers the overwhelming amount of noise our children generate. To borrow Charles Dickens' description from *A Christmas Carol*, "they were not forty children conducting themselves as one, but every child was conducting itself like forty."

"How was your workout this morning? Did you guys enjoy making yourselves miserable?"

My extreme fitness partner has returned, making my mornings complete. "Yes, we used our new 20 lb. vests, and our workout was gloriously difficult. We did ten rounds of fifteen burpees, fifteen kettlebell swings with the 35 lb. kettlebell, 45 seconds on the Rogue Echo Bike, and ten ab twists with a 25 lb. bumper plate. Oh, and at the top of each burpee, we rotated the 25 lb. bumper weight around our head. You should try it."

"I will not be doing that."

"Suit yourself. You're missing out. You could feel like you're going to throw up and hear your heartbeat pulsing in your frontal lobe. Anyway, look what I found," I hold up a picture from our wedding that had fallen from one of my journals. "The Portland Temple was in full eternal splendor that day. We were fortunate it didn't rain."

"We were lucky," he says.

"What was your favorite part of our wedding day?" I love asking him about his favorite moments because he does not volunteer the information.

"You."

"Okay, that's a given,' I can't suppress the grin spreading across my face, 'I mean, did you like the temple wedding ceremony, lunch at Fuddruckers, or our reception the best? Remember how I forgot to try my dress and bolero jacket on together before the wedding, and they were different shades of white? And that the bolero was too short and had to be awkwardly safety-pinned to my dress? Remember how my hair looked stringy at the ends, and I dyed it the wrong shade of mahogany red a few days before? And remember how I didn't care a bit? I would have married you wearing a potato sack and a piece of twine as my wedding ring."

"Yes," Eric looks up from his computer screen with his aquamarine eyes looking a little misty.

"I'm still not sure why you married me,' I confess as I curl up next to him, slipping my arm through his as he adjusts his hands so he can keep typing, 'I was a bit of a moody mess. Remember how I thought you were a distance runner because you are built like one, but it turned out that you don't run more than a few miles at a time? You tricked me when we ran up the Ridgeline trail in Eugene, and you beat me to the top even though I ran the entire way, and you didn't. Lucky for you, I couldn't see you walking because the multitude of ferns obscured my vision. Plus, you have long legs, and I have proportionately short femurs. Did you know I have short femurs? If my femurs were normal size and I didn't have a squatty neck, I would probably be 5'8" instead of 5'6". Well, almost 5"6. Remember how we walked the trail a few weeks later, and I told you about my family, and you got confused but just smiled and nodded like my childhood was normal?"

"I didn't know what to say, and I liked listening to you talk. I still do." He kisses the top of my head and adjusts his arm again.

"Mom! My body is starving, and the pee-ooches are annoying me. Come out now." Vivian sticks her head in our room with furrowed brows and a slight frown, the expression she wears when she can't understand why everyone else doesn't comply with their part in her program.

"Hi, Vivian." Eric gives Vivian a wave.

She waves back with a mischievous grin, "You're my big, fat daddy."

"Dad. I'm Dad, not daddy."

"I will call you Dad or Father,' she turns to leave, taking a deep breath as she prepares to announce to her siblings, 'Hey, guys! Dad said you can call him Dad or Father, and Mom said we can have chocolate chips for breakfast. Satisfied with her interpretation of the brief exchange, she slams the door.

"Did you ever think you'd have a little girl as wild as Vivian?"

"No."

"I suppose I should go out and stop them from eating chocolate chips for breakfast, but then I would have to alter my breakfast plans, so I don't look like a hypocrite. On the other hand, if they want pancakes, Bruce or Fiona has become rather adept at making their food. That's the secret to raising independent children – keep the kitchen open at all times with the shared understanding that if they want something, they have to get it or make it themselves. That's also why Oliver eats a diet of foods that belong to the beige family: crackers, noodles, bread, and cookies."

"He occasionally eats corn," Eric points out.

"Yeah, I may or may not have jokingly told him that he was going to develop pellagra if he didn't start eating more colorful foods."

"What's pellagra?"

"A disease that results from a severe niacin deficiency. The symptoms include diarrhea, dermatitis, dementia, and death. A doctor in the South identified the disease a long time ago."

"Did you tell Oliver about the symptoms?"

"No, I didn't think he would appreciate it. As expected, he told me the name sounded weird and then asked for a corndog. I should work on my diet to set a better example for him. I don't binge eat like I used to, but I could eat more fruit and vegetables. Oh well. Hey, do you know what's going to happen in a few weeks?"

"USC might win a football game?" Eric is possibly the most positive and devoted USC football fan to walk the earth. After every loss, he comes up with a scenario that, no matter how improbable, could allow them to go to a championship game.

"Unlikely. It's something even more exciting than USC football!"

"What's that?' Eric looks down at his USC t-shirt, one of many. Most of his t-shirts bear the USC logo, while the rest support Anaheim Duck hockey or Manchester United soccer.

"Church! General Conference, to be specific. We get a whole weekend of listening to our Church leaders. Aren't you excited? I took that Saturday off from work at Massage Envy to make sure I could listen. Instead of doing bodywork as a massage therapist, I will be doing spiritual work as a Tessa."

Eric smirks and shakes his head. Whenever I mention terms from the massage therapy world, recount a work-related story, or a break room conversation, he looks just as confused as when we first met, and he learned about the world of bodywork. Admittedly, the profession attracts a fascinating group of empaths, all energy and feelings, meridians, and trigger points. Eric's naturally cheerful and logical personality does not operate on the same frequency.

"Are you shaking your head at the necessity of spiritual work?" I ask.

"Nope, I am just shaking my head at you."

"Because I'm outrageous?" I smile, hoping he says yes.

"Yes. And the most beautiful woman in the world." I still look down and blush when he gives me compliments. I still have a hard time believing that he thinks I'm beautiful up close; before I met Eric, most men thought me only attractive from a distance.

"Speaking of outrageous, can you believe I just said that General Conference is something to be excited about? Remember when I used to hate the word? Do you remember, after Vivian was born, I said I was never going to go to church again because it was too painful?"

"Yes."

"And do you remember all my nuclear family drama and trauma? How it consumed me until I was hardly functional?"

"Yes, that happened many times, and it made me sad." his ever-present smile begins to fade.

"But you still loved me? I made your life hard with my mood instability, rage, and depression."

"Yes, I loved you. I still love you."

"Why? I was a mess?" Unfortunately, I do this all too often, unsuccessfully pressing Eric to admit the sadness I caused him.

"You were also wonderful," he says.

"Do you remember how you prayed aloud every morning, asking God to help me know how beautiful and wonderful I am? That meant a lot to me, even though I didn't tell you."

"I still pray for those blessings," Eric's smile returns, wider than before. I rest my head against his shoulder for a few more minutes before responding to the fight erupting over who is in charge of the chocolate chips.

The Sorrow

I Wish I Had Faith

I wish I had faith in something, anything, a reason for burning. I've been writing about death and dying since the second grade. I want my life to be more than exhaustion and heartache, but what is want against fate? I want to find God, but He doesn't exist or love me. I don't know which is worse. If I operate under the assumption that He lives, He purposefully sent me to hell and thereby did not love me. What father sends his beloved daughter into the lion's den? No shield. No armor. I was utterly exposed and dependent upon beasts with blood on their fangs and scars down their backs. God doesn't love me, nor does anyone else. I'm nothing but a burden, an annoyance, a girl that's too sensitive and too weak.

Why do people say, 'too weak'? Too little weakness? Too much weakness? Apparently, a suitable amount of weakness exists. I wonder who determined the appropriate daily value. Heaven's nutritionist, I suppose.

Even when I was cute, chubby, and innocent, my parents didn't love me. My mother abandoned me when I was four. My father remarried, and neither he nor his wife showed affection unless you count emotional manipulation and other forms of abuse as acts of charity. And God certainly didn't make time in His busy schedule to check on me, send angels, or save me.

When I was a kid, I thought graduating from high school was like walking through a mystical doorway—no more chaos. No more tiptoeing through rooms and floors made of eggshells, wondering who would administer punishment. Every morning, I asked my parents the same silent questions,

"What shall it be today? Passive-aggressive shaming and silent treatments, sexualized accusations, or did the Spirit reveal something new? How about one of you shoot me like you shot the dogs, while the other one does nothing to stop it, and we can all get this over with. Then, I'll be gone, and you can go back to congratulating yourselves on your parenting skills or playing the victim. Whichever paints you in the best light. You choose. I won't be around to protest."

Wisdom suggests that moving away from the place that holds my pain would be a great start towards healing, but I return every time I try. I have lived in or around Eugene, Oregon, most of my life. A city too small for a carpool lane but too big for one zip code. The running community affectionately calls this place Track Town USA thanks to the legacies of Steve Prefontaine and the University of Oregon track team. Presently, I am a nineteen-year-old college student having an existential crisis instead of the time of my life. According to some arbitrary equation of who is allowed to experience tragedy and the corresponding turmoil, I have no reason to complain. I have a job, a car, health insurance, an apartment, physical health, and enough money to meet my needs. Still, as if in defiant opposition, as soon as I start towards new beginnings, an ugly concrete wall shoots up with reminders of who and what I am, written in graffiti, in paint extracted from my veins.

I find a few scraps of solace in the studies of philosophy and psychology, and take as many classes as I can at the University of Oregon. The search for explanations and possibilities gives me a glimmer of hope that life is more than people inflicting misery upon each other. I'm not sure if the other students seek to understand the human condition. Attempting to discern between outer presentations and sincere states of introspection wearies me. Why did I give myself the job in the first place? Too many people live in disguise as if they are no more interesting than the box they're trying to squeeze inside. Imagine a room full of cardboard boxes, each the same size and shade of brown—what a snoozefest.

Earning an A in philosophy is easy, regardless of interest. You only need to know how to restate what has already been written in a way that confuses people. Behavioral observation makes even the slow classes interesting. Thankfully, quiet is not an appropriate adjective for my summer class full of students testing prevalent mannerisms and speech patterns, deciding which ones will gain adoration and celebration. Their search for approval leaves little room for theoretical discussions but plenty of space for social criticism. I've tried striking up a conversation only to get a mouthful of sand when I was hoping for an ice-cold lemonade after a ten-mile run on a hot day. Maybe my response to their conversations is just as disappointing.

Philosophy 204 is in an old building at the University of Oregon, which means no air conditioning. We enjoy the sun glaring through the windows, creating a sauna because the old, browned blinds do little to keep out the rays. Add the luxury of the heat-ripened smell of must and mold, native to the Pacific Northwest, wafting through the air, and we essentially have class in a five-star hotel. No matter, the smell won't linger in my nostrils. Body odor will soon take over.

We are small in number, and half of us pretend we don't see each other, which is silly, as we're four weeks into the semester—a small group of friends formed towards the back a couple of weeks ago. Even among self-proclaimed equality soldiers, social hierarchies don't take long to assert themselves. They may strut differently than their parading counterparts, but the preening and forced laughter are the same. I wonder what it's like to find an accepting social group amongst peers of a similar age. But then I'd have to pretend I'm interested in their incessant drivel about fleeting trends and drunken parties.

My attempts to locate any visually compelling distractions are futile. Brown blinds, brown desks, brown walls - this place could use a makeover. Do they have makeover competitions for outdated and smelly college buildings? The athletic department has money to spare. Between the Escalades, the uniforms, the fancy facilities, and the athletes' tutors, they could surely donate money to a university improvement fund. No matter. Maybe the administration wants to preserve authenticity: Mildewed and musky authenticity.

Our instructor, Maria, glides into the room with the glory of a sunny day on her face. Her nose instinctively crinkles at the foul odor in the room, and just as intuitively, she smooths it out. She looks too young to have been teaching long. I assume she is a Ph.D. student trying her hand at igniting purpose into the lives of budding young adults. But, unlike other Ph.D. students I have had the misfortune of 'learning' from, she is genuine about her quest for purpose.

Maria is a small and nimble woman who likely spent her childhood in a ballet studio. Her shoulders never roll forward; her hips never jut out to the side after standing in one place for too long. She has complete control of her body. But, on the other hand, her dark hair has a mind of its own. Curls fly every which way around her hairline, staging a desperate attempt to free their fellow tresses from the mound of curls tied in a high, messy bun on top of her head. A smattering of freckles across her cheeks magnifies the unique caramel color of her eyes.

"Welcome back to class, everyone. Today, we are resuming our conversation about the chief good. Does anyone remember what Aristotle postulated?"

"Uh, that there is a chief good?" A dark-haired and gangly guy answers, delighted with his cleverness.

"Yes. What else? What is the chief good?"

"Happiness. Trying to find happiness," someone from the back of the room blurts out.

"That's a great place to start. What is happiness, and how do people go about finding it?" Maria seems almost desperate for someone to provide an indisputable answer. Whether we're the student or the teacher, we're all looking for the same thing, which stands to reason that the answer is relative. Happiness is an old treasure map - so many treasure seekers and no treasure.

"Some people look for happiness in religion." The gangly guy says the last word with a sneer and glares at the woman wearing a hijab, sitting on his right, as usual. The glare must be his favorite facial expression; he wears it every time he answers a question. I wonder what happened to him to make him so hateful towards a woman he doesn't know. Today, however, her head snaps up, and her back straightens at the words 'happiness in religion.' She looks like she's bracing herself against a blow that's knocked her down before.

"Yes, millions of people have looked for happiness in religion since the beginning of recorded history. Why?" asks Maria.

"No idea. My guess is they cling to the delusion of an Almighty Creator because they are not smart enough to think for themselves." The gangly guy says.

A man in his early thirties with tired eyes and a Ducks baseball cap responds, "Your answer makes some pretty significant assumptions about the intellect of religious individuals. For example, Martin Luther translated the Bible from Latin to German to make the sacred book available to all Christians, not just the ones in power. For his act of kindness, which benefited humanity as many illiterate people learned to read using the Bible, he was excommunicated by the Pope, outlawed by the Roman emperor, and constantly criticized."

"Wasn't Martin Luther a religious leader? He wanted people to follow him and remember his name; that's why he translated the Bible. His idea worked because we are talking about him hundreds of years later. The excommunication and outlawing came because he was a nut job, not because he thought for himself. Besides, no one's going to admit they need some priest thinking for them. Or whatever they call their all-knowing leaders. Plus, most of them have been brainwashed for so long they think they are thinking for themselves as enlightened beings, but they're only puppets, to include Martin Luther." The eyes of both men meet, and only one clenches their jaw.

"How do you know you're thinking for yourself? How do any of us know that we are thinking for ourselves? What's the litmus test?" Maria asks.

"For one, girls who think for themselves don't get married right after high school and have a million children. They only do it because someone tells them to, and they don't know any better. Their religion doesn't want her to know any better. Look at the statistics. The more educated a woman is, the fewer children she has. Why would people suffer and die for some unseen Being unless they are brainwashed into thinking there's a prize at the end, like a room full of beautiful virgins or treasures? All these devoutly religious people are quite selfish if you think about it. They want wealth and status in the afterlife for refusing wealth and status in this life."

"Are you saying religious people, particularly religious women, are uneducated and poor as a general rule?" Maria asks. I like Maria's questions. She doesn't look like a challenger, but she is.

"I think you are the one making assumptions."

" I am trying to verify my understanding of your perspective," Maria says.

"Of course, there are wealthy and successful people who happen to be religious. I am saying devoutly religious people are scared of money because they think it's the root of all evil. Therefore, they think they are better than other people by remaining poor and guarding themselves against the evils of the almighty dollar. They also, 99.9% of the time, put a man in charge, which shows how much they value the leadership of women." He answers with feigned confidence as if he is shuffling through the files in his head for inaccuracies.

"Can you give me an example?"

He focuses his attention again on the young woman sitting next to him. "Let's ask the woman sitting next to me. I mean, you're probably married. Your mom and dad, well, your dad, because your people aren't too big on gender equality, told you who to marry, right? They didn't care about your opinion."

A memory from childhood threatens to wreak havoc on my mind like a boulder rolling over a trapped car.

"Yes, I am married," the woman has a resolute voice, which seems to surprise everyone, "I decided to marry my husband at eighteen." She keeps a pleasant look on her face. No anger, no shame.

"Because your father told you to, right? You had to choose between getting married or disgracing your family? Right?"

"No. I got married because I love my husband. I could not imagine my life without him." She refused to put her spirituality on the operating table to be dissected and dismembered. I like her.

The gangly guy's face begins to distort into something resembling Gollum - ferociously angry, deceptive, and determined to have the last word. I feel guilty for not standing up to his verbal assaults. But I don't know what to say. Religion destroyed my family.

A young twenty-something, voluptuous and fashionable without a hair out of place, narrows her eyes on the classroom arbiter of contention. "Excuse me. Um, I don't know your name. You're rude. How does her living her religion have any effect on you? Why do you care if she's married? Or are you bothered by women in general? Do you secretly wish you had a beautiful young woman as devoted to you as they are to their God? It seems like your problem hasn't a thing to do with religion and everything to do with what you think you deserve."

"What?! Are you a psychiatrist? I don't even know what you're saying right now." His voice begins to shake.

"Methinks thou doth protest too much." She raises her left eyebrow and tilts her chin to the left, daring him to respond.

Maria steps into the silent space the trendy woman created, "What about Aristotle's doctrine of the mean - the place between two extremes? Virtue and practical wisdom?"

The awkward and heavy silence presses in on my temples, so I raise my hand, "To me, the doctrine of the mean is another way of describing moderation, the space between two extremes. Too much or too little of anything lends to undesirable consequences - food, sleep, exercise, entertainment - to give more simple examples." I pause, realizing, as usual, my thought is incomplete, "Wait, now that I hear myself talking, those things are not superficial because they affect our moods, longevity, feelings, and coping skills, which in turn affect our ability to make wise decisions while upholding virtue."

No one responds. Did I sound like an uneducated dunce? I look at Maria, silently begging her to say something, to move the spotlight from me to her. She gives me an appreciative smile.

"Tessa makes a great point."

I hardly notice my surroundings as I make the mile walk back to my studio apartment. How could I have been a bystander as that gangly guy tried to shame the woman with devout faith? She has the right to believe what she wants without the snarls of someone looking for a fight. But she didn't look bothered. Her eyes didn't dart around the room for approval or in a silent plea for help.

I wish I were more like her. If I had her spiritual conviction, my life would be easier, or at least worthwhile. No more searching for purpose and wondering why I must wake up every morning—deciding which theory or ideal to follow from one week to the next. None of them fit every contour of my soul; there is always an uncomfortable seam or restricting neckline. Like ill-fitting dresses, they look better on the hanger. I want what that woman has - not her religion or lifestyle, but the will-not-be-moved look in her eye and the impenetrable armor she wears.

I wish I were devoted to God, to an omniscient and omnipotent being. But I must believe He loves me first. I won't find it in a church building because no denomination can say they have absolute truth, not even The Church of Jesus Christ of Latter-day Saints, no matter what they claim. I grew up listening to their sermons on the nothingness of man, our perpetual unworthiness before God, "less than the dust of the earth.[1]" If I, and we, are no more important to Him than dust, why does God bother with any of us in the first place? Creating a planet with billions of nobodies and unfortunates seems like a waste of time. People sitting in a pew to be told as much seems masochistic.

Nonetheless, millions of people worldwide sign up for misery and total manipulation. I'll acknowledge the Church's genius.

---

[1] Helaman 12:7 (The Book of Mormon)

Educated people of all types gladly throw away their wisdom as soon as someone says, "I felt prompted by the Spirit." No one can question a person's spiritual manifestation because there is no quantitative evidence to prove their claims. There are, however, scriptural accounts of people doing awful things in the name of the Lord, such as Abraham taking his grown son, Isaac, to the altar to kill him as a sacrifice to God. If God can command His prophet to kill his son, He can command anything contrary to His Ten Commandments. Plus, there are words from the scriptures to justify insanity, such as "And no man knows it except him to whom God has revealed it.[2]"

Even more than the claims that God talks to His children, I hate the focus on inadequacy, the unending rules, and regulations to keep my 'rebellious' soul in line. I mourn to think my Creator looks down on me, testing my strength and commitment by stripping away everything I hold dear. What will I have left if I give up all I am to know God - my dreams, hopes, and ambitions? A miserable life filled with poverty and tragedy, so He can teach me what an ungrateful wretch I am. If misery is the sign of a loving God, then I would rather He hates me. I'll take being ignored over being held in a fire, 'the refiner's fire,' they call it, while it slowly melts my flesh. How can a God who supposedly cares more about His children than all the sparrows in the sky allow me to be born into hell, forcing me to walk on shards of glass and jagged stone?

I don't want to listen to the doctrine that teaches parents to demand perfection from their children, to bring down merciless justice for the slightest infraction. An ideology in which a parent's dictatorship is backed up by the commandment to "Honor thy father and thy mother.[3]" The direct message to the children is, "If you feel like garbage because your parents treat you like garbage, you are choosing to feel that way. You are prideful and need to repent. Try

---

[2] Doctrine and Covenants 76:90

[3]Exodus 20:12 (The King James Version)

harder. Love them more by serving them. Understand they know more than you do. Oh, and by the way, the gospel is a gospel of happiness. Be happy. Having feelings other than happiness is a temptation of the devil. You will be relegated to eternal damnation if you are unhappy."

I don't need to put on a knee-length dress with a high neck and sleeves only to sit demurely listening to lectures on how worthless and inadequate. I understand the material down to my cells. My parents should get an award for excellence in teaching.

My dad, Oscar Knurre, attended every church service, social event, and service project at The Church of Jesus Christ of Latter-day Saints. Every Sunday, my dad, his second wife, Dolly, my two brothers, two sisters, and I loaded into the blue Astro Van with enough time to ensure an early arrival. Dad believed in strict obedience to God, which meant arriving early and ensuring his children behaved like well-trained service dogs. If social rules allowed, he would have worn a whistle at all times to keep us in line. After all, if children behave like loyal canines, their parents must be God-fearing, eternally righteous people, right? And aren't the people who praise God in church exempt from any further manifestation of their religious devotion?

Some Attention was Better than No Attention

Deep slumber is a delicious and allusive summer dream perpetually ruined by the stickiness of humid heat. Sleep deprivation keeps unwanted company until the average nighttime temperature drops below 50 degrees. Cooling options include a fan blowing around stagnant air, cold showers, and putting a bag of ice on my neck. Opening a window may seem like a viable solution. It's not. Whether this studio apartment complex has the structural integrity to withstand a four-year-old's attempt to blow out a birthday candle remains unclear. Buildings in questionable parts of town should be made with a sturdier medium, like granite. My decrepit living conditions enhance my sense of vulnerability. The premises invite the presence of perverts and predators. It seems my locked door would do very little to inhibit their intrusion. I sleep with one hand on a knife if they do get in. Plus, I'm crazy.

Why do I sleep with one hand on a knife? I am the omniscient nineteen-year-old idiot who signed a one-year lease for an expensive apartment, priced for its location rather than quality and surrounded by stoned and inebriated co-eds. Thieves of opportunity robbed me before I officially moved in because, as I said, I'm a nitwit. I moved half of my belongings over while still sleeping at my other apartment, without putting up curtains or closing the bathroom window. The front wall is mostly a window, so you can see the problem I created for myself. I am confident I gave the criminals a good chuckle of amusement over the follies of the inexperienced.

Unfortunately, exhaustion is the precursor to the emotional breakdown I call Wrath. I am trapped in a revolving door between this world and Dante's fifth circle of hell for the next six weeks unless fall convinces the universe to let it start early. Do other people find living so taxing?

Getting ready for the day provides a brief artistic distraction. First, I must always tie my brown-dyed-auburn hair up. I hate the feeling of hair on my neck - like a crawling lice infestation. Next, I must add color around my eyes to differentiate my facial characteristics. My face looks like a big peachy blob without it, including peach fuzz. I tried laser hair removal last year. I need a refund.

Uninspiring but practical neutral tones do not ring with creativity, but even the most vibrant palettes must have contrast. So, I use brown eyeshadow to color my eyebrows, shimmery beige eyeshadow, brown eyeliner drawn along the outer edges of my eyes to make them look farther apart, and brownish-black mascara. Black mascara looks too harsh against my pale and freckled skin. Finally come the earrings, the best part. Hoops, teardrop, and chandelier fashion jewelry afford me the illusion of a gypsy living the romantic life of never staying in one place long enough to become attached. Mysterious people, who refuse to be kept, are imagined as better than they are.

Looking put together while my insides resemble a competitive racquetball game has short-lived benefits. People don't treat me like I'm crazy, like they would if I had twigs and broken leaves stuck in my hair. Instead, most people are friendly until I start talking in rapid-fire and disjointed notions, vainly hoping they understand what I do not have the vocabulary to explain. I cannot speak fast enough to keep up with my thoughts, and they cannot respond fast enough to slow me down. I abruptly end the conversation once I see an understanding of my instability settle in their eyes. To be looked on with pity sickens me.

During the last few days, every conversation has been as slow, painful, and impossible as pulling melted Laffy Taffy out of my hair. If only a brain pathway were as easy to cut as hair.

***

10:35 AM and I'm in my philosophy class again. The mental reverberations are escalating. Words are whizzing around the musky classroom. They prick my nerves and make me squirm. Every offense to the English language is like the sound and smell of a dentist filing teeth. For the sake of preserving some semblance of intelligence, please stop using the phrase 'My bad.'-it's utter nonsense.
I cross, uncross, and swing my legs, manipulate my fingers, repeatedly braid and twist my hair, and shift my weight from side to side. Compulsively checking my watch does nothing to speed up the time. Must get out. Must move. We could have ended class early if everyone could shut up and stop asking the same asinine questions addressed ad nauseam throughout the semester. Idiocy abounds. My molars will fracture if I clench my jaw much longer.

"So, the paper for next week, what are we writing about again?" The red-headed girl who once asked to borrow my ID asks with feigned innocence.

I swear she noticed my squirming and decided to extend the discomfort as long as possible as retribution for her failure to acquire an ID that would get her into a bar. We're the same age, though I look older. My driver's license could do nothing for her, but I didn't let her in on that piece of information. I just told her no.

"As we have discussed . . ." Maria starts in on the seven millionth recitation of her expectations.

I throw my head back and then forward, slamming it down on my forearm as dramatically as possible, shaking it back and forth, a nonverbal "SHUT UP!" We are all adults, not second graders. Everyone has a grading rubric. Read it. For any student unable to read and assimilate the information, remedial classes at the community college are available. Plus, the classes are cheaper, so they can save money for their predictably long educational career. Most importantly, such students will simultaneously give this university - especially me - the benefit of not being here.

I hate this class, the heat, the smell. I hate feeling like I have a monster inside of me trying to stretch my soul's boundaries until I rip apart into undistinguishable heaps of flesh, broken hopes, and forsaken dreams. You need no further explanation if you have ever been perpetually exhausted while full of nervous energy. With concerns of classroom etiquette having stayed in my medicine cabinet, along with general civility, I shove my notebook into my backpack six minutes before 11:00. With every bounce of my feet, I make sure my heels audibly hit the ground while sighing deeply at fifteen-second intervals. My passive-aggressive fit does nothing. How disappointing. When the clock strikes the hour mark, I run-walk out the door despite the continued blatherings of the confused.

Stepping into the fresh air reminds me of breaking through the water's surface after trying to find someone's wedding ring at the bottom of a swimming pool. Being outside calms down the monster inside me enough to take a nap. I wish it would hibernate forever, find a new host, or implode with a breakdown so spectacular it leaves nothing to be salvaged. I want people to see it without seeing me, but we look the same, and no one can tell the difference.

The brief reprieve wakes me up to the beauty of the campus. Shades of green sprawl in every direction - soft grass, ferns, maple trees, and countless other foliage I cannot name but have seen all of my life. I head towards the Knight library to smell the books and drink the words of brilliant minds. Sometimes I read subjects I don't understand because the advanced vocabulary is like the pure majestic music of a cello to my mind.

Before I enter, I pause to absorb the regal beauty of the knowledge repository. Built in 1937, it maintains the original Art Deco and Romanesque design. I think of the skilled hands recruited to create such a noble edifice. Engraved in sand-colored stone are Greek words for university studies: Philosophia, Historia, Religio, Ars, Natura, etc. I wonder what scholars of the past would think of our current education system. Even more, I wonder what the billions of illiterate people throughout human history would think of library books unread, studies exchanged for parties, and advancement unappreciated or disrespected.

"Hey." A male voice startles me. I could headbutt him into unconsciousness for interrupting my silence.

I turn to see a guy from my class - quiet, pudgy, with a scraggly, dingy brown beard, and square glasses. His teeth need a thorough dental cleaning.

"Hello." Why don't good-looking men approach me?

"Um . . . uh. . . we are in the same class together. I'm Corey." He gestures towards the third-floor window of the building behind us. Sweat had soaked his underarms hours ago.

"Yes, I know."

"Well, I see you writing and drawing during class. Whatchya writing about?"

"I write about whatever I want." I'm nearly annoyed enough to explain to him why 'whatchya' is not a word.

"I think you're smart... um, I mean, you have good thoughts, I mean, ideas."

"What ideas are you referring to?"

"The ones about philosophy."

I want to roll my eyes as loud as ten thousand dice thrown on a card table, but he is trying hard to talk to me. Few people, men or women, try to speak to me unless they have to. So instead, I thank him, "I appreciate the thought."

"Are you busy? I'm on my way to lunch. Wanna come with me?"

No, I do not want to go with anyone who uses 'wanna' in place of 'want to.' But I haven't talked with a person around my age outside of class or work in months. Undoubtedly, his interests lie outside of intellectual discourse, given his unapologetic and primal assessment of my body. Still, a conversation is better than no conversation.

Against all wisdom, I relent. "Sure. Where?"

"McMenamins. You been before?"

"No, I have not, but I know the place."

"You'll like it. Trust me." He touches my shoulder with his fingertips, pointing me in the direction of McMenamins.

Why do people assert their trustworthiness so quickly? What if I hate American fare? My standard practice of not trusting males, especially males with soft baby hands, makes his declaration suspicious. Give me hands that look like they are used to hard work, and I might consider a trust.

As we walk towards the restaurant, he makes a good-faith attempt at sounding introspective.

"We shan't forget the need to ameliorate the condition of our lives through a divine search for the greater good existing in the island universe." He looks confused by the words coming out of his mouth. So disappointing.

"I don't know if divine searching makes our lives better." Talking to anyone willing to pay attention to me is what my life has become. Pathetic.

"Plato said . . . "

His vain attempt at sounding genuinely philosophical becomes background noise. I do not care about hollow recitations. I need authenticity. An exciting conversation would include what drives him, what causes him to question, and what questions he has. I cognitively understand the uncomfortable demand for deep conversations before a complete superficial vetting. Yet, I cannot cease my impatience.

Ten more minutes trickle by. Corey is carrying on about subjects he has not studied. I can't fault him for trying, but it grates on my nerves, nonetheless. How often have I wished I were more than what I am to impress someone? Am I this annoying? Perhaps if I wait long enough, he will stop posturing and start speaking his truth. While I have no interest in Dungeons and Dragons, I would rather listen to his thoughts regarding the topic if he likes the game. Here is a disappointing possibility; this is all he is, a human recording without original ideas.

We pass a cluster of pink and white rhododendrons. One flower has shades of pink, some yellow and white, too, dimensions created by contrast. Most people admit the grandeur of nature with its mountains, canyons, deserts, and rainforests. All extreme. All necessary. Yet humans seem uncomfortable with being different. We want to be like one another to impress or compete. How much misery do we cause ourselves by participating in such a practice? I speak against conformity, but am as guilty as anyone. Why else do I stand in front of the mirror pretending to cut the fat off my body with scissors? Do I want to be thinner, or do I think I should be thinner because pop culture tells me happiness lies on the lighter side, 130 lbs., when I'm on the heavier side at 155 lbs.? I was ten years old the last time I saw a number in the 130's between my feet.

McMenamins comes into view, a pub with an original 1960s hippy atmosphere. The artwork reminds me of new interpretations of older art, like American Gothic or an 1800s Adam and Eve painting. I appreciate the skill required to create such renditions, but I do not like them. The colors and lines overwhelm my vision and leave me feeling anxious.

"Where do you wanna sit?"

"Pardon?" Corey's question pulls me out of my thoughts again.

"Um, where do you wanna sit?

"I don't care what part of the pub we sit in so long as we are sitting in a booth." I try to hide my irritation at getting extracted from my thoughts.

We find a booth next to a window. Once again, the sun is making a nuisance of itself, this time making my left arm hot. Thankfully, my face is shaded. I hate squinting my eyes.

"I like your freckles." Corey nods towards my shoulders. I don't remember anyone complimenting my freckles before or paying attention to my shoulders.

"Oh, thanks. I got a lot of sunburns when I was little." I can feel myself blushing.

"I have a girlfriend,' he blurts out, 'I can tell you think I like you." What an assertion. I don't know how to respond. "Yeah, she's gone for the summer. Anyway, I don't want you to take my compliments the wrong way."

I nod. Maybe I was wrong about this sweaty man who appears to have an allergy to physical movement. If he has a girlfriend and tells me about her, he's probably just like any other man who can't keep his eyes from wandering. Still, I sense an unsatisfied hunger behind his eyes. Shrugging off my better judgment, I start talking. For an hour, I bounce from one thought to the next, hoping he keeps up. I must get all my disjointed ramblings out if this is the last social experience I will have for another four months.

Surprisingly, Corey doesn't seem uncomfortable - no squirming or continuously looking at his watch.

When I finally pause to eat my tater tots, one of my favorite foods, he says as quickly as possible, "What are you doing for the final?"

Irritation surges across my brain. Corey has no questions or comments about anything I said. A one-sided conversation, indeed. The fault is mine. I should have told him to interrupt me if he wanted to say something.

"I am writing a paper. Is there another option?" I am confused when people ask questions with implied answers, negating the necessity for asking in the first place.

"No. I mean, what are you writing about?" He answers with an amused chuckle.

His question reminds me of the vexing conversation I forcibly endured during class an hour ago. I pretend my fingernails are fascinating, so he can't see my face telling him to stop asking dumb questions. Having a glass face, as my aunt so calls it, is rarely advantageous. Most people know my opinion before I say a word. "I'm writing about the search for a greater good - the same topic you mentioned on our walk here. What about you?"

"Dunno."

'Dunno' is not a word.

He spins his soda glass around, periodically wiping down the condensation. "Hey, I was thinking," he pauses for a few awkward moments.

How marvellous. Corey can think. I refuse to give him the courtesy of helping him find his thoughts.

"I was thinking I can, um, I can read your paper. You know, good to have another person look at your stuff." He looks up while keeping his chin down, a selfish and disturbing prayer filling his eyes. I am probably paranoid.

And besides, I don't like people reading what I write, primarily if they refer to my work as 'stuff.' Writing is my sacred space, and I don't want it criticized. I get As or Bs on my papers, and that's all the feedback I need.

"We live in the same apartment complex. You wouldn't have to go out of your way or anything."

The hunger in his eyes begins to make sense. He's not just a man looking at any woman. He's been looking at *me*. My back stiffens, and I want to run. *Calm down, Tessa. You're paranoid for no reason. After all, he has a girlfriend, a point he was eager to make. Plus, the complex is one building with eight studio apartments. He wouldn't need to put effort into noticing someone. At most, he would need to be outside or look out of his window to see who lives nearby.*

I have never noticed any of my neighbours, and I live in the apartment on the ground floor nearest the road. Huh. I guess I am not as observant as I think. I look at Corey while he continues to spin his soda glass in nervous circles. I try to find something attractive about him, but I cannot. We could be friends, truly just friends. I will never develop romantic feelings for him, plus he has a girlfriend. So, there will be no underlying sexual tension or unrequited adoration for either of us. Perhaps allowing him to read my paper is not such a bad idea.

"Yes. I will let you read my paper." An unexpected and broad smile spreads across my face. Finally, someone wants to spend time with me after I talk at them for an hour.

"Great!" He smiles, too. Happiness mixed with relief. "Tomorrow at noon?"

"I work until 5:00 tomorrow. Can we do 6:00? I know it's Friday night, and you're probably busy. We can do it another time next week."

"Sure, sure. No plans. 6:00 it is. I live in number 4."

A surge of excitement propels me through my Thursday afternoon shift at Oregon Medical Group—the monotonous work of filing medical records and delivering faxed documents ticks by quickly. I get to talk to someone on a Friday night instead of reading a book in my apartment, driving an hour to the coast and back, or finding a movie to watch by myself at the Gateway Mall $1.50 Regal Cinema.

Upon awakening Friday morning, the excitement had been replaced with a sick uneasiness, the same feeling that made my back stiffen yesterday. I do not want to go inside his apartment, but I also do not want to spend another Friday with only myself for company. I have binged on loneliness long enough. He gave me no reason to be uncomfortable other than the hungry look in his eyes. Besides, what twenty-something-year-old man doesn't look like he wants to devour a woman? Pushing my concern aside, I put on grey slacks and a turquoise blouse and wheeled my bike out the door to begin the ten-minute bike ride. Driving a car on sunny mornings offends my senses.

Working as an office assistant is both simple and emotionally exhausting. Organizing files and data entry tasks are so easy that a tambourine monkey could handle the job. I suppose any repetitive task, done long enough, starts to feel that way. People, however, are unpredictable. Unfortunately, patients lean towards unpleasantness due to sickness, fear, or repeated blood tests. Doctors are demanding and impatient because they double-book themselves every fifteen minutes. The nurses and medical assistants are either friendly or cranky, depending on the degree of unreasonable expectations heaped upon them, resulting from the heavy patient load.

Because I absorb others' emotions, especially the feelings of those I am assigned to report to or assist, I leave the office crying no less than twice a week. The mix of frustration, anger, urgency, and sadness emanating from each individual creates an emotional cesspool deep enough to drown in. Yet, despite all that, today is different. Today, every condescending comment and an eye roll, every irritated and weary patient, doesn't affect me. Anticipation for the future makes the dreaded less dreadful.

I have forty-five minutes to analyze and reanalyze my clothing choices when I get home. Due to two consecutive months of eating recommended portions, my jean shorts fit nicely. They are not so short to be considered part of the Daisy Duke variety, but shorter than mom shorts. My upper body looks best in halter tops, given my broad shoulders, but I do not want too much of my back showing, at least not in front of him. I don't want him thinking I am trying to seduce him. I need something plain. The ribbed tank top from Old Navy is the winner. I should have bought the green one instead. Green is much more flattering. Why do I repeatedly try to wear maroon when I know it does me no favors? Further proof of my insanity, I suppose. Oh well.

Stepping back, I assess my reflection one last time. Enough body fat has melted off my collarbones to make them visible again. Collar bones and jawlines are the two markers I use for assessing body fat levels.

Disregarding the sense of dread mounting in my stomach, I pray to whatever higher power may be watching over me. God? I walk the few steps towards Corey's door, taking a sideways glance towards my car, noting the half-empty parking lot, my finished paper shaking in my hands. As soon as I knock on the door, I regret my decision. Before I can run back into my apartment and lock the door, he opens his. I pretend that keeping my hands behind my back is a natural way of standing. I cannot let him see my hands shake and mistake it for nervous attraction.

"Hi! You're here! Come on in."

"Hello, how was your day?" I force a smile—my prior imaginings of finally finding a friend begin to wane.

"It was alright, better now that you're here."

Because I do not know what to say when people give compliments, I smile once more and step inside. A putrid odor attacks my nostrils. I try not to wrinkle my nose. Greasy film covers the walls, and there are black specklings of mold beginning to form along the baseboard—dirty clothes, most certainly retrieved from the bottom of a damp hamper, reek of cheap cologne. The windows and blinds are closed. The air is stale. Odd for a summer evening.

I must have failed in my attempt at wrinkling my nose because he starts to explain why his apartment is a reeking disaster.

"Sorry 'bout the mess. Been busy." He is sweatier than the last time I saw him, like a wet sponge soaked in a sour nervous sweat.

"No problem! It's not that messy,' I lie, 'We can walk over to campus and sit on a bench if you prefer. Summer evenings are short-lived."

"No, no. I read better inside." His words have a halting quality to them.

"Okay, we can stay here.'' My response sounds more cheerful than I like. Why do I become more agreeable when I feel like something terrible is about to happen? The stenches are combining, and I may throw up. A lonely drive to the coast seems delightful right now. How can I get this interaction over as soon as possible?

"I brought my paper. Do you want to read it now?" I hold out my paper as far from my body as possible.

"Sure, uh, yeah." He seems confused, as if he forgot why he invited me in the first place.

I sit on his sagging brown couch while he sits on the other side of his grimy coffee table. He flips through the pages like he's checking for signatures rather than reading.

"Um, so, yeah, looks pretty good. You're good at this stuff." His sweaty hands leave marks on the paper, and he won't look me in the eye.

"Thanks. What do you think, other than 'good'?"

"Oh, I, uh. . ." Corey stands up and walks towards the front door.

What is this moron doing? He's probably getting a drink of water, and I am overreacting. I start looking around the room for pictures or artwork, anything to distract me from all the horrific scenarios playing out in my mind from watching too many Law and Order: SVU episodes.

While I am guessing how many layers of grime are on the coffee table, the deadbolt on the front door locks into place. The lights go off. Mercifully, the sun is still shining. The room is not entirely dark, only dark enough to be creepy. My body freezes while my ability to hear quiet noises increases exponentially. His feet sound like they are shifting from side to side instead of walking towards me. The old, panelled window would be too loud to open, nor would it open smoothly. I don't have anything to throw through the glass other than my body. If I screamed, no one would hear me over the buzzing of electronics and beer. Also, my voice doesn't carry very far. I bet the nastiness of this forsaken dwelling probably acts as a noise absorber anyway, like soundproof walls. Somehow, I need to get to the front door before he gets to me.

I snatch up my paper and wait for him to return. He will be between me and the front door if I stand up now. Space, I need space. I must wait until he leaves enough room behind him for me to run through. I'm sure I am faster than he is. His whale-like body can't move that fast. He only exercises his thumbs, judging by the video game stack in the corner.

I plaster an ignorant smile on my face when I hear him reach the corner.

"So,' he stammers, 'I um, I was thinking we could turn off the lights and touch each other." He stands still as if his suggestion were a natural progression from term paper editing.

Digging my nails into my hands to hide the shaking, I pretend like his behaviour is normal, even expected, "Oh. No. You have a girlfriend, remember?"

"Um, yeah, I do. But she's gone for another month, and she doesn't have to know. You are just so beautiful." His eyes dart around the room as he talks like he's afraid of getting caught.

"Does she have a name? I don't mess around with other people's relationships."

Why won't I tell him what a creep he is by spearing every profanity I know directly at his ugly face? *Do what you're good at, Tessa. Start talking nonsense, laugh like you've never heard yourself be so funny, and pretend like you don't know what's going on.*

My ramblings do not deter his attention. He repeatedly glances between me and the door, unsure of his next step. I slowly realize I am his first attempt at sexual assault.

Without a word, I make a beeline for the door, no longer interested in pretending like I care about anything except making it out of his apartment unscathed. I wish I could muster the courage to tell Corey to return to his home of fire and brimstone. If Satan employs him, I am sure his job requirements include, "Applicants must look like giant, dumb, fat garden statues."

I unbolt the door without fumbling my hands, a minor miracle, and sprint to my car a few parking spots away.

"Wait, Tessa,' he leans out of his doorway, 'I'm sorry. I didn't mean to scare you. The lusts of the flesh consumed me for a minute."

I turn around and acknowledge the talking festering filth behind me, walking backward until my trembling hand reaches the door handle of my silver Honda Civic. "Don't worry about it. It's nothing. I need to meet my sister. I forgot we had plans. I'll see you later."

As I pull out of the parking lot, I wave to him in the rearview mirror, the most disgusting gesture I have ever made. The fifteen minutes to the Valley River Mall are loud and bright. Is every Eugene resident out tonight? Adrenaline still surges through my veins as if it were a bullet without a target. I park near See's Candy as it's not a well-frequented area.

For an hour, I sob and scream, putting my purse handle between my teeth and biting with all 70 pounds of pressure per square inch available in my jaw muscles. The sorrow of my short life comes alive in my body like a rabid dog. It's clawing and snarling to get out, shreds of hope hanging lifeless between its fangs. Shreds, always shreds. Every drop of lifeblood dripping from its mouth condemns me. What happened was my fault. Why didn't I pay attention to how creepy he was in the first place? Why did I stay in his apartment, frozen by the worry of being impolite? Why did I try to make him feel better about being a disgusting predator? I shouldn't have been so excited about talking to him, not that I was excited about him per se. When will I stop being so starved for human attention that I accept attention from anybody? I am so stupid, so pathetic.

I open my silver flip phone and look through my contacts. I have no one to call, at least no one who will resist the urge to lecture me about my choices, how everything is my fault, and stop feeling sorry for myself. Worse yet are the awkward phone calls where I can sense the silent annoyance, "I'll always be here for you unless you truly need something. If you need me, for any reason greater than an artificial token of support, please keep that noise to yourself." Keep it to yourself. Don't ask for help. It's your fault—the soundtrack of my life.

Searching

Philosophy is over. I see Corey walking in the parking lot sometimes. I am alone, barely able to sleep at night for fear of being assaulted or robbed. Why are some people born in squalor and others in riches? Where is God in the unfairness and heart-wrenching experience of being human? How can God love all of His children unconditionally if He sends some to happy families and others to the shrapnel of a family long since blown apart? Where was God when my mother left? Where was He during the emotional manipulation, abuse, and friendlessness? Not that I deserved friends, I was not a very good one myself.

I search and see only His absence. If His love is unconditional and His power matchless, why are there millions of aborted and abandoned children? Why do so many children only feel their parents' hands when it comes down upon their defenseless bodies in wrath? What about sexually exploited children with depravity as their first memory? Statistics suggest that most victimized children will likely grow into adults with a subconscious penchant for seeking out more of the same abuses, thereby perpetuating the cycle of the worst human beings have to offer. I desperately want to be more than a mortal existence; I want to belong. Still, evidence suggests that whatever familial bond exists, it's fragile and dependent upon a measure of performance few people can maintain.

Why, throughout history, have people sought a higher power if one does not exist? Maybe we think ourselves intelligent and vital enough to be watched over by deities when, in reality, we are merely an observational experiment in a petri dish. I-We-You- can easily be thrown into a galactic trash can and replaced when the human experiment ends and the necessary data gathered. Our history is nothing of which to be proud. I cannot imagine the findings would be much for intellectual discourse between omniscient Beings. Eventually, every civilization ends in war, natural disaster, or internal battles fought in kings and governors' royal halls. In the meantime, we play a game I like to call "Who Can Cause the Most Harm." Kids are collateral damage every time.

Between unanswerable questions and being an emotional lunatic, I would rather not wake up most mornings due to a permanent sleep six feet underground. So, in a desperate attempt to recalibrate my life, I've decided to seek professional psychiatric care once more.

Dr. Meager, whom I found by chance while riding my bike through downtown Eugene's narrow streets, accepts my insurance. The last time I tried to get help, I saw a woman practitioner who promoted Eye Movement Desensitization and Reprocessing (EMDR) therapy. She asked me to think of a memory and move my eyes from side to side, following the index card she moved across her body. Theoretically, it should have minimized emotional and physiological responses to traumatic memories. A lobotomy seems more practical, but what do I know?

I arrive at Dr. Meager's office early. *Tessa, seeking professional help is a necessary step to healing.* Why? What can a professional do besides give some advice, talk about the top ten unhealthy thinking patterns, and prescribe a drug they are reasonably confident might work? Yes, I always fill out the requisite "how crazy are you" survey that reduces my struggle into a short series of questions, whereupon a diagnosis is given. The doctor pulls out their glasses labeled "bipolar," and I am nothing but a list of symptoms found in whatever version of the DSM manual they have on hand. I remain skeptical of the Diagnostic and Statistical Manual of Mental Disorders' ability to allow variations outside of the current version of normal without insinuating someone is sick. Maybe people are only different, and their way of existing makes 'ordinary' people uncomfortable due to our narrow social constructs of what makes someone intelligent and successful.

I walk through the doors into another sterile office; how cozy. Why can't the office of professionals who help crazies look more inviting, like the kitchen of a pleasantly plump grandma who bakes delicious food to keep her grandkids coming back? Pies and cookies are never about pies and cookies. They are a means of generational connection, in a better world than this one, anyway.

The office decorators made a valiant attempt to incorporate earthy tones into the decor with predictable faux ferns and lavender in the corner. A wall that reminds me of a less stimulating version of '70s avocado green emphasizes the other three khaki-colored walls' dirt and dinginess: semi-gloss and eggshell finish. I wonder if they chose two different finishes on purpose.

"Hi. My name is Tessa Knerre. I'm here for a 2:30 appointment with Dr. Meager."

A cheerful face painted skillfully with expensive make-up turns towards me, "Hello! Welcome to Dr. Meager's office. My name is Darla. I'm the one who asks for signatures, makes appointments, and deals with your insurance. I need your ID, insurance card, and a couple of signatures. I know it's tedious and annoying. But we have to do it anyway."

While entering information, Darla gives me a wink as her plum purple acrylic nails clack against her keyboard. Her words do not drip with artificial honey, as do most 35-year-old women well acquainted with tanning beds and high-end salons. Her cornsilk hair is in a high, sleek ponytail, which reminds me of a co-worker who says, "The higher the ponytail, the smaller the brain."

"Okay, Tessa, the last thing I need you to do is fill out this health history form. Go ahead and take a seat in the waiting room. Dr. Meager will be with you shortly. You can give him the form when he calls you back."

"Does he usually run on time?" I ask.

"Depends on the day."

"How about today? Is he running on time today?"

"Yes. Ish."

Ish. I clench my jaw and feign interest in a crack on the edge of her desk. I asked for a simple yes or no, and she answered with an 'ish.' Ish is not a word. Sort of, kind of, and somewhat are all acceptable options. Put 'ish' in the box of "nonsense-words-and-phrases-soiling-the-English-language.'" There are innumerable options to explain the status of affairs, and she chose 'ish.' Maybe she and Corey could play Scrabble together.

"Thank you, Darla." An insincere smile makes its way to my lips. To be fair to Darla, I work for a doctor who continually runs behind, and definitively answering a patient's question regarding punctuality usually ends poorly. I should have asked Darla how her day is going.

Dr. Meager is five minutes late. I alternate, crossing my legs and swinging the top leg as hard as possible. Swinging keeps me calm. If he takes extra time with a patient, it means he cares, right? Or doesn't respect other people's time because he thinks his schedule is the only schedule that matters. Six minutes late. Nine more minutes, and I'll reschedule.

"Tessa?"

There he is. Dr. Meager, twelve minutes late. I smile before looking up so as not to let him see the irritation on my face.

"Please, come in. The red chair is for you. Please, have a seat. Can I get you some water?"

"No, thank you." The ostentatious chair assaults my vision as it sits amidst soft shades of purple, cream, and white. How amusing that my favorite painting, *The Swing* by Jean-Honore Fragonard, hangs flawlessly in all its late baroque splendor behind his desk. A clash of style even for the clueless. We take our respective seats as he offers water and lifts the tissue box a few inches to ensure I know its location.

"Well, Tessa, my name is Dr. Meager. Can you tell me a little bit about why you're here?"

"Yes, after you answer a question to which I must know the answer post-haste, or I will be unable to concentrate. Why do you have a red chair in the middle of such a delicately decorated office? You have white eyelet curtains, for goodness' sake. You might as well hang a sign above the chair that reads, 'Crazy Person Throne.'"

"I like the color red."

"If you are so fond of the red chair, why am I sitting on the chair instead of you? I know I sound rude, but I must ask, or I will be distracted by the question for the duration of the appointment."

"Because I don't want patients thinking that I am putting myself above them. I want them to feel like my equal. Red is a powerful color."

"Normally, I would agree. However, in your office's confines, I feel like the red serves as a potentially shameful spotlight."

"We can switch seats if you like."

"No. I'll sit here. I disagree with your color choices, but this isn't my office. Also, The Swing is one of my favorite paintings, so we agree on one thing." Mild amusement appears in his eyes. I don't like to step above realism, but maybe he is not a horrible parasite growing rich in the misery of others.

"So, Tessa, now that I have answered your question, I need you to answer mine. Why are you here today?"

"I am here because I am tired of being trapped in my mind."

"What do you mean by 'trapped'?

"I mean, my mind won't stop. I can't relax. I can't control my moods, and I don't sleep. I want to sleep. I want to be normal."

"How long have you felt like this?"

"Since I was born, I suspect. I can't remember a time when I didn't feel like this. I know you are going to ask about my family history, so let me give you the bullet points."

Dr. Meager seems intrigued by my rapid-fire approach. He lifts his head off his knuckles, uncrosses his legs, and shifts towards his seat's edge, pen pressed against his yellow notepad.

"Go ahead. I'm ready."

"You may need to draw pictures," I warn.

"I'm pretty good at Pictionary."

I like this guy despite his perfectly pressed suit and pretentious black cufflinks. "I had the misfortune of being born to two people who were, in my assessment, mentally ill and bound for hell in a dilapidated truck with a frozen steering wheel. They thought having a million children was a good idea because what's better than crazy people having kids? My father's anger reigned supreme, my mother heard and probably still hears voices, and both claimed they were doing God's will. They divorced when I was an infant, after which a long and ugly custody battle ensued. Sarah, my birth mother, moved my older two siblings and me from Arizona to Oregon while my father was at work one day. He had no idea where we were for months and, at one point, hired a private investigator to find us, which he did. My mother and her two lunatic parents tried to change our names and birth dates.

Because my mother was mentally unstable, she couldn't keep her appointments for court hearings; therefore, my father was awarded custody. Next, they both married other emotionally unstable or insane people. Sarah's second husband convinced her that she was like the woman in the Bible, who gave up her baby when the king threatened to cut her baby in half after another woman claimed the child was also hers. Why is the Bible so violent? As any mother would, she turned to the Lord in prayer and received a witness from the Holy Ghost that she should indeed sign over her parental rights. A witness from the Holy Ghost is what members of The Church of Jesus Christ of Latter-day Saints use as an excuse for choices ranging from helping a neighbor to abandoning your children to being a pervert. Anyway, I was about four when she officially left and decided to have five replacement children with her replacement husband."

"Sorry, I don't mean to interrupt, but let me clarify: you have an older brother and sister who share the same mother and father?"

"Yes. Bruno is two years older than me, and Josephine is one year older. There are thirteen months between Bruno and Josephine and thirteen months between Josephine and me."

"Okay, okay. Let me write your sibling's names down." He takes the time to write down their names instead of initials. I like him a little more. "Your mother is Sarah, and what is your father's name?"

"His name was Oscar. He died in a motorcycle accident with his third wife a couple of years ago."

Dr. Meager looks up at me as if he wants to offer an apology.

"You won't see tears streaming down my face while reciting the timeline of a life defined by unchecked selfishness and deficiencies of conscience. Keep writing; there's plenty more."

"Alright, I shall keep writing."

"When Oscar married Dolly, his second wife, they began the most miserable marriage known to man. They were not attracted to each other, nor did they have compatible personalities. When Sarah signed over her parental rights, Dolly adopted me, Josephine, and Bruno. Oscar adopted Dolly's daughter, Sadie, who was also a year older than me. From their blessed union came my little brother, Emerson. I am three years older than him.

After thirteen years of marital strife, Oscar and Dolly divorced and promptly married others. Dolly remarried within days of the finalized divorce, Oscar within months. Eight months after Oscar remarried, he and his third wife died in a motorcycle accident, as I mentioned. She had three children under 18, and I feel sad for them. I only met her a couple of times, but she seemed good, too good to marry my dad. After marrying her, Bruno said Dad was a different man, but that could have been the honeymoon bliss of a new relationship. Unfortunately, they weren't married long enough to know different."

Dr. Meager holds his hand up, "Let me review. You have four siblings: two older sisters, an older brother, and a younger brother. The mix is a his, hers, and theirs scenario. Your biological parents divorced, your bio mom left and created a new family with her new husband, your dad remarried, they got divorced, and each remarried someone else. And your dad died. How did I do on catching the basics?"

"Pretty good."

"How old were you when Oscar died? Do you want me to call him Oscar or your dad?"

"Seventeen. Either."

"Who did you live with after that?"

"Oh, with my aunt and uncle. They hardly knew me when they invited me to live with them, but they do the right thing, no matter the cost, literally and figuratively. They are wonderful, and I paid back their selflessness by making their lives miserable, not on purpose, while I lived there."

"What makes you think you made their lives miserable?"

"I don't know. But I know I did."

"Alright, we'll table that assumption for now. We have a lot to work with here. I have a lot of questions, but since this is your time, you decide where to start."

"Why not start at the beginning? What was the first thing I said about a parent? I am not trying to be flippant, but my subconscious may be trying to bring the heaviest baggage to the surface."

"That sounds like a reasonable conclusion. You mentioned your father's anger. What do you want to tell me about his anger?" I appreciate his careful choice of words. 'What do you want to tell me?' leaves the option in my hands, whereas 'What can you tell me?' sounds like he already has the answer.

"He was angry. I mean, he didn't get angry; he was angry. Everything he did had the force of a raging beast behind it. He slammed doors, stomped through the house, and communicated by making demands or accusations. Fury oozed out of his pores when he slept. My dad might have been described as traditionally handsome were it not for his perpetual expression of irritation. He had a square jaw, expressive brows, dark hair, brown eyes, and high cheekbones. I think his nose would have been straight had it not been broken three times when he was a kid. Thinking of who he could have been makes me sad, but not that sad."

"Was his anger ever directed at you?"

"Why do you suppose I am sitting here in this lovely office with you on a summer afternoon instead of running along the Willamette River?" Asinine questions ignite my rage, an unfortunate family heirloom. I forget that people don't know what I know, so their questions are not stupid.

"Forgive my word choice. How was your father's anger directed at you?"

I'm not sure if Dr. Meager is being apologetic or patronizing. Right now, I do not care because forces within me are trying to push the pain out. So, I either talk it out here or pay the price later.

"Nothing was ever good enough for Oscar. No matter what I did, I should have done it better. I was always in his way or on his nerves. He didn't like that I used to cry. I cried a lot as a little kid. I was - am -rather sensitive. Then, when I was twelve years old, he told me I was ugly when I cried and didn't want to see me cry anymore. He had solid and sinewy hands and forearms."

"Strong hands and forearms? What did he do for work?"

"Welding and such. He worked for JCI out past Lane Community College. He was physically strong, which made his presence more intimidating. Scrawny men don't have the same effect."

He nods as he double-checks his notes. I straightened my back to check his writing pad for stick figures and thought bubbles. Neither. Only an information table with names, events, and outcomes.

"Your father, Oscar, was an angry welder who wouldn't - or couldn't - keep his anger under control. He said cruel things and had unrealistic expectations. So far, so good?"

"Yes. Add in Dad's religious devotion and zeal for The Church of Jesus Christ of Latter-day Saints as the center of his life. His religion justified everything he did. He was just another person claiming to be Christian, to be Christlike, by ruling with fear."

"How so?"

"We had a choice - unwavering disobedience or eternal damnation. Damnation, administered by Dad or his dear wife Dolly, which started the second we wavered from the path of righteousness." I can hear the contempt in my voice.

"The path of righteousness?"

"Yes, the straight and narrow way to heaven. Every mistake requires a person to admit their nothingness and wait for a flogging from God. My father didn't want to wait for God to do the flogging. He thought if he punished us first, the Lord would see him as a benevolent parent who raised his children to walk uprightly before the Lord." I pause, wondering how much to disclose.

Sensing my apprehension, Dr. Meager, in his deep, gentle voice, assures me, "I want you to say whatever comes to your mind. You don't have to edit yourself in my office."

I stare at the soft folds of the pale pink dress on the girl in the painting. How do painters make a picture look alive? A massive stone, half avoidance, half containment, threatens to lift off my chest and expose Pandora's box within. I can't let the ugliness out. It will smear its horrid rancor everywhere, show me as the monster I am. A tear rolls down my right cheek.

"Tessa?"

"What? Oh, sorry. I was looking at the girl in the painting. God likes girls like the one in the picture."

"Why do you say that?"

"Look at her. She has the luxuries of the world afforded to her with her elegant clothing and freedom to swing in a manicured garden with only white stockings on her feet. She wants not for adoration or a meal. The sun shines down on her happiness. Meanwhile, elsewhere in France, there are young women of the same age dressed in rags and wondering when they will eat again. If God is a generous God, it seems that His generosity falls on a small percentage of His children."

"Has He withheld His generosity from you?"

My unfocused gaze shifts from the painting to Dr. Meager's silver eyes.

"I was born into hell and told it was heaven. My father was insane, and my mothers are either deranged or passive-aggressive she-beasts masquerading as meek little lambs. I don't want to be condemned for withholding forgiveness. Yet, every time I rationalize Sarah or Dolly's behavior or explain to myself why I have no right to harbor ill feelings, another millimeter of my heart gets seared into volcanic rock. I'm slowly dying in my attempt to feel anything but hatred for them. When I hate them, I feel strong. When I try to love and forgive them, I feel worthless, like a punching bag punched empty."

Dr. Meager's fascination with human behavior begins to show through as he tries to control the questions surfacing on his face. Not a bad thing, I suppose, given the magnitude of family discord I spewed on him. Does he want to help me, or have I become a new case study?

"What more can I say? It sucked. That's it." My words come out more abrasive than intended.

"Nice try, but that is not it. Your life is not a scientific observation with a simple bullet-point summary. 'It sucked' tells me nothing. Many things suck - slamming your finger in a door, misplacing ten dollars, and broken-down cars. Given your way with words, you can do better than 'sucked.' Try again."

My brain shifts from irritated to belligerent, then back again, "I was abandoned by my mother. I was devastated and confused, with no recourse for comfort or compassion." The harshness in my voice does nothing to dissuade him. I keep talking.

"When Dolly adopted me, they changed my name. I remember learning to respond to Tessa."

"What was your name before they changed it?"

"Shanay. Shanay Dee Knurre."

"Do you know why they changed your name?"

"My father hated the name. He also hated Sarah, who chose my name. So, when I was adopted, he took the opportunity to change my name. I don't like the name, Tessa, in case you were wondering."

"Oscar and Dolly changed your name when you were adopted. Interesting. What are your thoughts about the name change?"

"All I remember of the name change decision is wanting to be called Rose or Princess Rose. Later, when I was twelve, Oscar told me he changed my name because he wanted to get rid of anything that reminded him of Sarah, then added that I looked so much like her that he could not stand to look at me. A few weeks after his Hallmark-worthy compliment, I asked him if he ever thought Sarah was pretty. Without hesitation, he told me, "You can't be pretty when your cheekbones are in your eye sockets.""

"What he said was cruel, very cruel. I'm sorry," Dr. Meager starts to get the look of pity on his face.

"Don't you say it. Don't you dare say you're sorry. I don't want pity or apologies."

"Alright, no sorrys. I am curious why you don't like your name?

"Because it is ugly? Because it is a daily reminder that everything about me was offensive to my parents? Never mind my physical presence; the very thought of me offended them. So please, do not waste your energy trying to tell me you think my name is better than what it is. Your opinion will not change mine." I cringe at how bratty I probably sound.

Why is it socially acceptable, even expected, to convince others of what they think and want? Have generations of such a bizarre practice helped further the condition of the human race? Or, are we crippling ourselves by allowing one arbitrary definition of shoulds to suffocate a spectrum of thought we are uncomfortable with considering? I wonder if the artist behind the Kleenex box on Dr. Meager's desk gave up any artistic ideations to create something so, well, so ordinary and expected.

"My parents had a talent for making their irritation and disdain of their children household knowledge. Dolly bemoaned anything that required her effort and attention. I dislocated my finger when I was in third grade, and she huffed during the drive to the hospital about the inconvenience. She even looked down at my hand and said with unbridled contempt, 'Well, which finger is it?' The top digit of my left ring finger was bent backward."

"Those are terrible things for a parent to say and do. They truly are. But, let me ask you this: have you considered their actions as evidence of their sickness? Their unhappiness? Have you ever thought that perhaps their inability to show love had, and has, nothing to do with you?" His eyes seemed to be pleading with me to understand.

"No. No, I have not." I am stunned by the thought. "How could it have nothing to do with me if I was on the receiving end of it?"

"I am not saying their choices did not do harm, great harm. I am saying they chose their behavior because of their illnesses. Sarah didn't abandon you because you offended her, and Oscar didn't change your name because you cried too much. They were sick, Tessa. You are no more responsible for their decisions than the sun's rays are responsible for being restricted by blackout curtains."

Dr. Meager sits back in his chair, letting his words hang in the air like surgical tools. I wish they would shatter on the floor. The scalpels are threatening to lance open my beliefs.

"Do you remember your biological mother?" He gently prodded.

"I do. Yes, I do remember Sarah. I briefly lived with her after my other two parents divorced about four years ago. She's crazy."

"We'll get back to your most recent interaction with her. But, right now, I am asking if you remember her from when you were little, before she signed over her parental rights?"

"Yes. I do." My angry shell makes an audible crack. "I remember Sarah. She was the most wonderful person in the world." A small smile came to Dr. Meager's lips. "Tell me all about her."

"Before I met her as a teenager, I couldn't recall how she looked. I knew she was small-framed, 5 2, with brown hair and blue eyes."

"Brown hair and blue eyes like yours?"

"Yes, like me, at least the brown hair and blue eyes part, though my hair is darker, thicker, and curly. Hey, how can you tell I dye my hair? Anyway, no matter how skinny I am, I teeter on the heavier side of normal, so our body types are different. Sarah and I also have the same long fingers." I look down at my hands, one of the two body parts I don't criticize every morning. The other is my nose, straight like my dad's probably was, but smaller, like Sarah's.

"What I remember the most about Sarah is how much I loved being with her. She let me punch down bread dough and eat popcorn with milk for breakfast. If ever she raised her voice, she apologized right away. We played dress-up, went to the park, went swimming, you know, normal kid stuff. She adored my siblings and me, as I imagine most mothers adore their children. She wanted to be with us. Or at least she made a good show of it. After the divorce, we were with our dad most of the time. I guess two and a half days of putting on a show isn't too telling of reality. Maybe when she sent us home, she collapsed in her chair and cried about how hard we were to handle. I thought she loved me with her whole heart. But she didn't. If she did, she would not have left."

"How does the difference between your belief and her actions make you feel?"

I snap my eyes from my fingers to Dr. Meager's eyes. "Are you really asking me, 'How does that make you feel?'"

"I am. I know how it sounds, but I need to know."

"Betrayed, betrayed by Sarah and Dolly with their meaningless words."

I pause for a moment, waiting for him to respond. He looks like he is rapidly searching through all his mental medical files to find the evidence-based proper response.

He's taking too long. No matter. I'm fighting to break the ropes and chains that have kept me prostrate. I am telling the truth today - the truth that causes other people to cringe - the facts that leave me accused of being unforgiving, as if I am responsible for the consequences that come when parents abuse a child.

Determined to bleed the anger out of me, I use my ugly words, "I hate my mother. I hate all mothers. They are liars. They slap with the hand that is supposed to feed and yell with the mouth that is supposed to offer words of encouragement and butterfly kisses on broken skin. Mothers are the poison killing the souls of their children who are searching for the love they were never given. No one tells them they are okay, so they use someone or something to make them forget. Forget the times they were told of their incompetence, their failures, their unworthiness. I hate mothers. I hate women. I hate Sarah, and I hate Dolly even more. At least Sarah was never cruel, mentally unhinged, yes, but cruel, no."

"Why do you hate Dolly so much?" I can feel the hands of rage suffocating me and, for a moment, believe he can see them, too.

"As a general observation and according to every other psychiatric care provider I have had the pleasure of meeting, emotional suffocation looks a lot like insanity. But no one thinks someone fighting or gasping for air after being trapped underwater is insane. No, they offer the helpless victim an oxygen tank and take their vitals. Yet, my trauma and necessity for healing bring not sympathy but irritation and a swift 'get over it.' How can I trust you not to tell me the same thing?"

"I cannot speak for the other medical professionals you have seen. But I do not see insanity when someone reacts rationally to an irrational situation. Now, please, tell me. Tell me why you hate Dolly."

"I hate her." My legs stop moving, and I look up through a furrowed brow with my chin down, "for not hugging me, just a hug instead of a hostile glare. That's all I wanted. Love. Affection. I hate that woman and her passive-aggressive martyrdom. I hate what I must deal with because of her. I wish I could purge her out of my soul, sterilize my body from the infection of her eyes, and the poison of being ignored. Everything was always about her, except responsibility, which was always about someone else. She was always so put upon and took no joy in her children. She hated us and made no secret of her feelings. And I hate that I still want her approval."

"What must you deal with because of her?"

"This!" I wave my hands on either side of my head. "My broken brain! Every time I tried to get close to her, she rejected me. 'Hey Mom, I want to be a published author by the time I turn 12.' 'What makes you think you can do that?' 'Hey Mom, I want to sit and talk to you about my day. I'll even sit outside of the kitchen while you make dinner, so I am not in your way.' She announced the new rule that no one could talk to her while making dinner the next day. I reminded her of her dinner rule a couple of years ago, and she said she was so stressed out that she needed the time to herself. She had every school day to herself! Who was she with while we were at school for six hours a day? She didn't go to work.

When we got home from school, she would close herself in her room except for a couple of days in the fall and Valentine's Day. During the fall, she would sometimes make pumpkin chocolate chip cookies. Those were always delicious. Valentine's Day, though, was the best. At least before we moved to Junction City, where the depths of hell gaped open, and our rickety home got sucked in."

"Tell me about Valentine's Day."

A small, unintentional smile begins to form, "I think she liked Valentine's Day more than any other holiday, except maybe her birthday. I think she was a woman always looking for romance - some dashing man to come to whisk her away on his gallant horse and give her life meaning. So, anyway, when we got home from school, there would be a well-thought-out pile of treats on the table for each of us: homemade heart-shaped sugar cookies with thick frosting on cute heart plates, a Lindt milk chocolate bar, and other festive baubles. I mostly remember the cookies, and Lindt is still one of my favorite chocolate brands.

She would make a good dinner, too. I mean, she always made dinner, but she would make something new or something more expensive than what we could usually afford. Sometimes she made a meatloaf with homemade rolls - a delicacy compared to macaroni and cheese with hot dog chunks. She seemed so happy, like she was walking on hopes. I don't know if she had ambitions other than her children growing up and leaving the house."

"You truly believe she took no joy in being a mother?"

"Yes. I 100% believe Dolly took no joy in being a mother."

"Don't you think her effort to make Valentine's Day special showed she at least felt something happy?"

"I think her Valentine's Day efforts meant she wanted, for scattered and brief moments, to feel something happy."

"Do you have a relationship with her now?"

"It's on and off. Sometimes I feel obligated to have a relationship, only to be reminded that Dolly is still Dolly. She's still incapable or unwilling to give of herself unless it's convenient. Dolly still writes passive-aggressive letters and emails. Oh, that's the other thing about her - she cannot communicate face to face about anything sniffing of disagreement. She has a gold medal in strongly-worded letters."

"Do you read her emails and letters?"

"Yes."

"Why?"

"Because I hope she'll sincerely apologize for being mean and tell me she loves me."

"Has she apologized before?"

"If 'I'm sorry you feel that way' counts as an apology, then yes." My face feels hot, and my breathing is shallow. I wait for a reprimand or a lecture about being dramatic and too emotional.

Dr. Meager doesn't say anything, and I don't have anything left to say. So, we sit in silence for a couple of minutes with the oversized clock tick-tocking in the background.

"Tessa, thank you for finding the courage to share your emotions with me. I don't think now is the time to analyze everything you just told me because you seem as in awe as I am of what you let yourself say. Is today the first time you have said what you truly believe out loud?"

I nod. I'm scared. My energy is depleted, and I want to take a nap.

Dr. Meager keeps a kind smile on his face rather than the uncomfortable, artificial clown smile of someone who met crazy for the first time. He takes a black composition notebook from the organized-by-size bookcase behind me. I don't like people reaching behind me.

"I want you to take this notebook and write down your unfiltered thoughts, even if it means using words you think may hurt other people. Use words like you used today - you do not need to show them to anyone, including me. Will you write?"

Dr. Meager's journal offering reminds me of the red, hard-covered journal my parents gave me for Christmas when I was ten. The Church of Jesus Christ of Latter-day Saints encourages journal writing, so naturally, my parents made sure we were well-equipped. We wouldn't want to be caught without them should the Lord return to Earth. I still have the red book with JOURNAL written in gold lettering, filled with Valentine's from my classmates at Coburg Elementary School, and professions of love for whatever cute boy caught my attention. Frequently, I wrote about boredom or questions about why my parents hated me and what I could do to earn their love.

The Church also encourages Family Home Evening (FHE), wherein families set aside time on Mondays to endure structured family time, complete with individual assignments. The seven of us rotated through prayers, song, scripture, lesson, activity, and treat assignments. Dad gave himself the additional duty of bringing our sinful behavior to our attention, enumerating why we were not good enough and the need to repent. He would cite the Book of Mormon, "For behold, if the knowledge of the goodness of God at this time has awakened you to a sense of your nothingness, and your worthless and fallen state.[4]"

---

[4] Mosiah 4:5

Utilizing his genius, Dad decided to combine the heavenly practices of journal writing, FHE, and crying for repentance. When he asked me to bring my journal out to use during the lesson, I knew I had no choice. With the vain hope for approval always intact, I thought he might tell me how proud he was of me for keeping a journal since he didn't. A smile spread across my face as I thought of being a godly example to my father. Surely his praise and acknowledgment would follow.

As I placed my deepest secrets into his hands, I felt joy for finally earning a moment of approval. Then, we gathered on the couch and floor as we usually did, waiting for him to preside over our family meeting.

Dad's brown recliner sat between the front door and the staircase while the wood fireplace glowed hot behind it. He took his rightful place as head of the household on his throne and began his lesson. I was so excited to hear the positive things. I was sure he was about to say something, so I hardly listened to what he was saying. Perhaps if I had heard, I could have called upon my defense mechanisms to weaken the blow that followed.

He read my entries aloud to everyone, scoffing and scolding me to my shock and shame. "Love? You love Sam Jones? Why do you love him? Do you think he loves you?" A mixture of disgust and exasperation coated every word.

I looked around the room, silently pleading for help. Josephine looked at me with pity, Sadie played with her hands, Bruno was in complete agreement with Dad, and Emerson was off in his imagination, playing basketball with Michael Jordan. Dolly, in her usual way, watched without attempting to intervene. Her eyes had the same dull effect as they always did when it came to witnessing Dad humiliate me. I later realized that her hypocrisy would have been on full display had she said anything. She read my journal regularly.

"Tessa?" Dr. Meager's voice brings me back to the present, "Will you write?" His hand stretches towards me again, offering the black notebook.

"I already keep a journal," I am telling the truth. Pen and paper are my reliable confidants.

"What do you think about devoting this one exclusively to thoughts and feelings about your Sarah and Dolly? You may not live with them, but they control your life."

I want to argue with him, to tell him how they mean nothing to me and how nothing I do has anything to do with them. Isn't 'nothing' what I was? To both of them? The lie sticks in my throat. Dr. Meager's eyes plead with me for the second time today.

"Yes, I can write. I can write about my two maternal units. I mean, not anecdotal facts about their lives but how I feel about them."

"Remember, write your thoughts also."

"Are thoughts and feelings not the same thing?" Dr. Meager's side smile returns, "Well, for you, I suppose they are."

"When shall I make my next appointment? It looks like our time is up." I prefer to end the appointments and to suggest future ones - it makes me feel like I am in control.

"I want to see you in two weeks."

"Sounds good. I will schedule with Darla on my way out."

***

Riding my bike home is as exhausting as running the last mile of a half-marathon. The traffic lights are a blur, I am swerving over the bike lane lines while my arms shake, and I can feel my heartbeat in the back of my head. Thankfully, my apartment is only a couple of miles away. I think I have some rice or popcorn I can make for dinner. The human interaction required to obtain food, even two minutes of ordering a mocha and an iced lemon scone from a barista, seems like a Herculean effort. On days like this, I wish I liked meal prepping, but I cannot commit to wanting on Monday what I make on Sunday.

As I turn the corner into my apartment complex, I notice my Honda Civic has yet to be stolen—a daily surprise. I expect to lose anything or everything at any given time. To expect a loss is to protect me from the shock of it.

Getting the key into the door takes seven times as long as it should, the failed attempts doubling the speed of the pulsing in my head. Once I lock myself inside, I let my bike and helmet fall to the floor as I collapse on my bed, my chest heaving with every violent sob that escapes. Mucus and tears mix with reckless abandon, soaking the corner of the cranberry and eggplant-colored comforter I used to think was pretty. Why did I say so much? Why did I allow myself to place hope in some stupid therapy? Rather than feeling relief, I am in a bitter fight or flight panic, worse than usual. I should have kept the conversation with Dr. Meager to an intellectual analysis of my parental units. An analysis is safe. Introspection is fatal.

All I have ever wanted is for someone to love me, God, a friend, one bosom buddy, one kindred spirit. One! Yet, I feel alone while surrounded by people. Ironically, I push away the people who see me as worthwhile, like Theodore, whom I briefly dated a year ago.

He liked me so much that he invited me to go bowling with his family. I agonized over what to wear, eventually buying a blue long johns-inspired shirt from American Eagle. He told me how pretty I was and patiently taught me how to bowl. He asked about my ambitions. Nothing I said was the wrong answer. He adored me even with Josephine in the room. Josephine is brilliant and can smile when she has every reason to frown. People love her, men especially, probably because her muscles are as strong as her brain. When we were younger, before life fell apart, and we ended up in different homes and high schools, I was 'Josephine's Little Sister.' Yet, while she attracted male affections, I repelled them. Crazy only looks fun from far away. Also, despite repeated attempts, I cannot pretend.

I assumed Theodore would forget I was in the room once he spent time around Josephine. Josephine's usual twinkling charm danced around her the first time he came to our apartment, but he was oblivious. Instead, Theodore kept looking at me as if waiting for my smile made his heart flutter quickly. Shortly after that, he invited me to

Thanksgiving dinner at his parents' house. Naturally, I agreed and immediately headed to the Valley River Mall to find a refined outfit to wear. Within the chaos of an eclectic clothing store, I found a sweater that reminded me of a mermaid. It was a cable knit sweater, the color of seafoam green and accented with holiday shimmer, complete with a subtle layer of lace behind the scoop neckline. Not wanting to look overdressed, I paired the sweater with jeans.

Theodore almost seemed proud to introduce me to his parents, who appeared kind and gentle. His mom said, "You're right, Theodore. She is beautiful." After the feast, we went to see the movie *Rent*. I didn't know what the movie was about and wished I had chosen differently after the movie started. I could tell he lost interest pretty quickly if he ever had any. Still, we got to sit by each other and soak in the excitement of new attractions and imaginings of the last series of first dates. I ended our relationship a few weeks later, right before Christmas. Theodore's genuine affections and goodness scared me. I hurt him and hated myself for it.

Had Theodore given me attention for a week and then vacillated between treating me like garbage and a little better than garbage, I would have devoted all of my time and energy to him. The more incapable and unwilling a man is to love me, the better. Challenge accepted. Never do I win, of course. Someday, when I have a niece or nephew who wants to create a life sketch of crazy Aunt Tessa for family reunion entertainment purposes, I want them to make the following abundantly clear. I DO NOT like traditionally acceptable romantic advances such as the recitation of poetry, flowers, or cheap chocolates in an inexpensive box with a cheap ribbon. Instead, I pine after men who want nothing to do with me. I yearn for a man who is so in love with his reflection that he wakes up singing a theme song that he wrote for himself. In a word, a narcissist. But let me clarify this critical distinction: I want a narcissist who doesn't even find me desirable enough to be part of his fan club.

The First Essay

5:45 am. Swollen and puffy eyelids from a week of crying. Responsibilities. Time to get up. I can thank Oscar for the ability to suffer without stopping. Complaining and laziness were utterly unacceptable in his house. Complaining included everything from resistance towards his ridiculous mandates to developing opinions. "You don't have an opinion!" he said, 'but you better work hard. You're not a Knerre if you don't work hard." So far, I'm still a Knerre.

I may be industrious, but I promptly ignored his absurd declaration that I did not have an opinion and formed hundreds I knew I couldn't say aloud. Did he expect me to keep my thoughts to myself or remove them from my mind? How would one go about removing opinions as if they were a wart or a skin tag? Wouldn't attempting to do so require an opinion on how the removal should proceed?

After checking my phone, I realized today is Sunday, which means I do not work. Grateful for the reprieve, I sink into my pillow and start to close my eyes when I notice the notebook Dr. Meager gave me sitting on the nightstand. *Ugh! Tessa! Why did you turn your head to the left? You could have kept your head to the right and remained blissfully ignorant of that accusatory book with its taunting empty pages.*

Ignoring the book, I disappear into my imagination, a world where moods have no grip, and I spend my energy as an artist - a novelist, a painter, a poet. I laugh easily, and my life is full of people who love me like a daughter, a sister, and a friend.

A couple of hours later, I return to reality, like a grain of rice in a pressure cooker. After donning my new dress, a dark blue maxi dress with white polka dots, I stuff the black journal into my faux leather shoulder bag along with my three favorite pens and a highlighter. Starbucks is half a mile away, and there awaits the comforting smell of coffee, a fresh lemon scone, mocha, and the little round table in the corner.

While ordering, the barista asks me if I want whipped cream, and I wonder who in the world says 'no' to such a question. It doesn't matter. Nothing matters. With mocha and scone in hand, I write, honest and unedited.

***

Pointless Exercise in Mood Identification

This is my five hundredth Ugly Essay on a search for faith while being as huggable as a wolverine, plagued by thoughts of death and unanswered questions about the existence of God - the same sad song I have been playing on repeat. I am tired of hearing, talking, and writing about it, but here I sit. I was smart once. I tested into the Talented and Gifted program in elementary school based on high mathematics and reading comprehension scores. Twice over, my brain broke. Now, I'm an official idiot. Stupid. Worthless. Unlovable. Alone. Scared. Selfish. Small. Unforgiving. Fat. Pathetic. Ugly.

When I sit in the calm of a Sunday morning at the coffee shop, without mania or darkness pulling me in unnatural directions, I can examine my belief system without wondering the degree of irrationality. Although are any belief systems rational? And, if they are, according to who? Depending on time, place, and culture, anything could be distorted as insane or acceptable.

If God is real, I want to talk to Him and see Him. I want to know that somehow, someone controls all of this chaos. Yet, if I come to know Him, I must reconcile the reality of Him allowing terrible people to do terrible things to me. Why doesn't He protect children if He loves them so much?

I feel like I must go to church, probably because I went most of my life. At home, sitting on my bed is a brand new, unopened set of scriptures. I guess I feel like I need a religious book, too. Much of the time, the scriptures used by The Church of Jesus Christ of Latter-day Saints come in two separate books. However, a quad, which sits on my bed, is a book unique to The Church of Jesus Christ of Latter-day Saints - a scripture combination of The Book of Mormon, The Doctrine and Covenants, and Pearl of Great Price, and the Old and New Testaments. The pages are nearly thin enough to see through, with types so small that even those with 20/20 vision need a magnifying glass.

I bought the scriptures a year ago in the Deseret Book Store at the Oakway Mall in one of my desperate searches for higher meaning. I keep going back to religion like a dog to its vomit. Many members of the Church have their names engraved on the front cover of their scriptures in the lower right-hand corner. I used to have a quad with my name engraved on the front, but I slammed the book into a Rubbermaid trash can. A metal trash can would have made the slam more cathartic. So why do I refuse to donate this quad or throw it away? What do I hope to find within its pages? These are, after all, the same scriptures as the ones Dad carried around. The exact text, the same stories, the same drivel he used as an excuse to make life miserable. Burn it.

There it is! There is my extreme suggestion to an emotional crossroads. How predictable. Where would I burn the scriptures anyway? In the fireplace I don't have? In a beach bonfire an hour away? Or should I simply light it on fire in the bathtub and watch the pages turn to ash while the smell of smoke sends the other tenants of the building into a panic? Shut up. Just shut up.

One day, I hope to understand why fire and death are the constants I carry around. Igniting a flame with the intent to cause destruction is not in my nature. Neither is breaking things that are not mine. Maybe the Book of Mormon is responsible for my obsession with fiery death. So many people died by fire in the Book of Mormon:

a prophet, children, and women, to name a few. Burning alive sounds worse than drowning. However, nothing sounds quite as terrible as having each limb tied to a different horse as the horses gallop away in their respective directions. I would want my head tied to a horse, too, because I wouldn't want to be aware of my body bleeding out.

***

How's that for a mood entry? My mind, heart, and body are at war with each other in a fruitless search to find God, and it all ends in death.

Dissatisfied with the inadequate articulation of my inner world, I slam the black book and shove it in my bag. To distract myself, I take my usual Sunday morning trip to the discount bookstore. Used books smell like an escape. What can I read today? I'm in the mood for something miserable; sad books make me feel like I am not alone. Dr. Frankl's book, *Man's Search for Meaning,* ends up in my hand, as does *Frames of Mind: The Theory of Multiple Intelligences* by Howard Gardner. A book centered around the Holocaust and a text full of more theories. Perfect.

I finish Dr. Frankl's book by 5:30. People in concentration camps survived by identifying a reason for their suffering. What is the reason for my suffering? What is my purpose? Another inevitable nosedive into darkness follows the unanswered question I take in my situation. My apartment is void of human connection. I haven't a friend to call or who wants to contact me. I have books, pens, journals, a computer, a bed, and a few kitchen supplies. That's it. My spirit wants to crawl out of my body and go home to heaven. Can't God take me out of this world as an apology for sending me here?

As I sit on the edge of my bed, the lyrics of a primary song dance around my mind like the music notes in sing-alongs for kids, "Heavenly Father, are you really there? And do you hear and answer every child's prayer? Pray, He is there. Speak, He is listening. You are his child. His love now surrounds you.[5]" Sister Johnson taught this song to me before I was in kindergarten. She used a cardboard box and butcher paper to make a movie reel to help my primary class remember the words. "Heavenly Father, are you really there?" is a question I have sung ever since.

The scriptures, still wrapped in plastic, stare back at me as if pleading with me to look at the answer right in front of my face. My primary teachers taught me that if I read the Book of Mormon every day, my life would become joyous and peaceful, that "A man would get nearer to God by reading it than any other book." Joseph Smith, the man who founded the Church in 1830, is attributed to making the promise.

How desperately I want to believe in his promise tonight. I want to be near God. Right now, I do not care about what seems reasonable and possible, the limitations of human understanding, and the psychological explanation for religious yearnings. Maybe my father, mothers, bishops, and stake presidents had it wrong. After all, some church members were good down to their core. I could feel their kindness and inner peace radiating off their bodies.

I want to know God. I do. I want to be saved from the pit of despair I wallow in. Indeed, if Jesus Christ died for my sins and sorrows, He could find me. I wouldn't burn His fingers if He reached out His hand if He fought and won the battle against evil. What more could I do to His scarred hands? I don't have the power to make His scars increase in size or become more profound.

If I unwrap the book, I fear everything I have been running from will come swooping at my face until nothing is left but two partial eye sockets and a shattered nasal cavity. But, on the other hand, if I leave the book as is, my life will continue as it has. I know how to survive with the version of hell to which I have become accustomed. I do not know that I am strong enough to shoulder anything more, and

---

[5] *A Child's Prayer*, Children's Songbook

those couple of thousand pages of scripture are sure to flatten me. Can't I find God somewhere else? I have two bags of chocolate in the cupboard. That will have to do for now.

Put your shoes on, Tessa, put them on, and walk out the door. If you do not, the unrest from yesterday's religious indecision and the binge eating will remain, leaving you liable to burst into tears at the slightest provocation. You will get mad about some petty grievance, your hands will start to shake, and the urge to throw a computer through a window will almost overwhelm you. Then, you will start crying in front of one of the doctors or a patient, embarrassing yourself to the nth degree, again. Next, out of shame and worry, you will bring food to work, probably Hershey's Nuggets, to atone for your erratic mental condition. Since you will be the one to eat most of it, you'll make yourself sick, and the cycle will start again because too much sugar makes you crazy. Put your shoes on.

Regardless of the effort required to get started, I touch the fringe of freedom when I run, the one sure pleasure I have: inner demons and illness rest. Without the ability to move until my lungs scream and my quadriceps burn with an inexplicable, pleasing pain, I would be dead by now - dead a long time ago.

September is my favorite time to run, even with its high precipitation rates. If I were bothered by the rain, I would have chosen another sport years ago. The bliss I experience depends on how close I get to the edge of my physical limits. I must run faster, farther, or up a steep hill six days a week. If I had not sabotaged myself with food, I might have been fast enough to earn a track and field scholarship to the University of Oregon. Unfortunately, that dream died at the same time as my intelligence.

Many people associate running with punishment. I have seen high school cross country t-shirts with the words, "My sport is your sport's punishment," written across the back. The idea of running as a punishment makes me chuckle. What more punishment does a person need than playing a game with five to seven other people? Working with others requires trust and dependence, both high-risk behaviors.

Last week, the X-ray tech at work asked me, "If you run so much, shouldn't you be thinner? I know a lot of people who run, and they are all pretty thin." I laughed, explaining how I am built for working in fields and factories. The lowest number I have ever seen on the scale is 137 pounds. I was 5"3 and twelve years old. By eighth grade, I was fully grown at 5"6 and 145 pounds, which I would give anything to weigh again. Well, I would give anything except give up my dark chocolate and peanut butter habit. The ten to fifteen extra pounds I carry around seem worth it when my nerves need numbing. Why do 10 minutes of feeding on chocolate outweigh the 23 hours and 50 minutes I spend hating myself for it?

The sunrise sweeps away some fatigue as I lace up my blue running shoes, always ½ size larger than my usual size. Toenails can turn a deep, sickly purple and eventually fall off if the toe box is too restricted. I have lost the big toenail on my right foot three times, the pinky toenail once. Whether lost toenails, the sting of skinned knees, or another minor, blood-producing injury, the pain distracts and satisfies me. I do not go out of my way to hurt myself, but I also do not move out of the way when I see a thorny blackberry bush.

While grabbing my keys, I consider my running route options. If I lived closer to Ridgeline Trail, I would run the two luscious foliage-filled miles to the top of Spencer's Butte and back. I participated in cross country at North Eugene High School during my sophomore year. Our coach took us to Ridgeline a couple of times, complimenting me for my ability to run uphill. I was determined and hungry for success without ever being successful.

Unfortunately, practices went better than races. Performance anxiety started the day of the race, and by the time the gun went off, I felt ill. Generally, the 3.1-mile race became an unconquerable distance at the mile marker despite being the shortest distance I ran each week. Every swinging ponytail and slender-boned girl that passed me shaved off a layer of my confidence. Citing my sturdy bone structure as a weakness, I would give up racing, pull back, and wish that the wet ground would give way to a hole that could swallow me.

Since Ridgeline is unfeasible, I can take West 18th towards Chambers Street. The sidewalks in every direction eventually become pleasantly uneven and broken, eroded by tree roots and time. The comfort and confidence of putting one foot in front of the other wash over me as I run on the imperfect ground in front of imperfect houses. I imagine the homes are warm, the families happy. Imperfectness carries a natural glow that the illusion of perfection never can. Besides, supposedly perfect families are usually hiding ugliness.

Finding rhythm and breath takes a few minutes. Binge-eating hangovers are unpleasant to work through. Still, the extra effort creates another satisfying pain. The local runners have strides falling into two categories: gazelles or bulky and rusted old trucks. Those who run like a gazelle look as if their legs would immediately and seamlessly adapt to any terrain. On the other hand, the rusty old trucks, like me, look as if the energy output vs. forward motion are forever unbalanced, like wheels spinning in the mud. When I see my shadow, I am disappointed to see my legs have grown no longer nor my body leaner. I am breaking the body stereotype of distance runners, I'm sure. Solid, slightly overweight women will be running around the Olympic track in 2008, leaving their lithe competitors in confused tears. Maybe Nike will sponsor me.

My legs feel heavy because I am heavy, the sounds of nature failing to act as a personal metronome. How disappointing. When blood is weighed down by too much sugar and too little water, it flows like mud. The song 'Another One Bites the Dust' begins on my MP3 player, a welcome replacement to the bulky CD player I ran up until six months ago. The CD regularly skipped, making an unbroken 45 seconds of music a happy surprise. The '70s and '80s rock is my favorite type of music to listen to while pounding the pavement, awakening sleeping energy stores, and taking me to an alternate reality. I spend a lot of time in alternate realities, though never with magical people or supernatural creatures.

A mile in and 100 meters ahead, a man walks his dalmatian. I want a dog someday, not a dalmatian, but a fluffy dog with a happy face. The man ahead is old with the halting gait of someone who has recently had a hip replacement. A narrow sidewalk makes room for two an impossibility, so I do a sideways leap onto the street to get out of his way. He gives an appreciative wave and a smile as we pass each other. I do my best to reciprocate, knowing my sweat-filled eyes and red face are hardly the stuff of a friendly expression.

Unless I actively smile, I look angry, sad, or frustrated. I get tired of saying, "No, nothing is wrong. I am not upset, just concentrating." After my explanation, I force myself to smile and give a polite laugh. What is the purpose behind polite laughing? Maybe it starts when we are little and desperately want to be part of conversations between people we admire. We do not understand what they are saying, but we know they are laughing and want to laugh, too. Maybe politely laughing is a subtle way of saying, "I want to be accepted."

Suddenly, I am sprawled on the asphalt. Who trips over the air? After scrambling to stand and get back on the sidewalk, I knew I sprained my ankle. When I sustain a running injury, it's always one of my ankles. Neither looks too bad. I brush some pebbles off my thigh and try to resume my run. As soon as my right foot strikes the ground, I feel pain, but nothing unbearable. Happily, I carry on running, debating how much distance to cut from my route. *You're hurt, Tessa. Rest. You have time to walk home and make it to work. Do not turn a minor injury into a major injury. If you keep running, you are going to make it worse.*

Disregarding the warning signs, I chose to finish the five miles. I can feel heat flooding my ankle as the injury makes itself known. I know I should stop, but running will be impossible for weeks, so I might as well get in the last few miles. Each quarter of a mile hurts more than the one before. The final steps to my apartment complex are pathetic one-legged hops with my left leg as I try to keep my balance with the big toe on my right foot.

Never have I opened the front door so aggressively. A passerby might think the door is responsible for my injured ankle. I want to run in the morning. That's it. Such a privilege is too much to ask. So, wanting to stop any suggestion that life can have small joys, God parted the clouds and said, "Tessa looks like she might be enjoying herself; better put an end to that nonsense and remind her of her place."

If I cannot run or do any exercise requiring two feet, how can I maintain what little control I have left? How can I eat my emotions without gaining an extra 15 pounds? I run to stay slightly overweight. Now, in a few weeks, I will be average overweight. God wants me fat and friendless. Things could be worse. Dolly or Sarah could have knocked on my door.

Through clenched teeth and outraged tears, I reach down, take my shoes off, and assess the damage. Dark purple bruises start blossoming across my foot and ankle like watercolors on porous paper. Attempting to stand back up seems like a waste of energy due to impending nausea and shaking. Crawling ten feet to the bathroom sounds like the least unpleasant choice of movement.

The water in the apartment is never hot enough. I prefer temperatures as close to scalding as possible. A tepid stream is as good a shower as this forsaken apartment complex offers. After cranking the cracked, white porcelain handle to the hottest setting, I fight to remove wet, sticky, smelly, and salty clothes. With a disastrous display of athleticism, I clamor into the bathtub, knocking over bottles promising silky skin and luscious hair, with my right elbow and hip taking the brunt of my body weight. The drops begin sprinkling against my back, making rivers between the caked salt along my waist and shoulders. The fresh chafing on my inner arms and chest starts to sting. I do nothing to alleviate the pain.

I may be injured, but I vehemently refuse to arrive at work looking unkempt. I recently purchased a jersey knit dress from Forever 21 that will foot - haha - the bill. Brown does me no favors, but the dress has buttons. I love buttons. Maybe the ladies at the office will be so busy fawning over how in vogue my dress looks that I will be able to get away with rolling around in the desk chair. One benefit to moodiness and quirkiness is people's general disinterest when I act abnormally. I might get away with putting my foot on my desk in the name of the injury protocol known as RICE (rest, ice, compression, elevation). So long as I avoid the female doctors, I should be okay. Once ready, I hobble to my car, thankful Corey doesn't seem like an early morning person. I cannot let him see that I am injured.

***

Dr. Green pulls in at the same time I do. Odd. He's rarely on time. No matter. Thankfully, he doesn't bother with obligatory small talk. Instead, he keeps his eye on his target, his blinders up. As soon as he gets past the front desk, I'll go inside. I plan to clock in, set up my desk, and sit down before the other ladies arrive in hopes they won't notice my ankle and start asking questions.

I swing my legs out and breathe deeply as the initial pain of setting my foot down washes over me. My teddy bear moccasins - as I so call them because they remind me of a teddy bear I once had - are trying to give my still-swelling foot more room. Maybe finishing my run was a bad idea. Oh, well. I limp towards the door and around the clinic, making my requisite stops to pick up charts and reports. Once I see my desk, a feeling of relief rises. My ankle feels hot.

"Excuse me, Tessa."

I startle. Why do people insist on getting my attention while standing behind me? And, more importantly, why is Dr. Green near the reception desk?

"Yes, Dr. Green. Do you need something?"

"You're hurt." He nods towards my feet.

"I rolled my ankle while I was running this morning. I'm fine." I move my injured ankle behind me as best I can. "

"No, you're not. You need an X-ray."

His eyes are the color of brown sugar, with tiny strands of genuine concern laced throughout. I nearly protest, but who am I to tell a doctor what does and does not need an X-ray? "I'll see if I can make an appointment for the After-Hours Clinic tonight."

"No. You won't. You'll come with me right now. I have time since I got here early. I had to drop my daughter off at school since her car broke down last night."

I look at my watch. The other girls won't get here for another 20 minutes. I can't leave the front desk un-womaned.

He picks up the phone and enters his nurse's extension without hesitation. "Lydia? Yes, I need you to come to the front desk and stay here until the next receptionist arrives. Tessa needs an X-ray. Bring a pair of crutches." I expect a smile to accompany his kindness, but his face remains stoic.

The X-rays reveal there is no break, only a strain. Except for this, "only a strain" will keep me off my bike and out of my running shoes for weeks. I spent the rest of the day making my co-workers laugh as I rolled from place to place in my chair. Working as a receptionist is far from a dream, but working is its own medicine. As I pull into my parking spot, I see Corey outside his front door, arm around his girlfriend, watching me pull in. He must not know that I am unable to walk or run. The fear I felt a few weeks ago twists in my stomach. I put the car in reverse. A pepperoni and pineapple pizza from Papa's Pizza sounds like a delicious dinner. I call Josephine, hoping she can spare a night away from her college studies.

"Hey, Josephine. This is Tessa. What are you doing for dinner? I'm headed to Papa's Pizza. My treat. I know you're busy, so don't worry about it if you can't. I have a book in my purse so I can read it while I eat." When I offer to pay, she is more likely to say yes.

"Why do you go to restaurants to read books? Don't you have friends? Pizza sounds good. I'm pretty hangry since I missed my afternoon snack. What time will you get there?"

"I'm on my way now."

"You move so often, I don't know how far away you are this time."

"I do move all the time, don't I? I live right across the street from the music building at the university." While her comment is more of a dig than an observation, she is correct.

"I don't go to your university."

"I know, but you've walked around it plenty of times."

"Tessa, how many minutes will it take you to get to the restaurant?"

"Fifteen."

"See you soon. Make sure to get a booth."

"Will do." When she says she will meet me somewhere, I do what it takes to give her what she wants.

The last time Josephine and I spent time together, we ran ten miles and bought a flat of peaches afterward from Lone Pine Farms. We were so hungry and thirsty that we bought three times more than we needed. We enjoy ourselves if we are running or hiking and no one else is involved. She tried inviting me to her boyfriend's parents' house for Sunday dinners for a while. I was an embarrassment.

Papa's Pizza doesn't look too crowded when I drive into the parking lot. I can see an empty booth as I eek towards the entrance on my fancy new crutches. Thank goodness. Sitting in a chair at a restaurant feels so exposing.

"Tess, wait up!" Josephine runs to catch up, though a slow walk would be sufficient given my current speed. "What happened to you?!"

"I hurt my ankle while I was running this morning. The good news is I can trip anyone I want with these crutches without being suspected of malicious intent."

She looks at me with concern and confusion. She doesn't understand my sense of humor.

"Don't worry; I am not going to trip anyone."

With an exaggerated roll of her eyes, she opens the door for me. The smell of brick oven pizza almost makes me forget the fear pit in my stomach. We order a large pepperoni pizza, half with pineapple. I grab the Parmesan cheese and red pepper flake shakers.

"Give me those, would you? We don't need you falling on your face because you try to do everything yourself." I resist pointing out that she does the same thing.

When the pizza comes, we both inhale a couple of slices in a matter of minutes. Unfortunately, I won't have the luxury again until I am back on my feet. If I can't exercise, I don't eat a lot, one of my rules. Or so I tell myself.

"So, what's the prognosis for your ankle?"

"Annoying." I try to stop my lower lip from quivering

Josephine starts putting on her proverbial Big Sister Super Suit. No one wears it better. "What's wrong?" She sets her square jaw with the single-minded determination that earned her scholarships and honor roles.

I tell her about Creepy Corey. Her face contorts into disgust.

"I'm afraid to go home,' I admit tentatively, 'I won't be able to get away from him once he realizes I'm a sitting duck. There are other weirdos, too, wandering around and waiting for an easy target. One dude told me I could ask him for help if I see him walking around at night."

"How do you come across these people, Tessa? No man would dare speak to me that way."

"I don't know. I'm a creep magnet, I guess. I can't stay at my apartment, and I can't leave either. I still have ten months left on the lease." My voice gets louder and higher with every word.
"Calm down, don't get hysterical. We have to think of a logical solution. Do you have any friends who need a roommate?"

"No. No friends."

"What about Granny and Pa? I bet you could move in with them?"

"I don't want to move in with my grandparents. I can take care of myself."

"Really? You're going with that story?"

We roll our eyes at each other simultaneously. We don't look like twins, but we look similar enough that people have gotten us confused if we're not together. We both talk with our hands and make the same facial expressions. We are different, though. Josephine is fitter, tanner, smilier, smarter, and all the other positive -ers. Except moody and crazy, those are my -ers.

Driving Memories

"Tessa, we're driving over as soon as we box up the rest of this pizza. You know they will say yes. Offer to pay rent if it makes you feel better."

With Josephine's final judgment, we drive to Granny and Pa's house in a part of town I try to avoid. The homes are quaint, the streets well-kept, but bitter memories of fractured relationships scream too loudly. I would almost rather risk the predators around campus. Almost.

The drive from Papa's Pizza on Coburg Road to my grandparents' house takes ten to fifteen minutes. As usual, when I drive into the parts of town that hold the most sorrow, my mind drifts back towards the voices and feelings of unspoken memories. The silence forced upon them by the refusal of others to acknowledge their validity enrages them, and collectively they make the monster I can barely contain. They never sleep, and they never stop.

To my family, my trauma exists if they think it should. If they've forgotten an interaction, I'm making it up. They dismiss me by accusing me of being hurtful and unforgiving so they can continue, absolved of all consequences. So, I'm quiet, knowing the monster without a voice will destroy me. I wear the chains of silence around my neck; I cut them into my skin, I howl and wail when no one can hear me. I fail my classes, and I beg for love from people who want nothing to do with me. Yes, I house the unspoken pain of generations so others can be free, knowing I will never have the luxury. And, if I start to talk, they only need to yank the chain until I choke.

If I move in with Granny and Pa, an inner battle will erupt between what I feel and what I am told to feel. Any progress towards stability that I have gained will be the first casualty. They will ask why I don't talk to Dolly, their daughter. My cute and sweet grandparents would only get upset and defensive if I told them the truth. What parent wants to hear the ugly truth about their child? Josephine tried once, and Pa said she "didn't know what she was talking about." That was the end of their relationship. Never again did Josephine come to them as a granddaughter.

Any interactions between them are now as polite as two strangers meeting to discuss the purchase of a piece of farm equipment. I cannot bear to hear, "you don't know what you're talking about" one more time. Why do people outside of emotional abuse and neglect claim to know more than the abused and neglected? So, I let them believe the story they tell themselves: Dolly is a selfless angel, and that Josephine, Bruno, and I are ungrateful for her sacrifice. After all, she married our father and adopted us when Sarah left. We should be better children. (By 'better children,' they mean interacting with Dolly according to her rules and expectations. Perhaps Dolly should have thought about the consequences of her parenting choices before the opportunity to change the outcome had passed.)

Granny and Pa's defense of Dolly means they love her and know a side of her I have never seen. They are good-hearted people, and I cannot fault them for believing their daughter to be better than I know she is. Or maybe I am wrong because I'm too emotional.

When Dolly considered divorce after our family self-destructed, they supported her. When she decided to stay married to Dad despite having every reason to leave and should have left, they supported her. Or did they? I've never asked. Two years later, when she met a new man at work and finally filed for divorce, they supported her still. For the most part, Dolly seems happy now. I'm glad she got out of the absurdly unhealthy, abusive, and incompatible marriage she sludged through for thirteen years. Yet, Dolly's deliverance does not erase what she said and didn't say, what she did and didn't do. Why do I wish she had loved me?

While Dolly claims she left Dad for Josephine's sake, I don't believe her. She started caring about her relationship with Josephine right around the time I realized she had romantic inclinations towards another man. She used Josephine as an excuse. My proof is this: after Josephine went through puberty and developed her talent to make others feel special and happy, Dolly told her to stop. Stop laughing and smiling because to flirt was to disgrace the family. (Why are girls often accused of flirting and utilizing their deceptive feminine wiles when they are simply friendly? And why are feminine wiles deceitful?) Stop running because Josephine wasn't "running fast enough to do anything." Stop blooming. Stop shining. We were expected to achieve but not to shine. Oscar and Dolly reminded us regularly of our worthlessness, each in their unique way.

On top of Dolly's efforts to silence Josephine, Josephine never had a childhood where her only concern was exploring, playing, eating, and avoiding naps. Josephine's childhood ended when Sarah left Dad. She took on the role of a tiny mother, like so many traumatized older siblings. Once Sarah listened to the Holy Ghost and abandoned us, Josephine's heart was ground to dust. She was six. Josephine never wanted to play dolls with Sadie and me. Nor did she join us when we filled my hamper with toys and clothes and dragged it behind us like a pioneer handcart. According to our estimation, our dress slips were the closest thing we had to pioneer clothing. The lace and rosebuds on the slip made me feel so feminine and pretty. However, I kept the information to myself, knowing that if Dolly or Dad knew I felt pretty in something, they would either take it away or accuse me of sexual motives, even though I didn't understand the term at the time. Shameful Sexuality. Maybe someone in the Church should write a book with such a title to expound on the sinfulness of being female.

Josephine sometimes irritates me with her bossy mothering, but I admire her courage. She was in 7th grade when Dad began entertaining the idea of moving to the country so his children could "learn how to work." (Apparently, working hard is something city folk cannot learn. I think Dad forgot he was raised in the city.) She started getting in trouble for getting male attention, so I suspect Dad's secondary motivation for moving to the country was isolating his daughters to hide our harlot ways.

Dad's drive to teach us to work approached desperation as if doing so was his singular purpose and mission. Well, almost his singular purpose and mission, next to preventing us from falling into eternal damnation. I instinctively knew he would do whatever necessary to teach us to work, even if it meant tying us in a straitjacket made with the fabric of fear and sewn together with guilt. He got the pattern from the jacket he wore.

***

As we merged off Belt Line and onto River Road, I remember my failed attempts at earning a track and field scholarship. The summer before my sophomore year, I worked ten to twelve hours a day driving combines at a local alfalfa farm. Each morning, I would wake up and run five miles. Then, once the school year started, I ran to seminary, a religious class before school. After seminary, I ran to school. I ran an extra mile after cross-country practice. I ran and ran and ran and barely improved.

I was in seventh grade when I first joined the track team. I asked Dad if I could join the team, knowing he would probably say no because it cost money to join, and money was limited. To my surprise, he said yes on the condition that I understood that if I was going to compete, I must work harder and longer than anyone else. To him, there was no sense in competing if you were not going to win. Because he wanted me to be a successful athlete, he told me I would know if I worked hard enough when I threw up.

Much to our disappointment, I was not a naturally gifted athlete and an embarrassment to the Knerre name. Dad had been an excellent athlete and wanted me to be the same. Initially, I gravitated towards distance events, like the 1500 and 3000 meters, even though I often ran the last lap alone and was humiliated, made worse by well-intentioned bystanders cheering me on. I still find "good job" to be a somewhat patronizing sentiment, as usually it's encouragement for subpar performance.

Self-inflicted torture appealed to me, so I kept signing up for track. By the time I reached the ninth grade, I was still slow and coming in among the last runners, but I was not always the last runner. So instead of running the 3,000-meter race, I focused on the 800-meter race. I told the high school track coach I could run 400 meters in sixty seconds, not possessing a concept of pace or time. She instantly knew I was lying, though I genuinely believed a lap in sixty seconds seemed doable. The memory makes me laugh.

According to my estimation, I worked harder than anyone else on the team. I pushed myself to the point of blurred vision and nausea. Hard work should have meant first place, or at least second. For me, it didn't. One evening, I could not keep the frustration and shame inside me another second. Against my better judgment, I went to Dad, lamenting my slow progress compared to the perceived success of other runners who "worked half as hard as I did."

I had never before complained to Dad uncensored. He listened for a few minutes until an irritated cloud formed in front of his eyes. "Tessa,' he said,' someone will always be faster, stronger, better, and smarter than you are. Get over it and get back to work." He shook his head as if trying to shake off a memory and walked away. I was astonished he did not do or say anything more. That day, I began to understand that he, like me, knew what it felt like to come in last.

Oscar grew up in a home he described as hell. If ever Dolly mentioned the volume and frequency of his yelling, he would say, "You have no idea what yelling is." In addition to coming in last, we shared another similarity. He was the third child of a tumultuous marriage that ended shortly after his birth. Whether he was a couple of months old or a couple of years old when his parents divorced, I am unsure, but his parents' decision initiated a series of events that left my father a shadow of the man he could have been.

Grandpa Knerre stopped visiting his three children when Oscar was eight. According to Dad, his parents fought with such unrestrained anger that Grandpa thought he was doing more harm than good by visiting his children. Dad said he remembered wearing cowboy boots and a cowboy hat when his father drove away. When we were at Grandpa's funeral, people whispered to each other about how much Dad and his father looked alike. I think that made Dad happy.

I wonder if Grandpa would have driven away if he knew the cruelty his youngest son endured. Dad's stepfather, Jim, was a heartless man. He regularly beat Dad with a belt until welts and bruises formed. One time, Dad picked up a belt, folded it in half, and started snapping it. Talking to himself more than anyone else, he said, "Jim always started snapping his belt before beating me." One time, Jim beat him so severely that he couldn't move. His mom said he deserved it.

The belt beatings, however, were nothing compared to the sexual molestations. A church leader and a family member did unthinkable things to Dad, robbing him of his innocence. When I imagine how helpless, scared, and manipulated Dad must have felt, I feel sorry for him. But then, I start to think that perhaps, as mean and angry as he was, he truly believed he was providing a happier existence for his children than he could have imagined for himself. Dad was also wild, full of restless energy and a racing mind. He once told his elementary school teacher that if she didn't want to see or hear from him for the rest of the day, she could "shut her eyes and close her ears."

Though Dad was who he was, not every moment was torture. My favorite times were when we lived in Coburg at the end of North Coleman Road before Josephine's body started to change. North Coleman Road was a paradise, and I am not using sarcasm for once. It was a dead-end road with potholes, gravel, and long-time residents, and at the end, the road opened into a mint field. When we moved in, our home was new, brand new, with three bedrooms, two bathrooms, and a backyard big enough for a garden, a trampoline, and a game of kickball. I am unsure how my parents could afford a new home because money was scarce. We wore hand-me-down clothes and ate free school lunches. I seem to recall a rumor of a benevolent man who made the purchase of our new home possible.

We were often the recipients of compassion and generosity when we lived in Coburg. For example, one Sunday, we pulled into the driveway after church to find a brand-new full-sized trampoline, still in the box, on our doorstep. Another time, our neighbors brought over Christmas mugs full of candy, one for each of us. However, my fondest memory of kindness came from a stranger. Our elementary school had a book fair every fall, around Thanksgiving. I knew we could not afford any books, but I would walk through the fair anyway, inhaling the smell of unturned pages, admiring their shiny covers, and hugging them to my chest before carefully putting them back in their place.

An older lady, who I believe was someone's grandmother, put her hand on my shoulder and offered to buy me *Little House on the Prairie*. I declined, knowing that if I brought home a new book, Dad and Dolly would accuse me of stealing or mooching off a stranger. Both sins carried the same weight. If I ever have kids and they have a book fair at their school, I will buy them whatever book they want. Even if they pick the most expensive option, I'll foot the bill. I'll save year-round if I must. I'll leave a donation, too, so a child from an underprivileged home can experience the exhilaration of a new book. Next to reading, playing outside was the pure joy of my childhood and an activity wholeheartedly encouraged by both parents. Dad added a long concrete slab to the left of the house, wide enough for another car to park and far enough back to build a shed while leaving us room to shoot hoops and use our roller skates. One of Dad's friends helped him lay the concrete slab. Emerson kept annoying them with his antics, so Dad's friend threw Emerson's action figure on the ground before they poured the concrete. Dad laughed.

The concrete was excellent for jumping rope, using the Skip-It ankle toy, and parking my bike. I loved riding my Schwinn banana seat bike with its blue frame, blue-black-gold striped seat, and mustache handlebars. Sometimes I rode with no hands, and other times I pretended to be a multi-lingual bus driver, stopping to chat with passengers from faraway lands. Outdoors was freedom.

Remaining indoors, however, felt like a dark prison where the only hope of sunlight came if, and only if, we achieved perfection. You can imagine how many rays of sunshine gleamed through the window under that impossible standard. When we inevitably failed, we were punished. Dolly's favorite forms of discipline were withholding affection and positive attention. Still, how I longed for her love! I carried the hope of gaining her approval and tried desperately to earn it, my heart rising and falling with every one of her resentful acts of caretaking. Almost involuntarily, I closed the opportunity window for developing a loving maternal relationship with her. Sometimes I pretend I haven't closed it, but I have. Who can regrow a severed outstretched hand?

After selling our home in Coburg and taking up residence in Junction City, in the house with blue and green sponge-painted living room walls, insanity, fueled by isolation and ignorance, was ignited. Were the memories not so painful, I might consider the four acres on Turnbow Lane lovely with its golden long grass field, clear stream, and a giant oak tree. There was a pond, too, a stagnant outlier. My singular memory of the pond involved Sadie pushing our fourteen-year-old neighbor boy in during the winter. Lucky for everyone, the ice was thin and the pond shallow.

Sadie was a feisty and free spirit, a girl of the elements, and unafraid of our father. She answered every inquisition with 'I don't know,' or 'I forgot.' She had adventurous brown eyes as if constantly waiting for someone to trigger a booby trap she had set. I used to make fun of her as retribution for her tattling and preferential treatment from Dolly. How I wish I could recall my words. So many times, I have spoken words of whose weight I was ignorant.

Our stream, surrounded by blackberry bushes on either side, split the property into two sections. The stream flowed a few feet lower than the ground on either side of it, necessitating a haphazard bridge made of one splintered slab of wood. Until Dad attempted to eradicate all the blackberry bushes on our property, the ones by the streams were majestic in a wild Pacific Northwest kind of way. Once Dad purchased his clunky blue tractor, any building, plant, or land patterns were subject to being torn down, ripped up, or moved. Most of the time, he could manipulate our land without resistance. However, blackberry bushes are an unrelenting foe. He would have had more success had he sent Sadie to do the job.

The entirety of the architecture on Turnbow Lane, from the house to the barn to every wooden beam on the wraparound deck, seemed as if they could collapse if the rain came down too hard. They reminded me of a willowy, osteoarthritic woman. If I think about the similarities between our family and our house, the frail old woman nearly becomes the emblem on our family crest.

One spring day, Dad brought home a stack of wooden pallets as part of his "My Kids Must Work Hard" curriculum. He unloaded the pallets in our grass field and instructed us to take them apart with a hammer or crowbar. Once deconstructed, we were to drag the beam from the field to the far side of the house. Four of us worked hard while Emerson found a way to disappear. He had a talent for avoiding work without getting caught.

Once all the pallets had completed the journey from one end of our yard to the other, Dad lit it on fire. He gave us each a marshmallow to roast, a reward for honoring the Knerre name. I would be remiss not to tell you that Dad's work ethic was unmatched. He did not sit comfortably in a recliner while we labored. He either toiled at work or worked alongside us, though not on the same project. He put in long hours as a steel fabricator Monday thru Friday. Then, when he came home, he tinkered with his clunky motorcycles or drove around on his equally bulky blue tractor. He loved that old tractor almost as much as he loved his red Dodge pick-up. Engines were his love language. Or perhaps he preferred engines to people because engines are predictable and controllable.

Dad had little appreciation for calm and quiet hobbies, especially reading. He did not care for books other than scriptures unless written about a prophet of The Church of Jesus Christ of Latter-day Saints. I doubt he understood much because Dad was a painfully slow reader, unable to read fast enough for characters to come alive or for facts to come together cohesively. I recall unintentionally embarrassing him during family scripture study in second grade when my reading level was higher than his.

Many doors of opportunity were closed to him due to his academic disadvantages. The competition of the professional world has no space for low literacy. More importantly, sharing ideas, exploring history, and being swept up in someone else's story were luxuries he had never experienced. His world was small. A few people have remarked that Dad lived his life with a chip on his shoulder. I believe, in large part, the chip came from being an uneducated but intelligent man. Not wise, mind you, but clever in a way that falls outside what America traditionally acknowledges as brilliant. He could look at a structure and figure out how to build it. Bruno inherited his gift.

While my father felt the sting of humiliation regarding his education, he was proud of me by the time I was seven. In perhaps his most significant act of kindness towards me, he told his friend and Grandpa Knerre, on separate occasions, that I was smart, citing my quick reading and mathematics comprehension. Dad did not say kind words for the sake of flattery; I remain unconvinced he was ever acquainted with the language of compliments, having received cruelty throughout his childhood. So, when Dad said I was smart, I sewed his words into the fabric of my identity. The last few years, I seem to be ripping the words out one stitch at a time.

If Dad were alive today, he would most assuredly be ashamed of my condition: mentally and emotionally unstable, without faith, and taking safe classes while avoiding math and science. Math used to be fun, specific, and orderly. Now, if I enrolled in introductory algebra, the professor would cover my quizzes and tests in red ink. My brain is akin to a sieve, mathematically speaking. To be fair, my ability to assimilate new information took a nosedive in the seventh grade when my parents' diet of mental illness and abuse neared the tipping point of no return. A deeper dive followed a few years later.

***

In any case, here I am, pulling into Granny and Pa's driveway, having processed more history than I prefer. It happens every time I drive down River Road, like the Ghost of Christmas Past
Granny and Pa live in a cozy three-bedroom, two-bathroom house on a nice patch of land. Pa keeps the front yard beautiful with a Japanese maple in the middle of a manicured lawn. The backyard is full of the fruit of his green thumb: raspberries, green beans, tomatoes, radishes, and corn. He makes the best canned green beans. Granny tends to the inside, which can only be described as a giant doily. A clean, pristine, never a thread out of place doily.

"Well, Tessa Shanay!" Pa is standing on the porch before I get out of the car. Pa must have seen me pull up while sitting in his navy-blue recliner, where he reads and watches country westerns. His plaid shirt and wrangler jean-clad self walk towards me as fast as his 79 years will let him. I love my Pa. In his heart, he will always be John Wayne with a mustache. There are moments when, for his sake, I wish I could love Dolly like he thinks I should.

"And Josephine, too." He tries to sound excited.

He gives me a big squeeze and thinks about giving Josephine a side hug before patting her on the shoulder. Roots of pain begin creeping up her neck. She slashes them down with an almost indiscernible shake of her head and focuses on the reason we came.

"Pa, as you can see, Tessa has hurt herself."

"I see that. Whadya do? Get hit by a goat? Taken out by a dog?" His jolly grin brings a smile to my face.

"No, just running."

"Getting hit by a goat sounds better."

As we walk inside, Granny greets us, immediately concerned. She's 4'11 with enough sass to take down a giant. I cannot remember a time when she looked undone. Today her blouse of choice is striped with navy and white.

"Ummm, I have something I need to ask," I don't know how to transition into my question smoothly.

"And? Let's hear it." Granny is not one to wait.

"Ummmm." I can't get the words out. I don't want to be a nineteen-year-old living at their grandparent's house.

"Come on, Tessa. Out with it." Pa looks like he already knows what I am about to ask.

Josephine lets out a loud sigh, gives me an exasperated side-eye, and explains, "Tessa hurt her foot and can't get around very easily. She lives by herself, and there are men with shady intentions in her complex. Can she move in with you guys?"

"I'll pay rent, food, and utilities." I quickly add.

"'Course ya can. How 'bout you pay $350 a month for everything? You don't have to worry about buyin' your own groceries." Pa says, still smiling.

"Thank you! Thank you!" Uninvited tears spring to my eyes.

"Don't knock yourself over! You'll use the guest room."

Josephine nods in satisfaction, having done her sisterly duty. Her head nod reminds me why emotional abuse is so hard to describe. How can I tell the implications of a smirk, a self-satisfied smile, or a furrowed brow? To some, they carry none or minimal weight. But to a child who is perpetually silenced, they are akin to a slap across the cheek.

"I'll be here tomorrow afternoon, right after I pack my things," I promise.

"Okay, Tessa Shanay. I'll make spaghetti and green beans with bacon," Pa promises back.

"And I'll get the room ready for you," Granny adds, with a twinkle in her eye as if she has a plan greater than moving blankets and furniture around. I'm confident she will hang a picture of Jesus Christ on a wall.

The Second Essay

I subleased my apartment within a week of moving into Granny and Pa's house. A small miracle. I put an ad on Craigslist, and thankfully, an English professor responded. He needs a place to stay during the week while teaching at the University of Oregon because his home and wife are in Portland. I know he will take good care of the place. Fellow students were also interested, but they ran a higher risk of trashing the apartment, and I would pay for the cleaning fee at the end of the lease.

Today I have another appointment with Dr. Meager. I hate driving when clouds cover every patch of blue sky, and the rain dumps down. It reminds me of when Bruno used to fill up a five-gallon bucket with water and empty the freezing contents on my unsuspecting head. Nonetheless, a calming drizzle of rain is acceptable so long as the season is fall and the month is October. Without the cool fall air and mist, driving in gray weather makes me carsick, a chronic ailment since childhood. Even exciting elementary school field trips left me feeling queasy and groggy.

As anticipated, the short distance between Westmoreland Family Medicine and Dr. Meager's office brings on the beginnings of a headache. How lovely. Doubtless, I should do this more often.

Darla's sitting at her desk, looking underwhelmed with her same high ponytail and clickity-clackity nails. Today her nails are the color fuchsia. Why the color fuchsia?

"Hi, Darla. I'm Tessa, here for my 1:30 appointment with Dr. Meager." I try to sound as pleasant as possible.

"Hello, Tessa. How are you today?" She smiles in my direction without looking at me.

"I'm at the psychiatrist's office, so my mental status is not ideal. However, I could be worse. I could be trapped in severe depression, watching the blood run down my arms after purposefully slicing my skin open so that I could feel something other than my aching heart. Or, I could be a whole lot better, flying on the wings of mania, making grandiose plans for changing the world's injustices, and impulsively giving away the life insurance money I received after my father's death. But, at this moment, I'm here, and you are there, going through the motions of a meaningless social dance where I talk, and you pretend to listen."

Darla looks at me, confused, debating various responses. I give her a smirk, and she starts chortling, yes, chortling. Soon, we're both lost in a fit of laughter and chortles. I love funny moments in the middle of stressful days because they are always more amusing than they should be. Sadie and I used to have many such moments in the pews at church.

"You ladies seem to be having a good time,' Dr. Meager gives an easy grin, 'you may not need my help today, Tessa."

"Don't be ridiculous. Of course, I do. I have at least six essays written in this journal you gave me." I wave the journal around with unrestrained vigor. My headache disappears.

"Very good, very good. Please, come into my office."

"I see the red chair remains," I observe as I flop into it.

"Yes, the red chair remains, though you no longer seem opposed to it."

"Do you want to read what I wrote?" Further comment on his silly chair is a waste of my time and money. Also, need to get the feeling of apprehension out of my body.

"No, no, I will not read your essays. They are not meant for me." Dr. Meager smiles in his friendly way without a hint of expectation in his eye, which means he is not lying. I have not met anyone so skilled in the art of deception that they can convince their eyes to join in the charade.

Tessa just read one essay. Dr. Meager wants to help. Without his help, you have two options: either the tangled neurological pathways in your head untangle, or you die. Don't be an idiot. The neurological pathways in your head cannot unravel; they are not a ball of yarn. What help can Dr. Meager give besides a listening ear and validation? He is not your friend. Don't be stupid and vulnerable. Keep your mouth shut.

"Reading one of my essays seems like the most efficient use of time and energy. My inner demons will punish me later for my act of defiance," I'm both joking and serious.

"Yes, yes, if reading your essay is what you want to do, then, by all means, go ahead." Dr. Meager leans forward, pen and paper ready as if what I am about to read is as enjoyable as his day gets.

***

The Poison of Mothers

I don't know if God has a limit on how many times He will warn us before the balance of our pride comes due. I guess that His warnings increase in intensity and rapidity the closer we get to utter destruction. We probably think He's mean when He's trying to save us from unseen dangers, like a child who thinks their mother is mean when she yells in desperation, straining her vocal cords, and praying her child hears her before a moving car ends their mortal existence. The child, of course, doesn't understand the danger they are putting themselves in or the panic they are causing their mother.

God doesn't stop us. He doesn't stop parents from hurting their children. God only warns us, and sometimes I wonder if He even puts forth that much effort. "Sorry about that' He seems to say, 'I love you, but my love allows you to suffer to the point of wanting to die. I love you so much I will stand here and watch you writhe and suffer.'

So, thanks to Him, I equate love with disregard and torment. Romantically speaking, many times, I am attracted to people who I know will cause me pain. My superfluous pilgrimage through the swamplands of unrequited love has produced nothing but embarrassment and shame, but I appear comfortable in unpleasantness. I do not know how to navigate peace and contentment. Like the brackish water in swamplands that is not salty enough to be saltwater nor saltless enough to be freshwater, I live between two contradictory states. I am fiercely independent and chronically love-starved.

I wish to explain what it feels like to be love-starved and know you have no safe person and no safe place at the age of three, before preschool, and before you're potty trained. Do you know what it's like to sleep just below the surface of wide awake to avoid the surprise of getting pulled out of bed or enduring a verbal beating? Do you know what it's like to do something you're proud of and, upon telling your parents, be accused of lying because they think you are incapable of anything but disappointment?

Anger, born of betrayal, fuels my words. What do I want to prove? What do I want to tell people? Another story about a hard life? Sharing miserable circumstances to let other people in on the secret of my misery and corresponding social struggles has been a fruitless endeavor. They already know I'm socially inept. What is the point of anything? I used to want people to understand the pain to understand me. The noise of reckless emotions is so loud that I remain convinced that everyone can hear my instability. If I explain, then I won't seem crazy, right? Why do I call myself crazy? Why is being sensitive a bad thing? Why have I tried to shut it down over and over and over again? Being sensitive equates to weakness, and I haven't the emotional capital to be weak anymore. To be strong, one must either shut off all emotion or be born without it. But is the unwillingness or inability to emote a strength? What does controlling one's emotions look like anyway? Does it look like sitting down quietly and keeping your mouth shut while the people who have assigned themselves the role of The Logical One make the decisions? Is that self-discipline, or is that giving up? Why do we default to people who claim to have the answers instead of becoming part of the conversation? What is it about

The Logical Ones that makes their solution correct? Experience? Yes, experience matters. No one likes a self-proclaimed expert with less work experience than everyone else in the room. Am I the one who sounds like I think I know everything to other people? Probably.

I know a few things. I know how to read people and predict reactions and behaviors. I try to have compassion. Social engagement vacillates between exhausting and exhilarating, just like everything else in my life. I don't like not knowing what to do. I don't like floundering around like an idiot. So much of my self-talk revolves around being stupid.

I hate the word 'Mom.' At first, I didn't think Dolly deserved the title, and then I came to hate the title itself. Passive-aggressive emails, letters, notebooks, and whatever other communications she chose. I wish Dolly could have said things to my face. I wish she had looked me in the eye as if I were a person and not a legal matter or an unpleasant business document. How a mother looks at her children is how children learn to look at themselves. One time, Dolly was upset because I wasn't smiling enough. She told me to sit on the chair and smile. I was four. I sat on the ugly brown chair and smiled until my face hurt. After she had gone into her room, I kept smiling just in case she suddenly came out. I was happier when she stayed in her own four walls. When she came out, the room turned to eggshells, my heartbeat soared, and I felt on the verge of a panic attack until she went back into the room. (Maybe I have her to thank for my resting heart rate of forty-two. I should write a letter to the Olympic Committee and suggest living in a constant state of fear as a cardiovascular training program.)

I wanted Dolly's affections and attention. I wanted her to be happy. I know she was married to a man she did not love. I know she was treated poorly. I know she blames Dad for our family falling apart when she was equally culpable. She is admirably skilled in the art of rewriting history to remove all personal responsibility. But I wanted her to love me, and she would not.

Would not or could not? To help myself feel better, I tell myself that Dolly couldn't love me, as Dr. Meager alluded to during our previous appointment. Dolly had plenty of tragedy in her childhood, too.

Dolly didn't live her religion, but she sure shoved it down our throats. Her friend once told me that Dolly constantly hoped one of her past boyfriends would leave his family and run off with her. When I learned of her hypocrisy, any speck of respect I had for her was gone. Here, she used Josephine's horrible reality as the catalyst for divorcing Dad when, in actuality, she would have left him a long time ago if someone else had whisked her away. Whisked makes me think of eggbeaters mixing eggs and sugar when making chocolate desserts. Whisked is too kind a word for her. How about flushed away instead?

After her friend disclosed this information, I let out twelve years' worth of rage in a verbal atomic bomb. Dolly's friend promptly told Dolly of my wrath, leaving out the part where I learned of her true intentions. Dolly was furious. I never told Dolly what her friend said about her. Her selfishness and hypocrisy are as subtle as a New Year's Day parade.

One example of her force-feeding me a religious diet of shame via the guise of modesty is the time my seventh-grade track and field team took season pictures. I knew that many, if not all, of the kids would be wearing their track singlets without a shirt underneath, thus exposing their shoulders and committing the crime of gross immodesty. I did not want to be accused. So, I talked to Dad about the situation, and he did not seem bothered by sport-appropriate attire. After all, there are several yearbook pictures of him in his swim team photo wearing nothing but a Speedo. After a brief discussion with Dolly, they told me the decision was up to me. I saw no problem with the track uniform. Admittedly, I did not want to stick out in the team pictures either. I opted to forgo a T-shirt for team pictures and wear a T-shirt for my individual photo. When Dad picked me up from practice, he asked what I chose to wear and simply nodded his head when I told him. Since he was not known to keep his opinion to himself, I assumed he was okay with my choice. On the other hand, Dolly grilled me on my decision the minute I walked in the door. She sat with a menacing look in her eye, like someone who knows they get to inflict harm.

"What did you decide to wear for pictures?" Dolly asked, her face distorted into a forced half-smile.

"I wore my uniform without a t-shirt for team pictures and with a t-shirt for individual pictures." I knew my answer was not the right one regarding modesty choices, but it was precisely the answer she was hoping for.

"Well, we were going to have taco salad for dinner to celebrate you making the right choice, but since you chose to be immodest, we will have something else." She looked like she was repressing a smile.

I knew better than to respond, so I headed up the stairs to hide in my room and punish myself for being a bad daughter. Why did I wear the track singlet? We often had disgusting meals, like macaroni and cheese with mixed cream of mushroom soup, canned peas, and tuna. We didn't have a lot of money for brightly colored foods. Even the fruits and vegetables we ate were not far from beige on the inside - bananas and apples mostly. A dinner like a taco salad was a rare delicacy, and I ruined it for everyone.

I grew to hate the sound of Dolly's voice. She can play the victim and the perpetrator simultaneously. She either has untapped acting potential or is mentally ill. Or simply mean. I am confident that elements of all three options are present. But, as I said, she had her own set of struggles. The level of hate we have for a mother or father is directly related to the hopes they crushed, the affections they withheld, and the cruelties they administered.

When I think of Dolly's name and every pre-fourteen-year-old memory, I think of a woman who turned the title of 'Mom' into a bitter taste that I want to spit out of my mouth. I want to scream in her face, force her to look at the diseases she caused through the most robust magnifying glass I can find, so Dolly sees what she claims she cannot see.

Here are the words I would say to Dolly if I had the courage - Dear Dolly, I hate you. I hate your passive-aggressive nature. I hate that you somehow make everything about you. Your selfishness is unmatched. I wanted your love and attention and got snake venom in return. Instead, you shut yourself in your room, made exasperated sighs, rolled your eyes, glared, and were otherwise hellbent on being the most miserable mother a child could have. Perhaps not - the - most miserable, but you're pretty awful. Sure, convince yourself otherwise as you sit removed from the responsibilities of your former life. What was once a responsibility would now be an honor. You could be involved in the lives of your adult children. But, as we know, the commitment was what you hated. The thought of devoting your energies to anyone other than yourself was sickening to you. Have you ever been genuinely happy for someone else? Did you, even in its tiniest measurement, consider how your snooping, your snide remarks, your shaming, and your unwillingness to accept responsibility have led me, Bruno, and Josephine to resent you? Whatever narrative you have created in your head about being a friendly, gracious, gentle, or generous mother is 100% false. Imagine if you were kind.

We were starving for love and would have inhaled any morsel you shared with us. But, no, keep blaming Oscar as if you were not an adult, as if you did not secretly hope to run away with another man while you were still married. You did care about people; you were thoughtful, but only if it benefited you. I hated you for being mean to Josephine. You didn't protect her from the despicable things Dad did to her; you blamed her. Do you know that you started the entire anorexia situation with your comments about "stealing from the family" when we ate anything without permission?

Meanwhile, you were overweight, so who was squandering family resources? I hate you even more for how you treated Bruno and how you let your parents treat Bruno. You decided Bruce was Dad's carbon copy and told him as much. What was your reason for telling Bruno something so hurtful? To shame, silence, and manipulate behavior, like you always do. He knows you hate Dad, so you essentially told Bruno that you hated him when you made the comparison.

I do not recall one instance of you showing Bruno affection or approval. Not one. For crying out loud, you criticized him for wanting to be with his father when life in Junction City fell apart. He was all of 13! How was he to know the severity of what was going on? You responded with, *I'm jealous* when you noticed Dad's unhealthy affections for Josephine. You were a coward. A selfish coward. Bruno was a little boy when Sarah left, and he loved her with all of his heart. You could have comforted him, but chose otherwise. His father was ripped from him, too, in the aftermath of a horrific motorcycle accident.

You are so selfish, you cannot give Bruno the freedom to love his father without accusing him of being his father. Do you know how he apologizes for Dad's mistakes as if they were his own? Do you know how conflicted he is about what he would do to a man who violated his future daughters, as Dad violated us? He must reconcile that the father and friend he adores is the same man who caused significant harm. Surely you know something of abandonment. Surely you must know the desperate sadness that comes from losing a parent. Did you not know great pain? I guess you got what you wanted for years - to be left alone. You always wanted to be left alone with your emails and computer. But now, you think we owe you our appreciation and time. You probably feel justified in all you've done, or maybe you have conjured up new realities in a happy universe where you are the heroine, more like heroin.

As a kid, whenever you came into the room, I had the urge to pee out of fear. As an adult, I have developed nervous bowels. After every encounter with you, I spend the subsequent three days binge eating and emotionally falling apart. You were abusive and manipulative. I am sorry Dad was cruel to you. You did not deserve to be abused. But your relationship with him is not an excuse for how you treated me.

When your life gets hard, maybe you could make yourself the sign you made for Bruno, "Life is 10% of what happens to you and 90% of how you react." You wrote it on cardboard and put it in his room like the coward you are. He threw it away. You retrieved it. He didn't want your signs. He wanted your love. He desperately wanted you to like him, love him, praise him, and show happiness when he came home. He would have been loyal to you as he was to Dad if you had shown him any inkling of goodness. You could have been the source of so much good, so much healing. But you caused more pain than a house can hold. Let Dad's sins rest at his feet, but know you have plenty of your own. I am reconciled with how you treated me, but I loathe your name for you for how you treated Bruno.

After the sugar-induced rage, after the I-hate-yous and how-dare-yous have consumed the oxygen in the room, the source of the scorching heat reveals itself. Raw and bloody pieces hold the basic shape of the human heart; the outer edges of each piece look like scar tissue started to develop, only to be ripped through with what looks like a blunt and rusted knife. You are that knife.

***

Without pausing or looking into Dr. Meager's eyes, I close my journal and start talking.

"I was treated like a dog when I was little." I offer no transition. In my journal, I have written no essays about being treated like a dog.

"Do you mean that specifically or generally?" Bless this man for going along with my inability to slow down.

"Both." My jaw wants to move, to tell Dr. Meager everything, but the anticipation of pain holds my jaw shut. Dr. Meager waits. My need to fill the silence wins.

"The memory sounds like my father is the cause of me feeling like a dog. Of course, he was the one who said dog. But Dolly was the one who watched me writhe in pain without an ounce of compassion. I don't suggest my father is without fault; he had plenty, but given the option between fits of rage and calculated cruelty, I will take the first."

Dr. Meager begins writing on his notepad, *scritch scratch, scritch scratch.*

My brain takes my heart back to observe the first season of my history. I wish memories were erasable, not unlike Ebenezer Scrooge and his thoughts about the Ghost of Christmas Past. Unfortunately, Ebenezer had to sit with his conscience, and I sit with the deficiencies in others.

Taking a deep inhale, I begin, "This story happened before my name changed from Shanay to Tessa. One late summer afternoon, I heard Dad's work boots stomp into the dining room. My heartbeat began to race as my ears perked up to listen to the report of grievances Dolly recited to him.

"Shanay and Sadie were playing outside, and Shanay kept coming in with a bloody nose. I would wipe off her face, and it would happen all over again."

Sadie and I had been playing on the small hill in our backyard. She pushed me down every time I got to the top. The short journey down the dandelion and rock-covered slope aggravated my bloody nose. I did not bother trying to explain anything to Dolly. Trying to describe a situation to a person with their mind made up is a waste of time. I had hoped she would have forgotten about my bloody nose by the time Dad came home.

"Shanay!" His voice boomed down the hall like a military sergeant.

I scurried down the hall, being careful not to move so fast as to be accused of running. His deep-set eyes and prominent brow bone made him look intimidating without trying. That day, his face wore rage. Fear shot up my spine. I knew there was no recourse, no hope my stepmother would intervene. After all, Dolly was the one who ensured I would be punished by tattling on me.

"Explain to me," his voice, already loud, threatened to shake the house, "why you kept coming into the house with a bloody nose?"

I couldn't say anything. All I could do was pee my pants in fear. Anger turned into disgust once he noticed my wet pants and the puddle forming around my feet. I knew if I walked away, I would get in trouble for dragging my urine through the hallway. If I stood still, I would get in trouble for standing in my mess. I took too long weighing the options.

"Are you a dog?" He sneered at me. "Should we put you out in the backyard with a chain around your neck that says 'DOG' to let the neighbors know how disgusting you are?"

Like the woman she is, Dolly sat watching with as much feeling as a video recorder. Crying and feeling the sogginess of my shame, I hung my head in submission, waiting to be spanked or dragged by one arm and thrown into the shower. A couple of minutes passed, and no one moved or spoke.

"Go clean yourself off." Dad let me go, repulsed by himself or me, I do not know.

The bathroom was my refuge. I dug my nails into my arm to keep my sobs quiet. I escaped the worst of Dad's wrath already; I did not want to reignite it by letting him hear my weakness. How I ached to be held, to be soothed, and loved. I wanted a mother who loved me like the mothers I heard about in stories - a mother bear. But no mother bears were nearby. Sarah was somewhere else, fighting an unseen battle. By her absence, she was assuredly no better than her replacement.

My sobbing got louder after putting on my gray Snoopy sweatshirt and red sweatpants. I started pulling at my hair with my chubby fists, punishing myself for living. When I heard footsteps outside the door, I yanked harder. To my horror, but not surprise, the door handle turned. Dolly stuck her head and half of her body in the door.

"Shanay? What are you doing?" Her voice held the expected level of exasperation and irritation; her face reflected a lifetime of resentment and disappointment.

I said nothing, grateful for an empty bladder while maintaining a firm grip around wisps of unruly hairs. The hair I had already pulled out was strewn across the ground in an accusatory fashion. Dolly's eyes traveled from my face to the floor and back again. I wanted to die.

"Do you need some help with that?" Her face was somewhere between delight and self-loathing as if she loved inflicting harm but knew it was wrong.

I let go of my hair but didn't move my hand. With tears blurring my vision and falling down my cheeks, I further berated myself for being wrong, for making my parents hate me. I vowed to be a better daughter. I promised myself I would be obedient, keep everything clean, be quiet if I got hurt, and I would never, never, pee my pants again.

But the rules changed daily. What was tolerable one day was a grievous sin the next. I lived in fear of making mistakes and getting punished. My sleep was superficial and filled with nightmares. I had more accidents."

When the last words leave my lips, I stare at Dr. Meager in fear of punishment, disgust, or the soul-crushing opinion that I had no reason to be upset. Tears begin to form. I tried to summon the safety of anger to keep them at bay, but they fell down my cheeks in defiance. Crying is a character deficiency, Dad taught me. I didn't even cry at his funeral. All I did was pump my leg back and forth so fast I made the pew move.

Again, Dr. Meager was silent, but not in an "I do not know what to say" kind of way. So often, my love of words notwithstanding, there are no words to fill the hole exposed after pushing a moss and ivy-covered slab of concrete resistance and self-protection to the side. Words that follow moments of voluntary vulnerability are akin to sand in my eyes.

I move my attention to the Kleenex box sitting on the antiqued book stand next to me. Today, Dr. Meager chose a white box with what looked like pink pastel paint strokes. I bet white and pink remind him of an infant's frailty and dependence because his patients require the same level of attention. I don't know how many minutes pass, but enough panic begins to build that I can feel my heart pulsing in my temples and jaw.

"Tessa, why did your parents call you Shanay'?"

"Oh, I thought I told you last time. Shanay was my name until I was four or five, when Dolly adopted me and my older brother and sister. You know, after Sarah heard the Holy Ghost tell her that God wanted her to leave her children and start a new family with her new husband."

"Yes, yes, I remember that part of your account, but do not recall the reason Sarah initially chose the name 'Shanay.'"

"Oh. I see. Well, Sarah has two brothers, Shawn and Shane. Her family has French-Canadian ancestry. I guess she thought it sounded fancy. Listen, I can see my time is up, so I'll get out of here."

"You're okay to stay for a few extra minutes. My next appointment is not for half an hour." Again, he smiles warmly.

"No. Thank you. Not to be rude, but I don't have the emotional capital to handle any further conversation with you or anyone else right now. I need to leave. Now." My words are tight and choppy. I run out of his office and pass Darla before either can speak. I doubt I will ever go back.

The Love of Grandparents

Fun fact: Oscar and Sarah used a knife to get me out of Sarah's uterus a month early, as if I genuinely was a parasite or intruder. Don't panic. Dad did not perform a crude cesarean section. No, Sarah was tired of being pregnant. I was her third baby in three years; she was emotionally and physically exhausted, and asking Dad to break her water with a knife seemed like a viable solution. He obliged, and I was born weighing five pounds and, thankfully, without health complications. When I hear stories like this, I start to wonder how unhinged my decisions are, even if they seem reasonable to me.

Having a father with bizarre ideas seemed normal until I observed other fathers. For example, Dad once suggested burying our sinful media in the yard to show God we wanted to change. Another time, while we lived in Junction City, he brought home an enormous metal structure from work with the aid of a trailer. The structure was so tall you had to climb a ladder to get to the top. After placing the trailer at the bottom of our property, he invited the teenagers from church over for a Sunday evening of spiritual enlightenment. After everyone arrived, he climbed to the top of the structure in his blue bathrobe and pretended to be King Benjamin from the Book of Mormon. Dolly had even put a sign at the end of our driveway that said CTR Lane. (CTR stands for choose the right). I was mortified, while everyone else seemed to find him amusing and creative.

I know certain family members would like to take these stories and replace them with episodes of a popular TV sitcom, but I can't do it. I can tell myself and my family whatever I want, but the truth doesn't change. An eight-inch-long and ¾ inch deep laceration can be ignored, but it can't stitch itself together. The unchangeable source of so much anguish lies in the events between 2000 - 2002. I have tried multiple times to bring up the events during my appointments with various therapists. I test them with a drop of what I want to pour out, like hair dye on a test strand. But, something about their response, with all the compassion and empathy they can muster, makes me wish I hadn't said anything. Unfortunately, I didn't make it far enough with Dr. Meager to test him. And besides, I designed the test to fail.

My pain is mine, and I want to protect it - like a fragile ball of spun glass - red and gold, unmistakably and painstakingly made for demanding attention. Spun glass can only be made after the regular glass is heated to two thousand degrees. I think. Two thousand degrees. The year two thousand. Fascinating. I remember hoping for all the fears of Y2K to come to fruition. Instead, much to my chagrin, the power stayed on, the television kept blaring, and the phone line worked. Our family would have to trudge forward. But, had the world stopped, and resources become scarce, we would've been fine. Knerres work hard and don't complain; we would have survived feasting on the chips on Dad's shoulders. By clinging to known pain, I prevent further pain from unsuspecting sources. If I keep my heart to myself, no one can break it. If I keep my academic performance low, I won't be embarrassed when my best attempts fall short. If I don't write, my books won't get written, and no one will criticize me. If I keep myself slightly chubby, I can shut down my ambitions of athletic greatness. All my dreams can remain if I keep them to myself and let other people believe that mediocrity is all I can accomplish. Living small and scared only hurts me, I know. Other people don't care about my choices. What I am or am not doing, what I am or am not achieving, has no impact on anyone's life if I'm behind them. People like to be better than their peers; prettier, funnier, smarter, and more accomplished. I will oooh and ahhh and pretend like I could never do anything so remarkable as to have my name written on a degree or certificate. I did get an award once: The Most Inspirational Award.

In tenth grade, I joined the swim team because my legs and ankles hurt after cross-country season. The swim coach had been my dad's coach twenty years earlier. He saw my last name and assumed I would be as great an athlete as my father. Ha! After one flailing, beached whale attempt to complete a lap, the coach understood he was not working with a swimmer. Instead, he was working with a suffocating mass of blubber.

Nonetheless, I tried my best in the slow lane. I swam for ninety minutes during every practice with hardly a break. During intervals, we theoretically got a break between sets. I was so slow that I could never finish the interval within the allotted time, so I got no rest. During swim meets, I swam the 500-meter freestyle. I came in last but once and entertained everyone first with my belly flop into the water and second with my awkward flip turn. I still can't dive off the blocks. Or a diving board. Ducking my chin towards my chest is where I drew the line. A jump, or dive, requires a momentary loss of complete control. I am willing to take emotional plunges without a glimmer of concern for where I end up, dangerous or otherwise. But a variable-controlled dive into a pool that could not dry up or move to the left was too much. I had to look straight ahead to ensure I started the race without a painful slap into the water.

During the end-of-season banquet, an assistant coach called my name to come forward and claim the Most Inspirational Award. She praised me for coming to practice and working hard. Her kind words were code for, "Tessa is an awful swimmer. She has no idea what she is doing. But she keeps coming and trying again." I was not offended because I was an awful swimmer, and I don't mean that in a self-deprecating-I'm-actually-pretty-good sort of way.

For once, I had no emotional connection to my performance. My performance fell far below mediocre, and I didn't give it another thought, whereas, after a foot race, I made myself sick with ceaseless analyzing and chastisement. I forgot which stroke I was supposed to be doing during one swim meet as soon as I belly-flopped off the blocks. If I started with the wrong kick, I would get disqualified. Wanting to avoid disqualification, I allowed myself to start sinking to the bottom until I could see the other swimmers ahead of me and identify the proper kick. I laughed at myself until I climbed out of the pool. The swim team in the tenth grade was the only time I experienced the joy of doing something for the experience and not the outcome.

Pa believes I have potential. My charade does not fool him. On Fridays, he often asks me what I am learning and doing. I hold up my payday shopping bags full of clothes from clearance racks to our collective disappointment. Pretty outfits that will fit me when I lose ten pounds are just another way I shut myself down.

I am currently taking Writing 122 and Danish 101, but neither is interesting enough to report to Pa. The only notable take-home from class is the appearance of my writing professor. She looks like a giant blueberry with blue sweaters, blue polyester pants, blue necklaces, and blue eyes. When I am as old as her, I'll give up on fashion and wear shades of green, except olive green. Olive green makes me look like I am losing a long battle with tuberculosis. My writing professor's passion for blue reminds me of my beloved fifth-grade teacher. I cannot remember a day when she did not wear purple. I loved her, but not as much as my fourth-grade teacher, who made me feel intelligent and capable. Every kid should have a teacher like her.

I am glad to pay Granny and Pa $350 every month, or else guilt would ruin the pleasure of collecting pretty textiles. Thankfully, Granny also appreciates trends and sparkly adornments. She loves seeing what I bring home, though we have conflicting tastes. I like color and adventure, while Granny prefers a more classic wardrobe. Pa may think I spend too much money on clothing, but he enjoys watching me and Granny share special moments. In addition to admiring pretty things, we watch *Law and Order: SVU* or *NCIS* five nights a week. Pa usually makes us popcorn or gives us scoops of ice cream. Granny regularly leans over and says in a girlish whisper, "He treats me like a queen!"

Granny's Love

"Tessa?" Granny's inquiring voice startles me; I've been wrapped up in Man's Search for Meaning all morning, my second reading in a few months. When I'm home, Grammy checks on me in thirty-minute intervals if I'm in my bedroom. I prefer solitude on Saturday mornings, but her house doesn't offer that amenity.

"Yes, Granny?" Granny's drying a bowl with a rose-colored towel as if she does her dishes in the hallway every day.

Her green cotton pants and white V-neck embroidered with red flowers around the neckline make her look like a summer Christmas. Her poofy hair looks like a halo, and her delicate gold necklace lights up her face. Sometimes I think Grammy's face radiates light as if she has a candle behind her eyes. "Tomorrow is Sunday. Are you going to go to church?"

"No. I am not going to church. The Church is not for me." If she sees my scowl, she'll initiate the same merry-go-round conversation we've had thirty times. So, I pretend the ceiling is as fascinating as the Sistine Chapel. I briefly lived in this room six years ago, after Dad admitted himself to the psychiatric unit at Sacred Heart Hospital. Grammy has since updated the hideous orange shag carpet to an acceptable light blue. "Tessa, just try it. The singles ward starts at 10:00 at the Institute building next to the University. You have all these nice dresses to wear." She gestures towards my closet full of dresses and other pretty attire. I do love getting fancy, but I needn't subject myself to misery to do so.

"I know when it starts. You've told me about it every Saturday for the last five Saturdays."

"Well, I wasn't sure if you remembered. You really should go. I'm sure you will know some of the kids there. Since only single adults from ages 18-30 attend the Singles ward, you could make new friends."

"I'm sure I will know some people there, but that's hardly a reason to go to church. Isn't religion supposed to be about my relationship with God? I will go if I believe God wants me to be there."

"He won't tell you as long as you're not going. You have to go to know."

"I feel like I should know before I go. Sort of like getting an invitation to a party. You need the invitation in your hand to know the party thrower wants you to be there."

"God's sending you an invitation right now. You're just refusing to see it."

I close my eyes and clench my jaw before I throw out words like merciless knives. If anyone else were telling me such things, I would have gripped my book so hard that it turned into confetti. *Calm down, Tessa. Don't unfurl your anger on Granny. She loves you. The Church of Jesus Christ of Latter-day Saints makes her happy, and she wants you to love the Church because she thinks it will make you happy. Strike a deal - you go once, she drops the subject forever.*

"Alright, Granny. I will go to church tomorrow at 10:00, and only tomorrow at 10:00, if you agree to stop asking me to go." A boulder of regret instantly forms in my stomach.

"Wonderful! I know you'll have a good time." I've never seen Grammy so delighted with herself.

Stop. Turn back. Tell her you were joking or feign illness in the morning. Something! You can't walk into that building and talk to those people. Are you insane? If you're not insane now, you will be committable by the end of Sacrament meeting, and you know it. Good job, Tessa. Idiot.

Sleep failed me last night. If people drank soda pop full of apprehension instead of caffeine, no one would fall asleep at the wheel. I'll chat with the next food research and development scientist I see and give them my idea. It could make them billions. Granny and I stayed up late watching our usual mysteries. Every time the show made the end-of-scene sound, I thought of seven ways to break our agreement, but couldn't bear the thought of disappointment dampening Granny's smile.

So, here I am. Awake with regret and trepidation. The smell of trees shedding the heat of summer fills my nose. Leaves tired of the beating sun fall to the ground in relief while onlookers adore the colors of their death, including me. I want to run through the oranges, yellows, and reds as if I didn't hurt my ankle and wasn't twenty pounds overweight. Pa makes delicious food, and I eat my feelings. Was another outcome possible? Absolutely, but I lack self-discipline. Fat Tessa. Slow Tessa. Worthless Tessa.

Oh please. Get it together. Stop with the Edgar Allen Poe-ness and get dressed. In two hours, this is all over. No more church or talk about church. I may hate where I'm going, but I will look presentable while there. What does my closet have to offer? My choices have narrowed, as half of the dresses can't hide my gibbous - convex - bulging - gluttonous stomach. Of what's left, some are too low, others too short. Most are too colorful. What can I wear that is positively boring?

A maroon jersey-knit dress will have to do with its frilled V-neck, empire waist, and dainty matching buttons. I risk looking pregnant due to the empire waist, but the dress is loose. I'll take my chances. After an ocular evaluation in the mirror, I must improve my situation; I look like a walking nap. Hoop earrings and a big, curly, messy bun do the trick. I pull the soft adipose tissue around my chin up behind my ears. Five more pounds, and I can say goodbye to my jawline.

When I open the door, I can hear my grandparents in the kitchen, light-heartedly fussing at each other about dinner plans. Ten steps to the door, and I'll be out to the car before they can stop me and give me a pep talk. I would rather walk barefoot across a mile of freezing Legos than go to church. Seems less painful.

With my hand on the doorknob, I holler out, "Bye, Granny and Pa! See you after church."

"Tessa, you wait a minute." Dang it. Granny's standing in the kitchen doorway. "You have not had breakfast. Take some toast or yogurt." She diligently sees to my nutrition needs while Pa ensures my satisfied sweet tooth.

"I'm alright. I won't be gone long. I'll eat when I get home."

"It will only take a minute. I'll make you a piece of toast." Granny walks like she's the blue fairy from Sleeping Beauty. As I follow her into the kitchen, I take deep breaths, hiding my nerves as best I can.

"You'll have a good time; I know you will. The kids there are nice."

I want to say, "No, Granny. I will not have a good, lovely, delightful, pleasant, or enchanting time. My soul will be splintering into one hundred equally agonizing directions." But, instead, I smile, shift my weight from foot to foot, and fidget with my purse. My body and face give away the status of my emotional equilibrium every time, like devious traitors.

"Stand still, for goodness' sake. You're making me nervous." Her eyes twinkle with amusement as she hands me a piece of nine-grain toast with homemade strawberry freezer jam.

"Thanks, Granny. I'd better go so I can be on time." Pa taught me years ago that punctuality is a sign of respect; you're not entitled to steal other people's time.

"Slow down. You have plenty of time."

"Bye, I'll see you in a couple of hours."

"Aren't you staying for the entire block? Three hours?"

"Nope." I close the front door before I can hear another word.

***

I may not know north from south or left from right without considerable contemplation, or be able to give directions using street names, but I can get from point A to B using landmarks like bushes and mailboxes. "Take the street after the blue house with the silver mailbox, pass the building with red lettering, and the used bookstore will be in front of you. Kind of, not directly in front of you. It's to the right or the left. You'll know when you see it. There's a rhododendron bush near the entrance."

I want to steer my Honda Civic onto every side street I pass, trying to find a believable way to claim that I got lost. My grandparents know I don't have a sense of direction, and I can use ignorance to my advantage. But, no, I can't. I can't lie to Granny. So, instead, the toast goes uneaten, the autumn day unseen, and, evidently, self-preservation unheeded. I arrive at the Institute building in twenty minutes.

Rage and panic fill my chest. Nervous to furious without a step in between. The brick building of religion sticks out like a radish in a bouquet of roses. I can't go in. I can't. I will tell Granny that I can't do it. She'll understand. Wait, no, she won't. She doesn't know the darkness that lurks behind the suits and handshakes, the evils done in the name of the Holy Ghost and Priesthood. I want to throw up.

Blood drains from my face, and my hands begin to shake when I see familiar faces from middle and high school. *Here's hoping they don't recognize or remember me.* My whisperings only add noise to the warning shots firing off in my mind. Gritting my teeth, I step out of my car and put one foot in front of the other, my one worthwhile skill.

Run, Tessa, run. You are in danger. These people are not safe. They are devils who talk about Jesus. RUN! Like a war drum in my head, *RUN! RUN!* I can't run. I must stay. I told Granny I would attend church one time. I can handle an hour and ten minutes if it means she never asks me to go again. *RUN! RUN! Granny won't know if you tell a little lie - it wouldn't be a bad lie, just a white lie to make her feel good. What's wrong with making someone feel good?* Tears threaten to roll down my cheeks. Grammy may not know if I lied to her, but I would know, and I cannot disrespect my grandmother after all she has done for me.

It's 9:50. Church starts at 10:00. I'll take a fifteen-minute walk around campus to avoid conversations. Tardiness equates to disrespect, and if any institution deserves my disrespect, it's this Church. Besides, no one expects me, so I am not wasting anyone's investment. My heartbeat slows, and the beating drums fade as I walk in the opposite direction. But after seven minutes, I turn around.

Walking towards my fate as if stuck to a conveyor belt, I open the Institute door. *Why do you insist on making extreme statements? Sure, you'll gain seven pounds this week, cry uncontrollably, flail until you almost drown in the tidal wave of memories, and act as pathetic as you are, but how is that different than your usual behavior?* A full-blown internal bayonet battle begins. *You're fine. You're going for Granny, and you don't need to make this about you. You make everything about you. You're feelings, your moods. Your. Your. Your. Think of someone else for once.* Utter self-destruction is imminent. Oh well.

An audible sigh escapes my lips when I see an almost empty foyer. One man, who looks as scared as I am, sits in the corner. I half expect him to sprint out the front door as if he just realized that he's not chained to the chair. Chains. A Church of chains - handed out for free - they'll snake them through and around you, then promise you that you can be one of their puppets. Oh, they call it faith, repentance, redemption, whatever, but anyone with a functioning brain knows the hidden meaning behind those words. Prison. Manipulation. Abuse. *Tessa, perhaps your brain isn't functioning, seeing as you're here voluntarily.* I wonder what keeps that man sitting in the chair beneath the portrait of Christ. Maybe he made a promise to his granny, too.

The chapel doors are open, which means they haven't started blessing the Sacrament. Chapel doors always close for the Sacrament to prevent distractions from people walking in and out. I can hear a deep, even voice giving the announcements. Either the bishop or one of his two minions is talking. Why do bishops have to speak at all? Why does anyone need to know the bishop's name? Why can't they ensure the bills are paid, people fed, and shut their mouths? No one needs to understand what the Spirit tells a bishop because, if the Holy Ghost is real, and per their doctrine, the Holy Ghost can talk to people directly. Not that I ever want to hear from Him; He tells people to do irrational, paranoid, and psychotic things.

"By way of announcement, we will be holding a potluck this evening at 6:00. If you want, bring something to share. Otherwise, bring yourselves. We have plenty of food. Tomorrow night, we will have Family Home Evening here at the Institute building. This week we'll be playing board games." The man talking sounds as excited as a nurse explaining how to prepare for a colonoscopy.

"In preparation for the Sacrament, we will sing hymn number 188, *Thy Will, O Lord, Be Done*. Following the hymn, the priesthood will pass the Sacrament."

The pianist starts playing the music, slow, somber, and full of shameful memories; closed in a dark, cold, and empty church classroom, prohibited from sitting with my family in the Sacrament after making a mistake. I was eight. Sent to bed without food as punishment for falling asleep during church. I was four. Listened to my parents accuse me of seduction attempts before I knew what seduction meant. I was eleven. Experienced any kindness or affection after listening to talks on becoming like Christ. Never. Those talks always made things worse. *Why are you here? Go home. You don't need to sacrifice yourself for your Granny. She doesn't need to understand your decision to respect it.*

I know I'm inflicting harm. I do. However, I can minimize the damage if I let the words and memories roll over me. I'm a duck, a goose, a swan—water off my back. *You have a lot of problems, Tessa. A lot of problems. Mostly, you're an emotional masochist. Have fun without self-destructive life choices. Simpleton.*

The bishop and his counselors are sitting behind and to the right of the Sacrament table. According to my estimates based on unfounded hope, about five people will see me walk in and sit down. Though my discovery is inevitable, they can't send their minions after me if I leave during the closing hymn. I know how their schedule works. It's the same from here to New York, to Australia, and anywhere else in the world.

To clarify, the Church doesn't care about anyone as anything other than a number. They care about reporting satisfactory numbers to the Stake President, who passes statistics to the person above him, and so on. Then, they can all stand around, clapping each other on the backs and congratulating themselves for keeping all of Christ's sheep in the fold. I am sure church leadership is positively euphoric as they see how many souls are saved from Babylon - from the evils and temptations of this world. In reality, the Church has an entire hotel franchise, feasting and thriving on the forbidden city's uninhibited sins.

Their congregations are an excellent hideout for perverts, sociopaths, and psychopaths. When the magic words, *the Holy Ghost told me,* are all that's necessary to accept any and all behavior, the morally unhinged are sure to flock in abundance. Good people stay out of guilt and obligation. I can think of approximately three families who acted like their religion was a privilege and not a subservient sentence placed upon them out of accountability and responsibility.

I want to subscribe to a religion that teaches love, growth, and forgiveness in practice and not word only. I want to believe in God, Jesus Christ, and the Holy Ghost. Desperately, I do. Where is God? What is religion? A manufactured organization to categorize, ostracize, and manipulate? Civilizations have argued and warred over religion since the beginning of man. It seems like a waste of time and life if we don't need it. Never mind, I retract my statement. The obsession with theology has roots in control. Encourage the fear of incurring the wrath of the Almighty God, answer all questions with, "If you only have faith," and the job is done. No one asks. No one questions, and no one thinks for themselves. Brilliant plan.

"Do you want to come in? I need to close the door." A tall, wiry man with unkempt chestnut-brown hair looks at me as if he's repeated his question three times. He probably has.

"No. I don't, thank you. Sorry." While I sit in the foyer, I hum alone. After the song, the Sacrament prayers start. I laugh at the memory of a Sunday long ago when I learned where the source of the praying voice. Until I was nine, I was clueless and afraid to ask.

On the day of my discovery, I overheard a little blonde girl with bouncy pigtails whisper, loudly, to her dad, "Daddy, where do those words come from?"

I braced, waiting for her dad to forcefully carry her out by one arm with a harsh hiss of "Be reverent." Then, to soothe my nerves, I sang the words of a primary song, "Reverence is more than just quietly sitting, it's thinking of Father above," and telling myself that Heavenly Father doesn't hiss at His children. I feared for nothing. Instead of scolding the girls' curiosity, her father scooped her up and hugged her, "Do you see the table up there?"

"Uh-huh!" Her pigtails bounced with the beat of her rapidly nodding head.

"Well, how many boys break the bread when we sing the Sacrament hymn?"

"One, two! Two boys!" She squealed with the joy of knowing the correct answer.

"You're right. One of those boys kneels to say the prayer while speaking into a microphone underneath the table." He spoke so gently I couldn't keep my eyes closed and my head forward any longer. I didn't know parents talked to their kids with respect instead of disdain. I turned in time to see the dad look at his daughter with an emotion I could not name.

I guess the only funny part of the memory was how long it took me to figure out who was saying the Sacrament prayer. After the prayer ended, I glanced down the pew, looking at my father. Dad's face was permanently stuck with angry desperation and fear as if suffocated by the ashes of his dreams. I don't know for sure what his grand plans were or if he knew he could dream.

I got distracted staring at his arm, wondering why he had a raised scar on his right forearm when my scars were flat. After a few seconds, I felt his glare on my forehead and jerked my head forward, willing myself to sit still. I summoned my nine-year-old willpower to curtail the impulse to run my finger between the bricks on the wall—a crime of scandalous proportions. I knew not to swing my leg, manipulate my fingers, twiddle with my hair, or close my eyes. I had to be reverent, show respect, and set a good example. My parents acted as if everyone were looking at us all the time. Dumb. No one pays that much attention to anyone but themselves. I tried to obey the Ten Commandments and honor my father and mother, but they couldn't see me flick my tongue around on the roof of my mouth. I grinned with pleasure at my unseen rebellion.

Tessa, would you stop with the memory recall and go to the foyer? You told Grammy you would go, now get in there. If I were smart, I would stay in the lobby for the rest of the service and consider my obligation fulfilled. I need visual details to present to Grammy, so she knows I tried my hardest. Unfortunately, I've never been in this building, so I have no memory to dig through for imagery and metaphors.

Walking through the doorway, I can see the clear lines between the social clusters that form the congregation. How predictable. No better place to separate groups based on attractiveness, education, and income than at church. Their hypocrisy affords me the blessing of not sitting next to anyone, as they've left groups of unoccupied chairs that look like polka dots amidst the mass. *Keep your eyes down, Tessa. Only forty-five more minutes.*

"I am thankful for the opportunity to start our fast and testimony meeting by declaring witness of . . ."

Are you kidding me? You showed up for the fast and testimony meeting? You exceed your obtuseness every day. Congratulations. You're fat. Every first Sunday of the month is a fast and testimony meeting. Members are supposed to fast for two meals, donate the money they would have spent on food to the Church, and gather to testify of Christ. That's the ideal. What truly happens consists of a predictable rotation of the same twelve people droning on about complete nonsense while everyone else shifts uncomfortably in their seats. A few make a display of their admirable spirituality with their forced tears and expected explanations for walking up to the pulpit, "my heart was beating so fast I knew the Spirit was telling me I needed to come up here." Who will be the first brave soul today?

A guy with a familiar face stands up, six feet, brown hair, big though not unattractive nose. He looks sad rather than moved by a higher power.

"The last month has been awful."

Uh oh. Let the confessions and awkwardness begin.

"Last week, my fiancé,' he pauses to calm his shaking voice, 'the woman I was going to marry sta . ." he attempts to gain composure.

Why did he walk up there in the first place? Doesn't he have friends he can talk with? I support authenticity, but this is embarrassing. I want to hide my head in my dress until he stops talking. However, the cool kids have stopped preening, so there must be some interesting backstory.

"My fiancé stabbed me in the back." Faint gasps ripple through the crowd. I feel sad for him.

"I loved her, still love her. I don't know when I'll start dating again." His eyes suddenly dry up as he looks from woman to woman, trying to make eye contact.

My sympathy burns up. Mr. Overshare is using the pulpit as a dating service. Gross. For the next twenty minutes of the service, I sit with my arms folded tightly, alternating my crossed legs, and rolling my eyes with disgust. Soon, I can only hear my heart pounding in my head and can see nothing more than what's in front of me. Dark spots cloud my peripheral vision. I get the sensation that putting my head in a head vice would feel like a relaxing massage in comparison. *Sorry, Granny. I can't do this anymore. I tried.*

Stepping outside feels like surfacing after getting trapped in the wake of a boat, sputtering, coughing, shaking hands, and gasping for breath. That meeting can only be described as a cruel session of desensitizing therapy. Storm clouds have rolled in, and the raindrops wash down my face, mixing with my tears. Sparks of childhood trauma are now ablaze. I can't go home. I can't go anywhere. Or, more accurately, I can't go to anyone who feels like home. So, I guess I'll take a Sunday drive with loneliness and see where I end up.

Unsurprisingly, I end up at my favorite locally-owned coffee shop, ordering a large mocha. The smell of coffee, chocolate, and milk is like Xanax. Good thing, too, because I recently ran out of my prescription. I can get a refill if I go back to Dr. Meager's office, which I don't want to do. If one more person talks to me like I'm the disease and they are the cure, I'll internally combust.

Mochas don't ask questions or give automated answers. Neither does chocolate. Dark chocolate is especially quiet. The expensive kind is silent. When I look down, my mocha is gone, and I don't recall drinking it. The relentless pounding in my head hijacks all other receptors. I need more. More chocolate. More sugar. Anything to stop the madness. Have you ever watched yourself go mad?

Trader Joe's isn't too far away. They have my preferred numbing agent, dark chocolate peanut butter cups. Unfortunately, their side effects include feeling sick to my stomach, tired, moody, foggy, puffy fingers, and weight gain if eaten over a long time. But, right now, I don't care. I'll take the side effects if it means my atoms will stop ripping my soul to shreds. Even if it means I will want to claw my reflection out of the mirror.

As I walk into the quaint store with the swirly handwritten price tags and deal-of-the-day chalkboards, I vacillate between giddy and calm. I rush through the chocolate aisle and panic-buy a one-pound 72% cocoa bar, peanut butter cups, chocolate-covered fruit, chocolate truffles, and dark chocolate-covered marshmallows. I'm almost twitching while the slowest cashier known to man begins adding up my items. *Keep smiling politely, Tessa. No need to be rude.*

"Looks like you got all the important stuff." He's a portly gentleman with an almost stylish haircut and a sad yet kind smile. I can use a smile.

"Yes, yes. I do love chocolate." Watching him look over my excess brings guilt. I shift back on my heels and look out the sliding doors, willing the exchange to be over as soon as possible by digging my nails into my forearm that I'm holding behind my bike.

"Me, too. We all use something." He's looking in the same direction I am with weary and understanding eyes. He knows why I am buying chocolate. I know he does.

"Thank you so much!" I give him the most genuine smile I can muster, one pained soul acknowledging another. He gave me kindness when he was searching for it himself.

I drive to an empty park before I begin to feed, like an animal. Fifteen minutes later, I've eaten ½ the peanut butter cups, a row of the 72% chocolate bar, and at least ⅓ of the chocolate-covered fruit. There are only four chocolate-covered marshmallows left. Chocolate has fallen down my dress and covers my fingertips. I'm disgusting. But the pounding stopped, and my breathing slowed. I have peripheral vision once more. I'm ready to go home, prepared to explain to Grammy why I will never go back to church. I'll be cranky enough by the time I get there; she'll see my threshold for discussion used up and let me sleep off my sugar binge all afternoon.

Thankfully, the vertical shades are drawn when I pull in. They must be off visiting a friend or still at church. I can't remember if they have meetings to attend. Whatever the case, I can hide without explanation. How can I force myself to run seven miles but find that traversing the distance from my car to my bed is nearly impossible? I want to throw away my self-prescribed medication. *You can't. You need it. Now, go to bed and enjoy a long afternoon sugar coma. You deserve it.* Yes, sleep—my second drug of choice.

The Source

The Third Essay

"Come on in, Tessa. I am happy to see you again," says Dr. Meager.

"And might I add surprised? You give yourself away, good doctor; your smile stretched back farther than usual."

"Yes, your last visit was a year ago, and it ended abruptly."

"Yes, it did; thank you for pointing that out. But, I'm back now, though I cannot say for how long."

"How have you been?" he asks.

"Well, fine, I started going back to church again, and I hate it," I say as I flop onto the red couch as if it's sitting in my living room.

"Why are you going if you hate church?"

"It's complicated. I feel like I should be there while simultaneously feeling like I'm knowingly walking into the same burning building that killed my family, as if I'm on a suicide mission."

"Why do you feel like you should be at church?" he asks while handing me a bottle of water. He must have taken a professional development class that suggested handing patients a bottle of water to help them feel more comfortable.

"Thanks for the water. I don't feel obligated to go as if my Granny is guilting me into going. I feel like God wants me to be there." Looks like Dr. Meager got himself a shiny pair of black wingtip shoes.

"Does your granny go to church?

I nod, "Her entire life."

"But you don't go for her sake?"

"When I went the first time, about a year ago, I did. I told Granny I would go once if she stopped asking me about going. I went, had a panic attack, felt like dying as memories from the past accosted me like water erupting from a fire hydrant, binged on chocolate until I felt like throwing up, and fell into a sugar-induced coma for the rest of the day."

"And you went back after that?"

"Yes. I did. I'm still going. Every Sunday." I'm embarrassed as if I'm admitting to drinking milk out of the milk carton in someone else's house.

"That doesn't sound like healthy behavior, Tessa."

"You're right. It doesn't. But I keep going," I give Dr. Meager a wry smile.

"Interesting. May I be frank?"

"As long as you're not Peter," he gives me a smirk and a head shake, which makes me happy because that's the extent of the reactions I get from my brother, Bruno, when I periodically blurt out the most astonishing thing I can imagine. Bruno got tired of my game thirteen years ago, but I still play.

"You sound internally conflicted to the point of self-destruction. That concerns me."

"Concern, bother, worry, troubles, doodle-dah, kerfuffle, malarky barky. Do you like my shoes? They're not as fancy as yours, but they have a bow. Cute, huh? Have you ever thought about walking on tiptoe from one star to the next, as if you're bigger than the universe, covering bazillions of miles with a dainty step? In my imaginations, I am barefoot, and my hair flows down my back like a horse's mane in the wind. A wild, unbreakable horse in a tornado."

Dr. Meager leans back, the twinkle gone from his eye, replaced by the look people get when they recognize my instability. Happiness gone.

"Tessa, can you ple…"

"Stop. Don't. I'm leaving," a sob forms in my throat as I stand up.

"Please stay. I want you to stay. Would you mind telling me why you don't want to go to church?" his eyes have a pleading quality to them, and his question just relieved a compression valve. The compression valve that covers my mouth when my opinions are begging for freedom. The adrenaline surge recedes, and I sit down.

"Well, I did bring my book of essays. Let me read the one titled Junction City, Oregon - Where Families Go to Die."

"I like that idea, Dr. Meager leans forward once more, but his concern still stares at me, mocking, 'Please, whenever you're ready. May I interrupt if I have questions?"

"Go ahead. Ask away. Here we go, reading some of the worst memories of my life."

***

Juction City, Oregon – Where Families Go to Die

I have a recurring dream of unsuccessfully running upstream. I'm stuck no matter how hard I pump my arms and lift my feet. When I try to yell for help, I can't hear my voice. A swell of water comes around the river bend like a tsunami. I try to shout louder; my knees won't bend. Freezing water crashes on me, filling my mouth with millions of tiny needle pricks. I can't speak, but I'm still standing.

Often, I worry that I made up our familial trauma and implosion. But then, I remember that Child Protective Services, courtrooms, a restraining order, the psychiatric unit of Sacred Heart Hospital, and suicidal ideations for more than one of us were involved. So sure, we were okay if okay means staying six feet above the ground.

If leaders of The Church of Jesus Christ of Latter-day Saints had been Christlike in their dealings with people who commit vile sins, so much heartache could have been avoided. Do you know what it feels like to have your faith used against you? The Church is a big fan of mitigating the consequences of the sinner at the victim's expense in the name of forgiveness.

My father was protected and defended when he did horrible things. We were told that we needed to forgive him if we wanted forgiveness. If we, the kids, could be more forgiving, everything would be fine. Forgiveness equated to letting him back into our lives as if nothing had happened. Forgiveness always includes allowing the perpetrator to go their merry way because we wouldn't want them to feel bad. If they feel bad, we must be doing something wrong.

My family, generationally speaking, was taught this version of forgiveness, and the destruction doesn't stop. To anyone who suggests that I have more forgiving to do, that everything would be better if I could just soften my heart, please, Shut Up. You have no idea. You do not get to tell me how to feel. I realize that's a tradition in this Church. We protect the adults who choose poorly, who abandon and abuse their children, either physically or emotionally. Generations have told each other to be quiet, to let the predators keep doing what they are doing. At what cost? The predators are not the ones wringing their hands in despair or wishing for death when the mental anguish of trauma and victimization wages an internal war.

Let me see if I can simplify the unnecessarily complicated requests made to victims of predators and abusers, "Why can't you carry their sins on your shoulders? Why are you so stubborn? Do you want to be the one who takes away their freedom? Are you the one who wants to put the shackles on their wrists? How could you be so heartless? Oh, we see we have made you upset. There, there, we know you don't want to cause harm; it's not in your nature. You're too nice. So, stop whining and be a good girl. Heave their bags of transgression on your shoulders and help them out. Nothing would have happened if you weren't you. You should have been more like her. ('Her' is a code word for a magical girl who enjoys abuse and cannot be named, or otherwise described.)

Tell you what, we'll make a deal; you can stop hauling around their garbage when the burden gets so heavy it crushes you. Once that happens, you will only have yourself to blame for your weakness since you're too lazy to exercise your spiritual muscles. Oh, and we will still use your mangled carcass as a target if we need to redirect any misunderstandings. We are sure you have told other people of your misperceptions and given them a false representation of the Church. You're rather disloyal. You really should read your scriptures more. If you do, you can become as righteous as we are."

Here's a novel idea: Predators and abusers SHOULD suffer the consequences of their decisions. We are doing no one any favors by mitigating the consequences of their choices. Their conscience should hound them relentlessly. They should look in the mirror and hate everything about themselves. If their offense deserves prison, they should go. Should, should, should. Too late, too late, too late.

***

"What do you think is the motivation behind your church protecting predators and blaming victims?" asks Dr. Meager.

"I believe people don't want the Church to look bad. They don't want people to associate evil with the name of Jesus Christ. However, by protecting perpetrators, that's exactly what they are doing. I realize it's the people in the Church, and not Church policy, to protect predators and blame victims."

I keep going to church because the pure doctrine, the gospel of Jesus Christ, is simple - faith in the Lord, repentance, willing obedience to God, and the making and keeping of sacred ordinances and covenants that allow us to return home to our Heavenly Parents.

Six months or so, while I was deciding if God expected me to return to church week after week, I recognized that I had a choice. I either needed to go to Church operating under the hope that someday I would experience the joy and love of which Jesus promises, or stop."

"But, Tessa, if God loves you, why would He want you to knowingly walk into a traumatic experience week after week?"

"I don't know. The rest of what I have written is kind of long. Do we have enough time to read it?"

"Yes, we do. You're my last patient of the day, and it's only 3:30. Please, take your time."

**

Before moving to Junction City, Dad considered taking a job in Des Moines, Iowa. He said the Spirit told him we should stay, which I now find conveniently suspicious. But I could be wrong. After all, the Spirit told Sarah to leave me, her daughter, Abraham to sacrifice Isaac, and Nephi to cut off Laban's head.

Laban was a man in the Book of Mormon, an evil leader who had sacred records. Nephi and his family wanted the records and tried to trade their wealth for them. Laban said no and ordered their arrest. They fled. Nephi went back, found Laban drunk and unconscious, and God commanded Nephi to cut off Laban's head because "It is better that one man should perish than that a nation should dwindle and perish in unbelief.[6]"

The first time we drove to Turnbow Lane to look at the four-acre property, I thought it was perfectly romantic. The sunshine of late spring wore rose-colored glasses to dim the memory of the long and gloomy winter, and the countryside looked like something magical was happening. I imagined running freely through the grass fields with a daisy crown on my head, wading barefoot in the stream that cuts through the property, swinging in the tire swing that hung from the enormous oak tree, and enjoying a scrumptious apple in the boughs of one of the two apple trees. The old house was surrounded by a porch, though it looked so haphazardly constructed, I dare not call it a wrap-around porch. It was the connection path between the house and the detached garage.

---

[6] 1 Nephi 4:13

Above the garage was a room so big I could have done three cartwheels across the floor. Maybe more. Dad promised Josephine, Sadie, and me that we could occupy the space since the house had only three small bedrooms, all barely large enough for two twin-sized beds. When I threw open the single-paned door to my freedom, I instantly fell in love with the deep teal carpet and white handrail alongside the few stairs leading from the entrance to the room. I thought the room would be my sanctuary, away from Dolly's resentful eyes and Dad's turbulent moods. In that instant, I wanted to move as much as anyone else. I didn't care about attending a new congregation or a new school. Through the hopes of the unknown and the ignorant certainty that a new situation is a better situation, I couldn't recognize the freedom I would lose because I didn't think I had any to take. Most freedoms are imperceptible until they are gone. Few liberties are regained without a war that starts with intellects, followed by wills and ends with death. No one wins. My experience followed a similar pattern.

After Dad and Dolly made an offer to buy the house, we prayed the owners would accept. Dolly was excited. She usually made mouth-watering treats when she was in a good mood. Our wait did not last long; our offer was accepted. For one moment, and perhaps the only one of its kind, we all smiled. In retrospect, I don't know if Josephine's excitement was genuine. Unlike me, Josephine doesn't cover her body with her emotions like she just careened down a steep water slide, flowing with every color of paint known to man. She lives on the inside, intrinsically motivated, elusive, and immovable.

We first attended the Junction City Ward on July 5, 1998. Three teenage boys from that ward had died the night before in a tragic accident. One survived. Another teenage boy in that same ward had also passed away several years back. The air in the building was full of heartache. I wanted to leave. Arriving on such an awful day felt like we were demanding attention when we had no right to be there.

A man from our previous ward spoke during the sacrament meeting to compound our uncomfortable arrival. The man was a handsome, intellectual doctor who usually used a visual aid and complex language that put half of the congregation to sleep. Not me. I looked forward to his talks. The wise words and layered meanings delighted me. In my mind, I practiced adopting some of his words into my working vocabulary. Now and then, I discover that what I thought the word meant and what it actually means are two different things.

Unbeknownst to me, the doctor was a big fan of my father. He told the members of the Junction City congregation how wonderful Dad was and how blessed they were to have one of the "finest families" he knew to move into their area. Through a sideways glance, I could see Dad's chest swell with pride. He threw his shoulders back and sat as tall as he could without stretching his neck. Dolly was expressionless. We were not a fine family. We were a patchworked lie and the awkward center of attention.

I started sixth grade at Oaklea Middle School. I had expected Oaklea Middle School to be as wonderful as Coburg Elementary - a haven of learning and joy where the kids were generally kind, and the teachers were angels without wings. But, within days, I understood that Coburg Elementary's loving and supportive community was gone. Where I once felt like I was unique, special, and smart, I felt nameless and unimportant. No more haven. No more escape. No one left to believe in me. I have yet to properly work through the grieving process of that loss.

The room above the garage, the room I had hoped would be a haven for Josephine, Sadie, and me, was a short-lived reality. Dad and Dolly didn't like us to have privacy because we were "bad-mouthing" them. (I hate the term "bad-mouthing," along with "as a family," and "Mom.") Dolly liked to stand outside the door and eavesdrop quietly. I discovered her snooping tendencies when we lived in Coburg. More than once, I saw her feet through the crack under my bedroom door. When I saw them, I would start saying everything she wanted to hear or cease talking entirely. Lamentably, my spoken thoughts were enough to end our time in that big, beautiful room. Dad and Dolly tried to control not only what we did but what we thought and how we thought. They were stalwart members of Orwell's Thought Police.

Parental fear and paranoia notwithstanding, in time, there was a practical reason for moving out of the beautiful room above the garage: a wasp infestation. Dad noticed an inordinate number of wasps flying around the garage. When he pulled off part of the exterior siding, he revealed a wasp's nest that ran almost the full height of the wall. Hundreds of black and yellow striped wasps - I don't know if they were paper wasps or yellowjackets - with their alien eyes and needle-like stingers, swarmed around their nest with aggressive buzzing. (I didn't realize buzzing could sound aggressive until that day).

Before we knew of the wasp's darling abode in the side of the wall, I had been stung right between the eyes as I was walking out the back door. I grabbed the wasp and crushed it between my fingers when I felt the sting. The skin around my eyes swelled so badly I was almost unrecognizable for a few days.

Dad took the extermination of the wasps into his hands. He sent us inside, covered his face, hands, and body as much as he could, and sprayed the nest with poison. I watched as some wasps fled, some fell, and some went straight towards Dad. Thankfully, Dad's work coveralls were thick and his boots heavy. But some of those demonic pests still managed their way into his pants and gave him a venomous sting. When Dad finished the job, he came in and took a shower. He never complained, but I could see red and swollen wasp stings on his calves. Dad's pain tolerance was impressive. One time, he dropped a piece of hot metal down his work boots and sustained a third-degree burn. He didn't complain about the burn, either.

So, with my dream of the room above-the-garage laid to rest, the seven of us crammed into the house. Josephine, Sadie, and I took the downstairs bedroom, Emerson took the hall closet, and Bruno took the second upstairs bedroom. Going outside was the only escape. Our first winter was not terrible because we lived in the honeymoon period that follows the hope of escaping ourselves by changing locations. We had electric heating, but Dad insisted we kids take turns fueling the fire stove during the night. So, when my turn came, it was not uncommon for us to wake up to a frigid house; the temperature finally matched the mood.

I tried to keep the fire going, but was inexperienced with stoking a fire and exhausted from waking up in the middle of the night. Often, the fire was nearly out by the time I woke up, and I didn't know how to revive it. I would throw a couple of logs on top of the embers, add some paper on top of the logs, and shut the fire stove door. Every so often, one of us would accidentally close the fire stove flue, and smoke would fill the front room. Dad was pretty patient with us when we disrupted the heat flow. Eventually, Dad either woke up to take care of the fire himself or relented and turned on the electrical heating. Either way, our turns attending the midnight fire came to an end.

The honeymoon period was over and forgotten by February on the day I started my period. I had a vague understanding of what was going on thanks to my fourth and fifth-grade health classes. I apprised Dolly of my situation, afraid of what she would say due to a previous experience with my changing body.

When I was in fifth grade, with unsuccessfully repressed irritation, Dolly asked me if I had a bra. I was confused by the question for three reasons. First, I did not know I needed one because I did not realize breasts grow gradually rather than materialize instantly. Second, I did not understand why she was asking a question that I felt she should have already known the answer to. In addition, I did not have money or access to a store.

Dolly's irritation with my bra needs seemed to increase as we made a family trip to the Shopko on Coburg Road. The drive was a long, molasses-esque ten minutes. She led me to where the training bras hung and pointed to those that fell within the budget. I settled on a strip of elastic with two white and flimsy triangles. I felt guilty handing her my choice because I knew we did not have extra money, and I could do nothing to prevent the cost.

After telling Dolly of my menstruation cycle's beginnings, I held my breath and waited for another triangle bra response. To my surprise, Dolly responded with kindness. She showed me where she kept pads, explaining the need to use pads for my first couple of cycles. I nodded my head, hoping she would keep talking to me with gentle understanding, nearly convincing me I had simply misunderstood her for the past nine years. She encouraged me to take two showers a day if I needed to, citing the messiness of menstruation. Such an offer was pure generosity as Dad limited showers to three minutes per person per day. For the first time, Dolly gave me verbal permission to do something other than what Dad commanded.

Then Dad came home, and my bubble of hope popped. He entered through the back door like he always did with his heavy steel-toe booted feet and greasy coveralls from a day of working as a steel fabricator. The smell of steel is somewhere between charcoal and gasoline. I was standing in the kitchen, talking to Dolly, thinking we were going to start the mother-daughter relationship I longed for, when she turned to him and said, "We have another woman in the house." I instantly felt sick.

Whether the creepiness in the house had gone unnoticed by me up until this point, or if I initiated it, I don't know. Regardless of the answer, I felt sexualized by both of my parents from that day forward. Dad and Dolly analyzed my clothes for fit and suggestiveness. Dolly found out I liked how I looked in one of my two pairs of jeans. She immediately prohibited me from wearing my preferred pair of jeans more than once per week. Upon discovering my preference for a blue athletic sweatshirt, she applied the same once-per-week rule.

Josephine also experienced severe sexualization. She had purchased two soft, long-sleeved V-neck shirts; one was red with thin gold and green stripes, and one was solid gray. The V-neck on both shirts was modest, only one inch below her collarbone. Dad and Dolly might as well have called her a harlot for all the accusations they made. "Why are you trying to show off your body? Would you stand in the presence of the prophet wearing that? Your vanity is sinful." Dolly went beyond telling Josephine to hide her body; she told her to hide who she was; stop smiling so big and laughing so loud, stop being so flirtatious, stop shining, stop, stop, stop. If we had lived during the

Salem Witch Trials, Dolly would have accused Josephine of witchcraft and watched with pleasure as Josephine burned at the stake.

We had tests to pass to ensure we did not expose too much skin. An acceptable hem had to touch the ground while kneeling. For a shirt to pass inspection, we had to raise our arms above our heads and bend in every direction without revealing any midriff. Dad administered the test in our bedroom while he sat on Josephine's bed. Controlling me and Josephine became their obsession. I don't recall Sadie being held against the same scrutiny, but that doesn't mean it didn't happen. If we looked in the direction of the nineteen and twenty-year-old missionaries, we were accused of trying to seduce them. When we thought our situation was as bad as it could get, the day of pink frosting came. Dolly discovered that Josephine had taken a fingerful of frosting from a bowl in the fridge. In her usual way, she accused Josephine of being a selfish thief because eating anything without permission was considered "stealing from the family." With that repeated accusation hanging in the air, Josephine decided she was done being lorded over and stopped eating. If she were a selfish thief for eating, she would not eat at all.

What punishment could Dolly and Dad dole out for food consumption refusal? More withholding of affection? Doubtful, Dolly's eyes could not be duller. Forbidding time spent with friends outside of school? We could only socialize with kids outside of school at church or a church activity. Oh, and by the way, church activities are no guarantee of above-board behavior. A church door does not stop the vapors of teenage hunger.

Josephine was well-liked among kids at school and church. She was pretty, with a welcoming smile and endearing laugh. Her straight, light brown hair was generally cut at shoulder length, give or take a couple of inches in either direction, feminizing her square jaw. Her even-tempered and adaptive nature made her a people magnet. A traumatic early childhood made her nurturing, like a little mother putting on a brave face. Now, she was a brave little mother starving herself.

Josephine did not have much of an adipose tissue supply to start with, which made her weight loss noticeable. So, with the best of intentions and suspicion of doctors, Dad found a book on severe and sudden weight loss, or anorexia, as western medicine understands the condition. An assumed hallmark of anorexia is the fear of getting fat and the presence of body dysmorphia, or an inaccurate perception of one's body.

Once he considered himself sufficiently trained as an anorexia specialist, Dad appointed himself as the sole member of the medical staff responsible for treating Josephine's condition. After his thorough research, he formulated a reasonable treatment plan. He would spoon-feed Josephine ice cream in the evening while she sat on his lap and sent Dolly to the high school during lunch. Josephine had orders to meet Dolly in the car, where Dolly would watch her eat lunch and ensure she avoided unnecessary physical exertion.

Their efforts didn't work. Josephine kept losing weight. Can you imagine sitting in a car, alone, with a woman who claimed the title of Mother but treated you with contempt? Dolly often looked through the garbage to see if Josephine had thrown food away. If she found any, she instantly took to berating Josephine for dishonesty by asking condescending questions and looking at her with the same malevolent eyes I saw when I was three years old, standing in the bathroom and pulling out my hair. Dolly's behavior made her seem obsessed with finding opportunities to punish Josephine for resisting parental authority.

Because Josephine was not allowed to run at school, she tried running on Turnbow Lane. Dad and Dolly allowed this for a few weeks until they decided she should not be allowed on such a long leash. Determined to keep running, Josephine started taking laps around our four acres. At the end of one cold, wet, and muddy run, Josephine came into the house to hear Dolly make one of her typical snide remarks, "I do not know why you bother running when you run so slow. It's not like you are doing anything out there."

I looked from Josephine's face to Dolly's, convinced this was the breaking point where Josephine would make an equally caustic remark - words so hurtful they would wound Dolly's soul. Indeed, how I hoped she would. I wanted to see Dolly's face fall. I wanted to watch her feel the pain of being treated like a cluster of putrid blisters. My hopes came to not. Josephine said nothing. The next day, she left her uneaten banana at the top of the garbage can, no digging required, and ran twice as long as usual.

While Dolly's passive-aggressive conduct increased in frequency and severity, Dad's jagged edges seemed to be smoothing out. He spent a lot of time talking with Josephine instead of talking to her. I was confused by the phenomenon taking place. I never saw Dad sit and talk while smiling with my siblings. True, Dad and Bruno spent quality time together while working on motorcycles, but their hands were busy with a task that could serve as a distraction if they ran out of discussion-worthy ideas.

More bewildering changes started coming about. Instead of hiding when Dad got home, Josephine's eyes got brighter. Soon, she started running out to welcome him home. I was too young to articulate the sensation of dread building in my stomach, but I knew something was not right.

One Sunday morning, as we were driving to church (so many events occurred while driving to or from church), Dad asked if we betrayed him and Dolly by telling our friends or youth leaders terrible things about them. He told us we would not get in trouble for our answers. So, as usual, we took turns answering his question. I confirmed that I did not tell my friends or youth leaders terrible things about either of them; I simply recounted noteworthy instances of our interactions. Whatever assumptions my friends or leaders made were theirs. I had nothing to do with their interpretations of events other than telling them in the first place. I suppose my parents would have preferred a gag order or issued a mandatory lip stitching requirement.

To say anything about a family member, however accurate it may be, that paints them in a pallid light and is akin to betrayal.

Family members are loyal to each other. I later learned that they keep each other's secrets, no matter how dark.

Except for Bruno. With his self-appointed role as informant extraordinaire, Bruno gleefully reported any infraction. He vigilantly observed the boys we talked to, how close we stood to them, whether we laughed or flirted, in sum the weight of the shame we, by nature of being women, brought down on the family. While I often wrote of love in my journal, I was too shy to do much else. Josephine, however, was one to give hugs. She soon attracted the affections of a sixteen-year-old boy in our ward. At some point, they started exchanging letters. I do not know how Dad found out, but when he did, there were no more letters. Except one.

Josephine kept one letter in the pocket of her navy, light blue, and white rain jacket after relinquishing the others to Dad's custody. She never let me read it, I did not press the matter, but I esteemed her as a hero. Here she was, white-knuckling her autonomy, no longer caring about the consequences.

The thinner Josephine got, the gentler the attention Dad gave her. Within a few months, she had lost so much weight that she started getting bruises on her back from sitting in the chairs at school. Her face started to grow fuzzy white hair, hardly detectable unless she stood in direct sunlight. Dad said the white fuzz was her body trying to keep itself warm.

Around this time, Josephine and Dad's relationship made a devastating shift. Dad seemed to get jealous if we, mostly Josephine, received male attention. Dad would seethe with anger and tell us that we needed to be more obedient. We were vain, he said, and immodest because we spent too much time in the bathroom doing our hair. Therefore, he limited the time we could use the hairdryer and curling iron. Dolly insisted that this new regulation would reduce the heating bill. Josephine and I were further instructed to wear no more than one ring on each hand or one necklace. Additional fanciness would put us in danger of hell. Dad cited the scriptures to prove his point.

"Moreover, the Lord saith: Because the daughters of Zion are haughty and walk with stretched-forth necks and wanton eyes, walking and mincing as they go, and making a tinkling with their feet—Therefore the Lord will smite with a scab the crown of the head of the daughters of Zion, and the Lord will discover their secret parts. In that day the Lord will take away the bravery of their tinkling ornaments, and cauls, and round tires like the moon; The chains and the bracelets, and the mufflers; The bonnets, and the ornaments of the legs, and the headbands, and the tablets, and the ear-rings; The rings, and nose jewels; The changeable suits of apparel, and the mantles, and the wimples, and the crisping-pins; The glasses, and the fine linen, and hoods, and the veils. And it shall come to pass, instead of sweet smell there shall be stink; and instead of a girdle, a rent; and instead of well set hair, baldness; and instead of a stomacher, a girding of sackcloth; burning instead of beauty.[7]"

The Lord didn't want to smite us, Dad explained, which is why He put the warning in the scriptures. God wanted to save us from ourselves, and he, Dad, was in charge of making sure that God got what He wanted. So, I resolved to repent of my sins, try harder, and be better. "Honor thy father and mother," the Ten Commandments say. I knew I didn't honor either of them, which made me an ungrateful and sin-filled child of God. How could I talk to God if I were deliberately disobedient?

Wanting to keep a closer eye on us, Dad decided that Josephine, Sadie, and I should switch bedrooms with Bruno. His decision was absurd because the bedroom we were moving into had an A-frame ceiling, making the middle floor the only place where we could stand up straight, a space big enough for three cats or one

---

[7] 2 Nephi 13:16-24

human, no more. My parents thought the room was too small for my brothers to share; Emerson lived in the closet downstairs as an alternative to sharing the space with Bruno. If the room was too small for two boys, how was it big enough for three girls? What did we know? We were only girls.

One day, I was wearing an old skirt of Josephine's, a black and white checkered A-line skirt that was in no danger of rising above my knee cap. As I was bounding up the stairs, Dolly chastised me for my brazen choice of attire, "I don't want to see this much," she held up her fingers to indicate several inches, "of the back of my daughter's thigh!" I now think that one possible solution may have included avoiding looking up my skirt when I walked up the stairs. But that's not what I thought then. When it happened, I felt ashamed. I had failed her once again and told myself that I was no better than a haughty or arrogant daughter of Zion, destined for hell. Josephine and I were on the receiving end of endless accusations as if we had purchased unlimited refills. My seventh-grade track season ended with a doozy.

My final offense of the year occurred while at the district track meet when I bumped into a girl from church who attended a different school. She was a year older than me and always kind. She introduced me to her tall and skinny friend, John, right before he started running around the track to warm up for his event. So, of course, following social etiquette, I said hello and thought nothing more of the encounter.

A couple of weeks later, I came home to Dad and Dolly looking at me like I was the adulteress brought before Jesus. The biblical story may shine a light on the hypocrisy of throwing stones at a sinner while being a sinner, but, as per usual, the lesson did not apply to them. They were righteous Pharisees who needed to ensure their daughter, the adulteress, was adequately punished. Exhausted from the panic of predicting what accusation or punishment was coming my way, I waited.

"A boy from Harrisburg wrote you a letter," Dad stated.

"Who?" I asked. I didn't know anyone in Harrisburg.

"John," Dolly answered as if I should know the answer, "and we've read the letter. What did you do? Why did he write you a letter?"

"I didn't do anything. I met a John at the district track meet because he's a friend of a girl at church. We hardly spoke!" Their ignorance and audacity flooded my body with fury, blocking the usual heartbreak of being a constant disappointment. Tears refused to spring into my eyes. I wasn't willing the tears away; they simply weren't there.

"Why don't you read the letter?" Dad thrust John's romantic prose towards me as if I had dictated every word.

Have you tried reading the scrawlings of a teenage boy while being stared at like you were a lady of the night? I don't recommend it. After scanning the letter, which included such sentiments as, "You are so pretty that I got nervous looking at you and ran away," and "I looked up your last name in the phone book," sprouts of excitement sprang up in my heart. I had spent an unhealthy number of hours pining after boys who wanted nothing to do with me. (Oh wait, I still do that.) I didn't know what to think about a boy asking to meet me at the mall. An outright impossibility. Dad and Dolly cut my contemplations short by boring holes into my thoughts with disdain-filled eyes.

Unbeknownst to me, I was using my growing feminine form to purposefully seduce young men, as if a bad haircut, ill-fitting clothes, and altogether unattractive appearance were number one on a list of The Top Ten Things Men Want. It seemed to me then, and it seems to me now, that those who vehemently accuse others of unfounded, malignant crimes are the ones with the reddest hands.

I looked right back, mirroring their expressions. What did Dad and Dolly want me to do? Apologize? Wear a paper bag over my head? Become more socially awkward than I already was? Burn the letter in righteous indignation at the perceived impropriety of a boy writing to a girl? A letter that contained nothing salacious or threatening. I opted to say nothing and felt no remorse, guilt, or responsibility. At that moment, I didn't care what they did or said. Ignore me? Great. List all my faults? Perfect. Take away the privileges I didn't have? Wonderful. Send me outside to weed four acres of land by hand? It would have been my privilege. Anything to get out of those four forsaken walls was a joy.

***

"Wow, Tessa. I don't know what to say."

"There is nothing to say. My parents were so concerned about protecting us from the topic of sex that they taught us all about it. Dolly let songs play on the radio until halfway through. Then, she would turn the song off and tell us that she was testing to see how long we would listen to inappropriate music before asking her to turn it off. She would then explain what the lyrics meant. If she had to explain the meaning of the lyrics, how could she have expected me to know that the lyrics were sexually suggestive? And why did I get in trouble?

The Fourth Essay

"Hi, Dr. Meager. How are you?"

"I am well. And yourself?"

"Internally at war. I have been so angry lately, furious. Everybody makes me angry. I wish people would leave me alone, yet I want attention. I feel like I fight and fight to stay functional. Anytime I get tired, Satan's bloodhounds are unleashed as if they've been yanking on their chains all day, waiting to taste my blood."

"I'm so sorry. Is this particular war specific or general?"

I grip my purse handle so hard I'm shaking, "I live in the land of the devil. He's awake before I am, fighting for my soul. Where is God? I don't hear Him when I wake up. He stands back while Satan uses my mind as his personal playground. I don't have to do a single thing for Satan to show up, but for Christ to lift His finger on my behalf, I must pray, read my scriptures, go to church, write in my journal, think pure thoughts, do a bunch of service projects, and then - maybe- He might extend love. Maybe. If He's having a good day. If Jesus is so loving, why is He so slow to listen and impossible to reach?"

"Let's take a seat, shall we, and talk through this," he gestures towards the red chair, politely waiting for me to step aside so he can close his office door.

"I want all the misery out, and I don't know what more I can do to expedite the process. Jesus isn't helping. He told me to come to Him, and now He's nowhere to be found. I shouldn't be surprised; dangling promises in exchange for sorrow appears to be His preferred way of dealing with me." I cross my arms and slump in the chair.

"I don't know if this helps, but part of processing trauma is working through overwhelming, and often frightening, memories." Dr. Meager's eyes look like they've seen what I've seen, not that I'll ever know.

"I guess you're right. But where is Jesus in all of it? There are many days that I feel like I cannot subscribe to The Church of Jesus Christ of Latter-day Saints. Most days, I want nothing to do with the Church. I cannot rip myself apart for one more Sunday. I can't feel torn between those I love and this Church. I feel like I am betraying Josephine and my family every time I go."

"Why do you feel like you are betraying Josephine?"

"The Church betrayed my sister, so if I go to church, I am also betraying my sister. But if I don't go, I feel like I am betraying my feelings towards God. I am tired of crying, trying, failing, falling on my face, and standing up, only to repeat the process as soon as one foot touches solid ground. What does God want from me? I have nothing left to give. I hate feeling torn in half. I hate anxiety. I hate memories. I HATE it. I cannot do this. I am tired, and my emotions are burnt out. I feel like a failure. I should be better. Fear, masquerading as anger, consumes me. I hate my mood swings, I hate my lack of patience."

"Will you tell me how the church betrayed your sister?"

"I have an essay prepared, just for you." I wonder if Dr. Meager is religious because he seems comfortable with religious language. I'll ask him just as soon as I stop talking about myself.

***

Betrayal

I have sat on my bed for hours, morning after morning, trying to figure out the subconscious beliefs I must address. I can't figure it out. I can explain away any thought that starts to bubble to the surface, so nothing seems valid. Jesus Christ is not at fault for the poor choices of others. The gospel is perfect, but men and women are fallible. I cannot throw away discipleship because another's opinions or manipulations stand in opposition to what God teaches. He commands me to ask questions, seek answers, and knock on heaven's doors.

To give my brain a break, I started looking at old pictures and came across Bruno's freshman picture. I see the heartache in his eyes as he tries to smile. Then, one word comes to mind, and understanding washes over me.

Betrayal.

I thought Christ's love meant protection, literal protection from abuse. I thought His declarations of "I will not leave you comfortless" meant that He wouldn't leave me alone while violent sobs racked my body and thoughts of suicide swirled in my brain. Why did He stand by and let them hurt me if He loved me? Jesus, the Only Begotten Son of God who made blind men see and raised the dead, knew I was abandoned and treated like nothing, watched it happen, and did nothing to stop it.

If I knew one positive thing about my Dad, it's that he would have stopped anyone causing me physical harm, and he was my dad. My traumatized, broken, and fear-filled Dad. Christ, the omniscient, omnipotent being, stopped nothing. Where was Christ in the midst of tragedy? Where? I feel like we, meaning my siblings and I, put our faith in Christ, and in return, we stepped on a proverbial rake and got smacked in the face. Jesus, what's the right word, betrayed me. Yes, He betrayed me and made a fool out of me. And yet, I know it's not true. But it feels true.

Especially when I recall Dad's worst choices, Dad tipped the scale from eccentric and paranoid to insane. Before my eyes, as if I possessed the single working pair in the house, Dad began falling in love with Josephine. I don't know how to explain it any other way. He sought her company, held her hand, and kept her as close to him as he could. Please understand that my father was not a man of tender affection. I don't recall him hugging me, patting me on the back, or any other physical exchange that didn't end up with me crying or wetting my pants. If he was so willing to rip me apart for attracting male attention, he should have slammed his head into the mirror until he bled out.

One night, I woke up and witnessed a horrific evil. The following day, Josephine carried on as usual. To my utmost shame, I never broached her about the abuse she endured the previous night, or the daily abuse from both parents, one right after the other, as if they held whips and took turns slashing her to pieces with the measured beat of a metronome. Utilizing a dark creative license, my parents followed the scripture in Matthew, "Be ye therefore wise as serpents, and harmless as doves.[8]" Except I imagine their version said, 'Be ye therefore as poisonous as a serpent and the antithesis of a dove." How's that for scripture twisting?

Dad started to bring up his sexuality as one might comment on the weather. Odd comments and inappropriate questions abounded. On a drizzly and foreboding Sunday, Dad called me into his room. He was lying on the bed and gently requested that I lay down next to him. My body felt like bags of wet sand.

I should have run away or said I had to go to the bathroom. Instead, I lay down on the bed, terrified. Dad instructed me to face the wall and asked if I wanted a back rub. Before I said anything, his hand was up the back of my periwinkle sweatshirt. I fixed my eyes on the old, wrinkly-looking wall in a cold sweat. I wanted to scream at him, kick him in the face, and tell him to go to hell. Instead, I lay there and let him stroke my back from shoulder to hip. Finally, he told me I could get up and leave. I walked out of his room, not understanding what had happened, with my senses on red alert. Sounds incapable of volume adjustment got louder, my vision narrowed, and my legs filled with enough energy to run through the farmlands and forests of the Pacific Northwest until I reached the Canadian border. Other things happened, too, but I buried them with Dad.

---

[8]Matthew 10:16

Shortly after that incident, a lady from the church named Sister Janet Smith used her talent of observation and recitation of said observations to break the silence. Sister Smith was a woman who shared her opinion with many people and in as many ways as she pleased. She didn't care how loud she spoke or whether someone took offense, not that she was purposefully rude. One glorious rainy day, Sister Smith told Dad that the only reason we were so well-behaved was fear. She further observed that Josephine should have been in Sunday school, not in the truck with Dad. Dad was furious. Outraged. When we got in the car, he asked us if what Sister Smith had said was true. Were we obedient out of fear? All five of us said we were obedient because being obedient was the right thing to do. Bruno was the only one telling the truth. I don't know how the weight of our lie didn't crash down on Dad's head, but it didn't.

Dad's satisfaction would not last long. Sister Smith kept talking, and other people started to notice. The adult woman who led the youth program for girls subtly asked me if things were okay. I told them the truth. Dad kept denying that there was a problem. Finally, in a desperate attempt to convince people we were a happy family, he said to one of my youth leaders, "I dare anyone to find a family happier than mine." I had to stifle a laugh when I watched him make his false declaration that no one, not even he, believed.

A few weeks later, Dolly came to me one evening, looking heartbroken and helpless, asking if I had seen or heard Dad do anything. I told her most of what I knew. She sobbed a horrible soul-purging sob. I wanted to cry, too, but could only sit and watch. Within days, Dolly started making preparations for us to leave.

On a hot day in July, we loaded into our van and drove away from the old house on Turnbow Lane for the last time. On that heavenly morning of deliverance, Josephine, Sadie, and I knew we were leaving; Emerson was likely oblivious, and Bruno went to work driving combines. Dolly was scared that if she told Bruno, he would alert Dad, who would stop us. She also knew that Bruno would not want to come with her because he didn't want to go anywhere with her. Bruno always chose Dad because Dad liked him.

Dolly's disdain for Dad was not the only reason Bruno didn't want to be around her. Dolly spent a lot of time on the computer to cope with her life. Years later, Bruno told her that he wished she had spent less time on the computer and more time with us. She explained that she needed her email communications with her friends to cope. While I don't deny that her email correspondence was a lifeline to sanity, her inability or unwillingness to pay attention to Bruno cost her his trust. I wish she had taken the time to know Bruno as Bruno rather than as Dad's son. Had Dolly done so, she would have found a fiercely loyal son of her own. But, hads and woulds are high in energy cost and worthless in solving problems.

Before we departed from Junction City, Dolly arranged to stay at a different house every few days to prevent Dad from following us. One night, we stayed with some friends from our old ward in Eugene. For two or three nights, we stayed at the home of someone else who was out of town. Dad did not attempt to hunt us down. When he discovered our absence, he eventually landed in the psychiatric ward of Sacred Heart Hospital. Dad told me once that on the day Sarah left him, he ran through the streets screaming our names. I think he probably did the same thing this time, but worse. Before taking complete leave of his senses, he called our bishop as if the bishop could save him. The bishop and his wife watched over Dad, convinced of his innocence. Dad spent two weeks in the hospital, where his emotional age deteriorated into that of a child.

While Dad lived in the luxuries of Sacred Heart Hospital, we were bored and restless. The days were long and tedious. We had nothing to do since the houses where we stayed had long since passed the time when their walls held the adventures and imaginations of children. Once we got the news that Dad was in the hospital's psychiatric ward, we moved into Granny and Pa's house. They were away on a mission for the Church on an Indian Reservation in Arizona, so their house was empty.

To Dolly's credit, the police and Child Protection Services quickly became involved in our situation. The magnitude of the task before her, I cannot imagine. Yet, she seemed brave and unyielding. In the light of heroism, I wanted to love her, convincing myself that she had come to love me, that she was willing to protect me, and be the mom I desperately wanted. She even allowed us to start wearing fingernail polish.

Dolly brought us to the CPS building, where we were interviewed. Without realizing what was happening, I stepped into the world of pens scratching wildly on yellow legal pads, patronizing questions, and idiotic hope.

In August, the court issued a restraining order. Dad was not to come near us. When Dolly enrolled us in school, she gave them a copy of the order for their records. I watched her fill out the accompanying paperwork. Watching her write Dad's name and the reason for the restraining order made me feel exposed and raw all over again. Sitting with those feelings for too long is humanly impossible. So, I shoved them down where they couldn't bother me and soon found out that is humanly impossible, too.

With each passing day, tensions between Josephine and Dolly increased. Dolly was jealous of Josephine, and no change of scenery or removal of Dad changed that. Dolly liked to play loyalty games. She would question us, pit us against each other, and administer crap tests. I loved her and hated her at the same time. Not much has changed since then.

On good days, we were allowed to ride our bikes or walk to the local elementary school playground for forty-five minutes to an hour at a time. When we got back, we had to return to boredom - TV, listening to the radio, wishing I could go anywhere else but where I was. I hated being indoors when there was perfect sunshine to enjoy. I wondered what it felt like to want to be home. There were excruciatingly lonely nights when the sun laughed as it refused to rise. Most of the time, my grief funneled into anger, but on those nights, I sobbed and sobbed.

Sorrow filled my body until I felt like a helium balloon about to burst - except prison bars kept me in place. A walking brain prison. Self-harm seemed like the only relief.

Television became the numbing agent of choice, or so it seemed. The TV was always on, but that could have something to do with access to cable, which we had never had before. Some people regularly enjoy watching hours of television at once. I am not one of those people. I am especially averse to TV marathons in the middle of the day. I get a headache, feel grumpy, and otherwise find the experience unpleasant. As the day draws to an end, a movie or a couple of shows is more acceptable because productivity has earned it. Since there was rarely anything productive to do, the television was simultaneously a lie and a punishment.

Dolly gave me a moment of mercy one day. She asked me if I wanted to make a nine-patch quilt out of her fabric scraps. "Yes, yes, yes!" I thought. When she brought out her box of fabric scraps, I was in heaven as I decided which colors and patterns looked best. Cutting the blocks, sewing them, and ironing them was a feast for my creative leanings. Dolly taught me how to use the sewing machine and helped me when I made a mistake. Then, when I held up my first finished block, Dolly smiled. A genuinely warm smile. How my heart soared!

Shortly thereafter, my heart took a spectacular head-on collision into the cliffs of betrayal. Dolly decided to visit Dad while he was in the hospital. Why did she need to see him? What could they possibly have to discuss? I was sure a lawyer could mediate all necessary legal business. Unfortunately, Dolly bought into Dad's A+ manipulation because she was no longer sure about getting a divorce when she returned. Maybe she didn't buy anything; perhaps she wanted to stay with him. When he was released from the psych ward, she spent the night with him at Turnbow Lane on a Friday night. Yes, to Dolly, the same man who was dangerous enough to file a restraining order against was also worth spending a romantic weekend with.

Josephine had gone to a friend's house in Junction City that same Friday night and later told Dolly she was not coming home. Instead, she preferred to become a ward of the state.

For reasons I will never understand, CPS deemed our house dangerous enough that Josephine could enter the foster care system, yet safe enough for the rest of us. So for a few months, Dad had a probationary period where he was allowed to be around us but was not allowed to spend the night. During this time, he sold the house on Turnbow Lane and bought a place in the Santa Clara community of Eugene, about half of a mile away from Granny and Pa. The house was a typical suburban home, much more structurally sound and modern than Turnbow - three large bedrooms, two bathrooms, a spacious living and dining room. The front yard was well-manicured, and the backyard modest. My singular memory of the backyard includes Emerson depositing his newspaper route in the bushes on the side of the house and claiming he delivered all of them.

During Dad's probationary period, he was uncharacteristically generous with money. I don't know if they made money on the sale of the Turnbow house, but it seemed that our domestic financial situation got elevated from low-income to middle-class overnight. Almost every piece of hand-me-down furniture in the home got replaced - the couch, rocking chair, kitchen table, chairs, and bed frames were all purchased from the department store. In addition, dad got a new motorcycle, a yellow Honda Goldwing.

The stress of the previous year seemed to fade with all the fancy new things and sparkling promises of 'never again.' Unfortunately, the fading pressure was an illusion - as pointless as wiping condensation off a windowpane during canning season. I had one sliver of hope, one escape. I got a job babysitting a little girl for about a year, three or four days a week. I talked to her mom all the time, telling her of my home life. In retrospect, I think I cost her and her husband money, considering how much food I ate. Still, earning my own money and limiting my time at home protected me from completely falling apart.

Dad and Dolly made Josephine the villain, the scapegoat. Nothing would have happened if Josephine had not chosen to develop an eating disorder. They told us we were happy in Junction City, that our family had been excellent until Josephine ruined it. Families are supposed to be loyal to each other. Thus, to be faithful to Dad and Dolly, they instructed us to turn our backs on Josephine. One evening I was called into their bedroom and interrogated.

"Tessa, do you want to see Josephine?" Dad asked.

"Yes, I do."

"Josephine has caused this family a lot of harm. She's making us go to court and saying things that are not true," Dad continued, "we can't have that in our house. No one is to have any contact with her."

I wanted to laugh and cry. I looked at Dolly, imploring her to gather her senses and resist manipulation. Who could believe this nonsense? I saw what I saw, felt what I felt. There was no way in heaven or hell that I would take this dose of poisonous medicine to rewrite history and pretend like we were the inspiration for a Norman Rockwell painting.

Dolly's eyes were dark and empty. Her hardened exterior reinforced - the jealousy, the bitterness, and the inability to be happy for another's good fortune. Her betrayal took shape like thousands of pieces of scarlet-stained glass swirling into a dagger.

"Can you promise us that you won't have any contact with Josephine?" Dad's question was more of a command.

I looked once more from Dad to Dolly and back again.

"No." Dagger or not, I refused to bleed out in front of them.

Dad's eyes narrowed, his jaw set, and the veins in his hands began to swell with his predictably increased heart rate. "You will stay in this room until you promise not to see Josephine ever again."

I glared at them with contempt, refusing to speak.

Our glaring contest lasted for a few minutes. Finally, Dad dismissed me with a wave of his hand. I hated him. I hated them both.

Soon after the Josephine conversation, Dad started making rules about how often and for how long Sadie and I could visit Granny and Pa. Emerson and I had become accustomed to spending Sunday afternoons at their house, so naturally, Dad had to put an end to it. After all that he had lost, he still could not stand the idea of anyone under his roof developing a close relationship with anyone besides him.

Our one sure escape from home was any activity or meeting related to the Church. One night, we went to a youth fireside at a ward member's home. We came out to the car a few minutes late, and Dad was livid. He punched the clutch as hard as he could as his hands twisted back and forth on the steering wheel. When we tried telling him that we had had an inspired religious conversation, he gritted his teeth and yelled, "The Spirit leaves as soon as a meeting runs late."

After several more of these outrageous episodes, I couldn't contain myself any longer. I told a friend everything I felt, thinking our conversations were just between us.

Soon after, I got home from track practice one afternoon, and as I was about to turn down the hall, Dad stopped me. "Tessa, I heard that you think I'm going through a midlife crisis and that you punched and kicked the side of the house?"

I felt guilty on both accounts, and my face cannot lie. However, Dad knew the truth, so I would go down fighting. Dad got a sly look on his face like he was weighing the different punishments he could impose. While he was busy being proud of himself, I stated, with a break in my voice, "You are starting to be just like you used to be, who you promised you would never be again."

He sat with his mouth open, unsure how to respond.

Dolly, who was in her bedroom listening to our exchange, answered for him, "I've read your journals, Tessa! I know what you think of us."

"My journals are not your business!" I called down the hall, thankful for a legitimate reason to raise my voice. I wanted to scream in her face.

"I read your journals so I can get an honest answer about what is going on with you!" Dolly's cowardice was on full display as she kept the door closed, yelling from under her covers like the amorphous blob of personality that she was. My hatred grew with every syllable she uttered.

"Here's an idea: you could ask me!" I yelled back, silently adding, "You spineless, heartless, ugly excuse of a mother. If you're going to hide in your room, keep your mouth shut. If you could keep your mouth shut at all times, that would be fantastic. I. Don't. Like. You. You give me a headache, and your haircut is stupid."

Dolly said nothing more, and neither did Dad. I fully expected him to come within an inch of my face, finger pointed, and yell at me about how disrespectful and ungrateful I was. I looked behind me and saw the chairs sitting ever so neatly around the table. I wanted to pick one up and slam it against the wall, into Dad, and over my knee, convinced that if I felt the pain of wood splintering into and over my skin, I could be free from the war raging inside my brain and body. The knife sitting on the cupboard looked equally enticing. I was sure that some good old-fashioned bloodletting would rid me of the disease ravaging my youth and intellect. But I could not rid myself of my DNA.

I stormed into my room after that heated exchange and threw my bag on my bed. Within minutes, I heard a knock on the door.

"Tessa? It's Dad. Do you need new running shoes?" His voice was calm and sincere. Dad did not administer passive-aggressive crap tests as Dolly did, so I knew he was genuine. Oh, I should mention, they made a new house rule when we moved in. Dad was not to enter my bedroom.

"Yes, I do," I said, opening the door and looking at him. The rage drained from my body, leaving me with a massive headache and an overwhelming desire to take a nap. "I've saved enough babysitting money to buy a pair."

"Well, let's go to Big Five, and we'll see what we can find. Come on." He waved his hand and headed down the hall. I yanked my shoes back on and ran after him, knowing that when he said it was time to go, he meant 'go now,' not 'go in five minutes.'

When we arrived at Big Five, I shied away from the shoes that I knew were outside of my budget of $40. No Nikes, Brooks, Adidas, or Asics for me. I walked straight towards the section of New Balance shoes and found a decent pair in my size, white, blue, and silver, the most excellent pair of shoes ever to adorn my feet. (I had not yet learned to buy my running shoes a half size bigger than my regular shoes to prevent jamming my toes while running downhill and losing a toenail. I ended up losing three toenails before I learned my lesson.) When I went to pay for them, Dad told me to put my money away. I was speechless.

***

"So, what do you think?" I ask Dr. Meager.

"I'm still unclear on how the Church betrayed your sister."

"Oh, right. The Church betrayed my sister because they ripped out her umbilical cord to heaven, also known as her faith, wrapped it around her neck, and watched her swing. They cited her refusal to pretend like nothing had happened as flagrant disobedience to Jesus Christ's commandment to forgive. An unwillingness to forgive is a greater sin than whatever sin requires forgiveness, you see. Thus, blaming the victim for any fissure in a family relationship is practically church doctrine.

In the Church, when someone commits a grave sin, they go and talk with their bishop to repent. I don't know all the parameters for grave sin, but Dad qualified. Dad confessed his sins to the Bishop and Stake President. When Josephine went to them for spiritual guidance, they refused because they "needed to be there for her father." Oh, and I should add one small detail, one of them stood as a character witness for my dad in court."

"What?" Dr. Meager raised both eyebrows as his mouth gaped open.

"Oh, yes. It's true. One of our stalwart leaders stood up in court and defended my father's character. What character trait could Oscar Knurre have possibly possessed that needed defending? Can you imagine? The notion makes me want to throw up.

Oh, and a couple of years ago, Josephine and I were at Dairy Queen having lunch when one of the aforementioned church leaders walked in – a different man than the one who testified in court. This arrogant fool walked right up to Josephine and said, "So, have you figured out the world's problems yet?" I lost my appetite when I saw the smug look on his face. The worst part? Neither of us said a word as he sauntered over to the cashier, delighted with his cleverness."

"Tessa, what do you think forgiveness means?"

"Silence."

"Why?"

"Because how can I talk of anything other than superficial noise without the pain escaping? It cannot be done. If the pain escapes, I am labeled as unforgiving, which means I am more corrupt than my parents. Thus, I must be silent."

Dr. Meager stares at a piece of lint on the ground for a few seconds before shaking his head, "I was taught about forgiveness much differently than you were. Forgiveness has nothing to do with diverting natural consequences and everything to do with what's going on in your heart. A wound cannot heal as long as it remains infected, and remaining silent feeds the infection rather than cleansing it."

We sit for a few minutes as I bend the upper edge of my journal back and forth, not knowing what to say. Thankfully, Dr. Meager takes the lead, "At the risk of sounding trite, I want you to know that you and Josephine deserved better."

"Thanks. See you next week?"

"Yes, I will see you next week, and I am looking forward to it.

As I walk towards my car, I wonder if I can buy a serving size of ice cream instead of buying the largest size available and telling myself I will only eat part of it. I'm glad Dr. Meager lets me read my essays to him without trying to tell me how I should feel or how I should interpret events. I am going to try and emulate his conversation style – no blaming, lecturing, or shaming.

The Fifth Essay

"You've been crying," Dr. Meager says.

"Thanks for noticing. I've been crying for four days."

"Why?"

"Because I sat through another Sacrament meeting and Sunday School lesson that felt like hundreds of fishhooks simultaneously embedding my skin. We talked about God putting us in specific circumstances to learn the lessons we need to learn. That idea doesn't sit well with me because it suggests that people must suffer to become what God wants them to become."

"In your religion, the goal is to become like Christ, right?"

"Yes."

"Didn't Jesus Christ suffer? How can you become like Him if your life is free from challenges and heartache?"

"I don't expect my life to be free from challenge and heartache, just the particular brand of challenge and heartache that I was dealt."

"Tessa, I can almost guarantee you that everyone feels the same way about the hand they have been dealt. Hard is the constant. The variable is your reaction. I think we need to start talking about your reactions to your life. Please understand me. I still want to talk through the rest of your trauma, but Tessa, you need to start developing some emotional resilience.

"Emotional resilience? You mean I need to learn how to develop healthier thinking patterns?" I'm annoyed, but I know Dr. Meager is right.

"Yes. You need to develop healthier thinking patterns about yourself, your past, and your future. You cannot keep your focus on the past."

"Like Lot's wife from the Old Testament? God turned her into a pillar of salt when she turned back to look at Sodom after he commanded her to leave. Are you saying I'm going to get turned into a pillar of salt?" I want to laugh, and I'm not at all upset.

"No, not quite. I've been seeing you for quite a while now, and I think it's time we address the present. I worry that countless opportunities are passing you by. You seem to punish yourself by choosing insignificant and unchallenging paths. Tessa, you came to this earth to do great things, not take safe roads. I fully acknowledge the sorrow you went through, but you are not empty-handed. You're not. You have more potential than you can see. We need to start feeding it."

I'm quiet for a few moments, thinking through what Dr. Meager said, "You think I have potential?"

"Yes. I know you do. And so do you, but you're more comfortable where you are because it is what you've always known."

"Yeah, I can see that,' I admit, 'but I have two more stories to tell and only one essay written. Can I read what I have written?

"Of course. I want to hear the rest of your past; I do. But I also want to see you move forward. You're so young and capable that it's painful to see your power devoted to the past," Dr. Meager says.

I wince at his words, "I don't think I have many choices in the matter. The past has a hold of me. However, Victor Frankl survived Auschwitz and afterward wrote that anyone can be victorious over their circumstances. He called hard times an opportunity and a challenge. I can be victorious over my circumstances."

"Yes, you can. Remember, victory over circumstances is not an event, but an uphill climb."

I nod, "Can I read my essay now?"

"Yes, go ahead."

***

The Day I Met Sarah and Why I Should Have Remained in Ignorance

I chose to live with Dolly after she and Dad divorced because she was almost different after marrying her second husband. She was deliriously in love with him and had a smile on her face most of the time. She let me and Sadie dye our hair, paint our nails, and do whatever we wanted, including resuming contact with Josephine. Betting on her willingness to say yes to almost any request, I asked if I could contact Sarah. Dolly agreed, and I quickly wrote a letter to Sarah, hoping she would be as wonderful as the Sarah in my memory. I received a response within a couple of weeks. Inside the letter, Sarah included her phone number. I called that same afternoon. To me, Sarah sounded like an angel. I could hear the smile and excitement in her voice. She told me how she found my letter in the mail after a trip to the grocery store. She said she thought of Josephine, Bruno, and me every day and would forever regret her decision to abandon us.

I had hoped memories would flood my mind the first time I heard her voice. They did not. Instead, my ever-erratic heart felt like it was shocked by an AED. I felt stable for the first time in my life, as if the electric pogo stick I seemed duct-taped to disintegrated, and I stood on solid ground. The reprieve was as long as a whisper in a dream. Then the duct tape came back and coiled around me like a boa constrictor at the sound of her baby crying.

"Oh, that's my youngest. He's one year old. His birthday is one day before yours."

"How old are your other kids?" I asked.

"Three, five, and seven."

"I thought at least one would be older than that. You were pregnant the last time I saw you."

"I was pregnant; you're right. He was stillborn." An uncomfortable silence threatened to settle in, but she pushed it away.

"What do you like to do?"

"Run. I really like to run. I'm on the track team right now. Do you want to come to one of my track meets? I know you live in Wisconsin, but I thought I would ask."

"Yes! I would love to come to one of your track meets."

And just like that, we made plans for her to come and visit for an extended weekend. She stayed with my Granny and Pa; I didn't realize then what an interesting arrangement must have been for both parties. But they did it for me, so I shall forever be grateful. After hearing Sarah's voice, I was excited to see what she looked like. I knew she wasn't tall from what my father had told me, only 5"2. I started to think of her as a gentle elementary school teacher that all the children loved long after they had moved up several grades.

When Sarah arrived in Eugene, she immediately came to the house that Dolly and her second husband had recently purchased. Dolly thoughtfully arranged all of our schedules to ensure that I was the only one home when Sarah arrived. I wanted to look my best, so I naturally wore my metal-colored jeans and a worn-out baseball T-shirt. I never played baseball, have no interest in even watching it, but raggedy T-shirts were in vogue. Or at least I thought they were.

My curly hair was in its usual place - swirled in a messy bun at the crown of my head. I wore some eyeliner and mascara, and some silver hoops. I wanted her to think I was beautiful. The knock came. In the mirror on the wall, I could see the rhythm of my heart as my carotid arteries pulsed with the influx of blood. My hands were trembling as I opened the door. And there she was.

Everyone should feel what it's like to be looked at with as much maternal love and tenderness as Sarah looked at me. The mixture of grief, regret, and joy on her face left me with nothing to do but smile. So many hopes filled my heart - a hope that she would be everything I imagined - quick to smile and encourage me, a mother who did not use shame as a primary mode of control, and a mom who would show affection even after I made a mistake.

I instantly began searching for a resemblance between us because Dad thought we looked so similar. Unfortunately, we did not look as similar as he suggested, though there were enough shared physical characteristics to make a mother-daughter connection. In addition to standing a few inches shorter than me, Sarah had a slighter build, an observation based on her ankles and arms, since her floral, sky-blue dress was shapeless except for a thin tie in the back. With a dainty nose, blue eyes, and light, straight, brown hair with silver strands woven throughout, she looked like a gentle motherly figure from a children's book - a woman with many kids and no expectation that they act like adults. Sarah wore no makeup or jewelry, except her wedding ring. Her wedding ring stung- a reminder of her replacement children - the children she loved enough to keep. I quickly shoved those feelings down, though I should have regarded them as a warning.

I asked her if she would have recognized me had she seen me in public. Her stalled response answered the question, but she did say that my eyes hadn't changed a bit. The fact that she wouldn't have recognized me hurt, too, but seeing how much she wanted the truth to be something other than what it was, compensated for the pain.

On a Thursday, she came to my track meet. I desperately wanted to impress her with a miraculous burst of competitive speed, while I simultaneously did not care how the race turned out. As a result, I cannot remember my 800-meter time, but I remember feeling blissfully happy. She saw me as if I were a priceless diamond that had just been removed from its guarded glass case and handed to her. Dad was there, too. He came to every sporting event after he and Dolly got divorced, even though I either ignored or glared at him with unbridled contempt.

One time, I had a cross-country meet an hour away along a trail covered with a canopy of golden and red-leafed trees and a floor of softly packed, fresh-smelling dirt. Dad had left work a couple of hours early to arrive in time to set up his lawn chair near the parking lot to watch me race. The 5k wove around the perimeter of the parking lot, so his chosen spot afforded him the best view of me competing. Before the race started, I walked within two feet of where he sat and purposefully looked down at him as if he were the most disgusting maggot on the planet. When he saw my eyes, his shoulders slumped forward as he cast his down towards the ground, and I was glad of it. I'm ashamed to say that I almost spat on him and probably would have if others had not been around.

Dad didn't bring a lawn chair to the track meet Sarah was at. Instead, he brought his new, nameless girlfriend. She was thin, blonde, tan, and not from Eugene. When Dad saw Sarah, he got a flashback look in his eye and tried to leap over a hurdle, which he was in no shape to do. Though strong and naturally athletic, stress had rapidly added thirty or forty pounds to his solid frame. After the failed hurdle attempt, he ran around his new girlfriend in small circles, teasing her like they were two six-year-olds. She did not look impressed, and Dad seemed unable to stop. I did not approach them, but as Sarah and I walked off the track and towards her car, I wondered for the first time if Sarah had broken Dad's heart when she left. I knew he fought for Josephine, Bruno, and me, but I wondered if he ever fought for Sarah.

After the meet, Sarah and I drove to the coast for the weekend. First, we went to Florence and then up the Pacific Coast through the long winding roads, with either side a moving masterpiece of the cerulean, blue ocean or trees in every possible shade of green. The weather was clear and sunny, making the long drive less nausea-inducing. Next, she took me to an outlet mall and bought several outfits. Light blue, low-rise jeans from the Gap, two fitted t-shirts, one white and one bright green, a brown leather belt, pink capri pants, a white blouse, and a royal blue floral skirt and matching boatneck top with ¾ length sleeves. She may not have loved fancy, but she loved that I loved it. Interestingly, the fancy gene skipped over Josephine, too.

We stayed at a couple of different hotels, talking and getting to know each other. Sarah braided my hair, and I could see her crying as I looked at her reflection on the television screen. I told her the truth about what life had been like since she left and watched as every word hurt her, though causing pain was not my intention. She possessed a sort of frightened vulnerability, and I instinctively wanted to love and protect her.

As our visit ended, we scheduled a time for me to visit her in Wisconsin over the summer. Bruno planned to go with me, too. Dad did not want either of us to go, but he respected our decision. A few weeks before we left, we decided to fly to Utah and meet her at her parents' house because they lived in a massive home with plenty of room for all of us, and Sarah was leaving her husband. I remember her husband from when I was little, as he was the one who suggested that Sarah abandon us. He hated us, especially Bruno. His eyes and nose reminded me of a rodent, and his demeanor was one of calculated evil. No part of me believed that he had changed, so, without knowing any details, I completely supported her decision. I wondered if time with me had spurred a thought into action.

A week after Sarah had arrived in Utah and a couple of weeks before I was to leave, I spoke with her parents on the phone. I had no working memory of them but asked if I could move in with them. At the time, moving in with them felt like it would be an exciting and glorious adventure. They excitedly accepted my request, and just like that, within days of the school year ending, I flew to Utah to live with a family I didn't know. When I went to Dad's house to inform him of my decision, he begged me not to go, which fueled my determination to fly to Utah as soon as possible. Dad said Sarah and her family were not healthy people, crazy, he called them. In response, I told him to go to hell and stormed out of his house. I should have listened; I should have stayed with Dolly, pursued my dreams of becoming a track star, and left the past alone.

Bruno surprised me and flew to Utah with me. He stayed for one week. He had not interacted with Sarah when she was in Eugene, but, for some reason, decided to satisfy his curiosity about her. In retrospect, I wonder if Dad had asked Bruno to come with me as a protective measure. In any case, there was much excitement upon our arrival. Sarah's parents had opposed her decision to sign over her parental rights, and they had missed us ever since. Their faces expressed love when we saw them, but not quite as much as Sarah's. She was our mother, after all.

My maternal grandparents' home was the grandest dwelling I had ever been inside. The outside was fancy, with a half-circle driveway that passed by the front door. You could step inside the passenger side door from the porch and drive away without the necessity of backing up. But, as impressive as the exterior was, it did not indicate the number of rooms inside; it was a house built on top of a home. The entrance led into a fountain room, where all the walls were glass or sliding glass doors. A TV room, a kitchen, a beautiful main room used only to host guests, two bedrooms, two bathrooms, and an office made up the stairs. Downstairs had a spacious game room complete with a pool table, a kitchen, a dining room, a living room, three bedrooms, and a bathroom. Sarah's grandma lived down there. She never said much. The yard looked professionally landscaped. Sarah's parents drove a Hummer and a Lexus. They were at the top of their careers as nutrition supplement salespersons and thoroughly enjoying the monetary luxuries that came with it. Several years before I reentered their lives, Sarah's mother had been diagnosed with breast cancer. She attributed her recovery to a changed diet and nutritional supplements. This event seemed to fuel their lifelong obsession with their weight. I anticipated their daily morning announcement of how many pounds they had gained or lost since the day before, placing their self-worth on the altar of the scale. Not only did their current weight dictate their day-to-day emotions, but their weight from ten and twenty years ago haunted their memories. They passed their body shame to Sarah, a cursed family treasure as expected as a Christmas present.

Josephine was the next daughter in line to receive the curse. Though her days of starvation had passed, she was still obsessed with preventing the accumulation of adipose tissue. Shortly before moving to Utah, Josephine introduced me to the idea of eating 'clean' six days a week, followed by one day of eating an unlimited amount of junk food. I thought her concept sounded great because she was leaner than me, and who wants to be the fat little sister? The day I gave myself permission to gorge on honeybuns, kettle corn, gummy bears, and chocolate until I was sick felt exhilarating. The following day, I had my first sugar hangover. It felt awful. My running was sluggish. My stomach was hungry and nauseous at the same time. Yet, despite feeling disgusting, I instantly became a sugar addict and an indentured servant to the number on the scale. I guess I was the second daughter in line to lay my self-worth on the altar of the scale.

Moving in with Sarah's parents meant that I was exposed to other strains of disordered eating - weighing myself multiple times a day, telling myself, "Tonight will be the last night I binge. Tomorrow I will eat cucumbers, bell peppers, and raw spinach. Tomorrow I will be healthy and run ten miles, but tonight I will eat whatever I want, for the last time." I still tell myself the same lie, though, in the middle of shoving a pan of brownies down my throat, I believe it. Of course, 4,000 calories worth of chocolate makes the lies go down.

Sarah's parents adhered to a daily regimen of rigorous Super Greens consumption. They drank bottle after bottle of water mixed with a scoop of green powder, the color of dry alfalfa. The makers of Super Greens promised all sorts of magnificent palliative health benefits. Sarah's parents promised more miraculous cures from all kinds of ailments; anxiety, breast cancer, the common cold, and hopefully your personality if they deemed that necessary. The house diet was rich in vegetables and guilt to facilitate their clean eating habits. Since fruit contains sugar, it was discouraged. Never mind that it's nature-made, God-given sugar. At best, they gave fruit a condescending side-eye of disapproval. No one could enjoy so much as a morsel of bread or dessert without the pre-dessert warnings of indulgence, the eating dessert reprimands of gluttony, and the post-dessert regrets and morning weigh-in apprehension.

I don't know where Sarah's mother got her training, probably from some upscale sales rep with a talent for lying through their teeth. But she fancied herself capable of conducting blood analysis to determine a person's emotional history. She would extract a small drop of blood and analyze it under a microscope. Based on the shape of the blood cells, she could supposedly tell periods of trauma or illness in one's past. The spikier the blood cell, the more traumatic the history. When Sarah's mom examined my blood, it looked spikey and dark. I interpreted this as evidence that her analysis was correct because trauma defines my life. Sarah's parents believed that through the regular use of Super Greens, cells could heal, and health would return.

I wanted to believe them, so I embraced their theories and perspectives. I wanted to be healthy, thin, and perform at the top athletic levels. So, upon their well-intentioned advice, I did a three-day 'cleanse' where I ate nothing and drank only Super Greens. Three days with a caloric intake under 50. By the third day, I could do little more than lie face down on the couch. My vision was blurry; my head hurt; my cognitive function was wavering. But I did it! They were so proud of me. I had finally done something worth applause and praise. But the work didn't come without punishment. Naturally, after starving myself, I wanted to consume as much food as possible. So, I did what people do after they try to starve themselves. I ate everything in sight.

Being the thoughtful people they were, Sarah's parents ensured there was plenty of junk food on hand, chocolate, chips, candy, and pastries. I forced copious amounts of food into my body. My stomach felt like it was about to blow up, but I would not stop eating. I couldn't. As I stood at the kitchen counter shoving cookies into my mouth, I watched the clock as the minutes ticked by, eating as if all the food in the world would vanish at midnight. When I finally tried to sleep, I felt like I might die of a stomachache. I was, nonetheless, happy in this honeymoon period of living with people I had so often imagined. Sarah made sure I got my driver's license, a job, and enrolled in Mountain View High School, which had one of the best cross-country programs in the state. According to school boundaries, I should have gone to Pleasant Grove High School, but with the help of a kind family from church, I was able to go to Mountain View.

I started going to cross-country practices in the morning with a family of gifted track athletes. Two of the kids had graduated and left their legacy, while the other two were making theirs. Every morning, at 7:30, the cross-country team met at the high school and broke into groups according to gender and speed to run the required minutes. The girl from the family at church was kind enough to invite me to run with her and two of her friends. Little did I know that the three of them were the fastest girls on the team and among the top runners in the state. I tried with all my might to keep up, but my lungs and legs refused to cooperate with my ambitions. Being the thoughtful person she was, the girl from church didn't zoom off without me because she knew I had no idea where I was or how to get back to the school. The other two girls politely followed suit. By the end of our run, one of the girls said, "Next time, let's just run with the three of us. We can't wait for slower people."

My face burned, and my eyes stung with embarrassment. Once again, I was the one who was not quite fast enough to be good. Thankfully, no one noticed my embarrassment because my face was already red and sweaty from running. I knew I could not close the gap between them and me in a single season. However, I determined to make the gap smaller. Every morning, I ran as hard as I could for as long as possible; how very Steve Prefontaine of me. When I got home, all I wanted to do was take a long nap. I thought I had worked hard before but running with these girls made me feel like the harder I worked, the harder it got.

Aside from the initial expression of frustration at my lack of talent, my teammates were kind and good. We prayed before every practice and race, but we never thanked God when we received the blessings we had requested. I wanted to be around them and to be like them. They went to church, so I went to church. They spent Sunday evenings singing hymns to old people in a retirement home, so I did, too. For a few mostly happy months, I wanted to be at church and answer the questions like I had studied the Book of Mormon all of my life. I even wrote Dolly a letter, thanking her for letting me move to

Lindon, Utah, with Sarah and her family. I told her how I felt like I had been given a second chance. My feelings of disdain toward Dolly started to wane. I was happy that she was happy and, for a brief moment, forgot that she refused to love me.

Shortly after I had moved to Utah, I visited one of Dolly's friends, where I learned information about Dolly and her hidden disloyalty that I would have been better off not knowing. Upon hearing of Dolly's disloyalty, I instantly shredded the peace treaty between us that I had been drafting in my heart. Hatred and rage descended upon me like a locust cloud, devouring the happiness that had begun to grow. In my furious state, I articulated every scathing opinion and criticism I could think of to Dolly's friend. I seethed at the image of Dolly sitting on her moral high horse while playing the part of the martyr when she was a selfish hypocrite, a liar, and an opportunist. She never loved Dad, Josephine, Bruno, or me. Instead, she loved herself, Sadie, and Emerson. Dolly could have made them billions of dollars if Disney needed inspiration for the ultimate villain. Think about the character development: an unsuspecting, religious, non-confrontational, passive-aggressive, average-looking, occasionally fat housewife who will betray anyone, even the child of her womb, to get what she wants. She'll call herself Mother, and everyone within her reach will grow to fear the title. They will have nightmares of her vampirish tendencies. Only she doesn't feed on blood; she feeds on hope and joy. Everyone will be scared to be happy. And so, the smiles stop, the excitement, and dreams come to an abrupt halt, and the few unconquerable spirits will be bludgeoned to death by their own people in the name of safety. On second thought, perhaps Disney is not the movie production company meant to take on such a villain, as it might get a little too terrifying for children. In any case, I'm sure someone would be thrilled with such a screenplay.

Dolly's friend promptly gave Dolly a detailed report of my comments, omitting the part about me learning of Dolly's betrayal. Dolly was, of course, upset with me and wrote a strongly worded email. She couldn't believe I would say such mean and horrible things.

I was once again the ungrateful wretch of a child whose only intention was to make her life miserable. I didn't care what she said or how she felt for a full two days. I know I've written about Dolly's betrayal several times now. But, after some introspection, I think the hypocrisy hurts the most.

Dolly's mistakes aside, she did not have the capability to inflict the pain that came with trying to recreate the broken mother-daughter relationship that I had lost with Sarah. I never considered what feelings watching Sarah love her other children would awaken in me. There they were, living with her. They cried; she came. She listened to, hugged, and held them. A new breed, or a new intensity, of self-hatred was born. I didn't bother asking why Sarah kept her four younger children after leaving me behind like I was a broken and ugly old toy. The answer was already playing on repeat: You're stupid. You're ugly. Your mother could not love you. Do you think she loves you now? That she's changed her mind? She refused to answer when you cried for her until your body stopped making tears. And you were four. Nothing's changed. You're still you, still a second-class daughter, as if you even deserve that title. Daughters are cherished. Daughters are adored. You're not anyone's daughter. You're more of a maggot. Maybe a leech. Or Lice. Something gross and annoying. What did you expect when you moved here? You're still you.

I didn't tell Sarah how I felt because I could feel her daily sadness. When Sarah and I spent time together, we talked about the past like friends. She told me how she had left Dad, how her parents had helped her leave him, and how hard it was being married to him. I often wondered why Sarah didn't take us with her if Dad was such a horrible human being. What did she suppose would happen? She frequently talked about her memories of Josephine and Bruno. Her memories of me were not as abundant as I had hoped because I was younger. We probably spoke the most about our collective disordered eating. According to Sarah's parents, she was never thin enough. Her parents cited her father's ability to wrap his hands entirely around her mother's waist as the gold standard of weight in their house when she was a teenager. So, Sarah starved herself, binged, and her emotions followed the same extreme pattern. She didn't go on runs or go to a gym, but she walked. And walked some more.

As I talked and interacted with Sarah and her parents, I learned of the abuse she and her children had suffered at the hands of her second husband. Terrible, awful, nightmare-ish things. When I looked into the eyes of her two oldest children, I could sense that their innocence of ugliness had long since gone. Whatever they had endured would steer their future. But I told myself, they still have a mom who loves them. Knowing the Devil himself was reflected in the eyes of their father didn't matter to me. Nothing could be more devastating than a mother who doesn't love you.

I remember the last time I saw her as a four-year-old. Dad picked us up from her apartment on a rainy and cold night. He seemed weighed down but tried to smile.

"Did Sarah tell you guys anything?" Dad asked Josephine, me, and Bruno as we drove away.

"She said she love me!" Bruno declared. He loved Sarah with all his heart. Frequently, when she dropped us off at Dad's house, Bruno would run back to her car as soon as we got to the door and refuse to get out.

"Anything else?"

I looked around the van, scanning for something to focus on; anything would do. I thought I was about to get in trouble and decided to remain silent. Josephine shook her head while sitting up straight, and her hands folded reverently on her lap. She was wearing a red and white checked dress with a red ribbon tied in her hair—the picture of grace. I was wearing sweats, and my hair flew in seven different directions.

"We're going back." Dad whipped the van around with a different brand of aggression than what he usually used.

I got scared as he marched the three of us to Sarah's front door and hung my head down, ready to receive whatever punishment was coming. Dad pounded on the door as if he had tried to knock but couldn't restrain his fist from doing what it wanted.

When Sarah opened the door, I only raised my eyes as far as her pregnant belly.

"I am not going to be the one who tells them, Sarah. You are. This was not my decision." Dad's voice was full of sadness, and he sounded like he was about to cry. They must have been exchanging looks for quite some time because it seemed like an eternity before anyone spoke.

Sarah leaned down as far as she could and looked at us with a grief-strained face, "I'm not going to be your mom anymore. I'm going away, and Dolly is going to be your new mom. The Holy Ghost told me I need to leave, so I am following what God wants me to do."

With that proverbial punch in the face, Sarah gave us a final hug before we walked back to the car, stunned. Dad quietly loaded us into the van with his jaw clenched and hands shaking. I was surprised when he didn't get mad as I stumbled over Sadie's feet and fumbled with my seatbelt.

As we drove away from Sarah, her husband, and their baby for the second and final time, I put my chubby hand on the window and silently cried, my tears coming faster than the rain could fall. Within an hour, I went from believing I was Sarah's treasure to knowing I wasn't worth keeping. God didn't want her to keep me.

"Hey, do you guys want to go to Dairy Queen?" Dad asked. I saw him wipe something off his cheeks when I looked forward.

How can I explain what it feels like to have your heart dissected in real time? Well, it's closer to the exquisite pain of abandonment or verbal and emotional abuse, but more specific in its target. In the case of watching Sarah love the four children she chose to keep, it felt as if she took a searing hot blacksmith iron and placed it directly on my spine until my skin melted and my vertebrae turned black.

By the time fall was nearing an end, my brain had broken. Every academic concept fell out of my brain. I couldn't remember mathematical concepts or write coherent sentences. I knew I was in trouble when handed a math test and could not answer one question. Not one.

Later that week, a boy on my cross-country team laughed while regaling other teammates with his story about the stupid student who turned in a test without answering a single question. He was the math teacher's assistant for a different class and must have heard her say something about the tragedy of students who can't perform. I wanted to tell him that I was the stupid student he spoke of because I wanted him to stop laughing and telling other people about my incompetence. I said nothing. My grades and hygiene tanked, and my weight went up. All I wanted to do was sleep and eat.

One time, during art class, my cognitive function was so discombobulated that I couldn't see, and then I fell off my stool. My muscles were weak. My mind was in a fog. I went to a couple of track meets where I thoroughly embarrassed myself and my coaches. Mostly myself. During an indoor track meet, I was so slow that I came in worse than last place. I came in at least 50 meters behind everyone else, maybe more. I say 50 meters to make myself feel better.

I was wearing knee-high Valentine socks to ensure impressive visibility. After telling the coaches of my personal record (PR) in the 800 meters from the previous year, two minutes and twenty-seven seconds, I crossed the line like a child caught in a lie. I couldn't look them in the eye any more than I could bring myself to cheer for the other runners. I had no misplaced understanding as to my responsibility for my overweight and awful condition. I was trying to fill a gaping wound inside my soul with food. Finally, I couldn't run anymore. It was too hard, and it hurt. I was a lethargic blob, gross and repulsive, a happiness vampire, a stormy cloud smothering other people's sunshine.

I wanted to cheer for the flawless girls on my team with their slender, muscular bodies, glossy ponytails, and genuine smiles. In my ignorance, or perhaps my selfishness, I assumed their families wanted to be a family. I envied them to the point of intolerance. Being around them was painful, their kindness shining a bright light on my flaws, a microscope on what I had lost -my family, my mind, and my will to live.

When my friends seemed glad to see me, I thought they were making fun of me. Paranoia became one more whip in a long line of taskmasters. I was sure they were making fun of my weight gain, my chronically terrible short hair made worse by bleaching and dying my once flawless curls between black and orange, an unintentional orange but orange, nonetheless. As a lover of fashion and getting fancy, my once cute wardrobe started to morph into something comical as my waistline expanded. I vacillated between a size eight and a size fourteen, with half the poundage going to my jawline.

Sarah moved out of her parents' house and into an apartment with her kids. The three could not cohabitate because they shared a rawness that could not satisfy both parties. I stayed because I shared a different rawness with Sarah. Because I moved from downstairs to the main floor of my grandparents' grand home, I thought we would have more interactions. Of course, they were friendly, making me dinner and ensuring I got to work and school. But they commented a little too often on my weight. Sarah's mother told me that I looked *jowly*, like a bulldog. How wonderful. That's the second I've been compared to a dog—an animal. When I was a kid, Dolly and Dad adopted dogs only to get rid of them. One went to the dog pound, one was given away, and two got shot.

I shouldn't leave the explanation there as if there was no reasoning, however rational or irrational, I don't know, for shooting two dogs. When we lived in Junction City, the golden retriever and the black lab had gotten into the chicken coop while we were gone and ate all the chickens. The chicken coop was a make-shift placeholder. Dad destroyed the sturdy chicken coop when he took down the barn. The makeshift one was four posts and some metal mesh acting as a wall.

Upon cracking the case of the disappearing chickens, Dad determined that the dogs needed to die so they wouldn't wander off to the neighbor's property and eat their chickens. So, he dug them a grave, put the dogs inside, and shot them with the neighbor boy's gun. Unfortunately, Dad was not a good shot. One dog died instantly, and the other did not. The bullet went through her eye. She leaped out of the grave and raced around the property, making the most horrific noise I have ever heard come out of any living thing. The man living in the trailer up the road yelled, "WHAT ARE YOU DOING?!" No one answered. Thankfully, the dog was caught and put out of her misery within a few minutes. Dad, Bruno, and the neighbor boy filled the dog's grave. The next day, I made a tombstone out of cardboard scraps and set it against a rock at their burial site.

***

"Oh, Tessa. That's, wow, that's, um." Dr. Meager says.

"It's my life."

"How long did you live with Sarah's parents?" he asks.

"I lived with them until I finished my junior year. After that, I moved back to Eugene, Harrisburg, actually. Josephine had married by then, and I planned on staying with them for the duration of my senior year of high school and through college. Those plans changed, too. I'll finish writing my essay about the final tragedy and bring it in next time."

"I like that plan. Out of curiosity, what are your plans when you leave here?"

"The usual; buy more chocolate and candy than most people eat in a month and shove it down my throat."

"What do you think about making a plan to do something else?" he says.

"And what would that be? Go on a run? Read a book? Sit in my car and speak positive affirmations into the universe?"

"No, no, none of those things, though all are good alternatives to making yourself sick. Have you tried to pray? Since you believe in God, why don't you pray to Him and ask for His help? You could even write a prayer down in your journal to help focus your thoughts."

"Your suggestion is interesting. A girl at church suggested the same thing to me the other day."

"You don't need to write anything as long as your essays, but you could write a sentence."

"You know I never write only a sentence," I say, smiling.

"So, to be clear on the plan, when you go out to your car, you are going to sit down and write a prayer, however brief, before doing anything else?"

"Yes. I can do that. I'll let you know how it goes next time I see you. I'll write a book full of my essays and prayers someday. You can count on that."

As I walk towards my car, the post-appointment emotions begin to swirl like dust in a tornado. When I sit in my car, I am disgusted by the wrappers yet feel desperate to get more. But, if I have few redeemable qualities, at least I do what I say I will do, so long as I must report back to someone else. With pen in hand, I open my daily journal, which is different than the black one Dr. Meager gave to me.

***

Dear Heavenly Father,

I've reached the end of my rope, again. Where are you? Why must the search for you be so hard? Why aren't you easy to find? Hell's bells are ringing, and sleep is my only escape. I tell myself that food is an escape, but it only fuels my instability. I have no idea why I am so angry right now; I just had a productive appointment with Dr. Meager. I am furious; can't you take it away?

I hate this life. I do. I hate that I cannot let things go and simply be grateful for all I have. I can feel the clicks in my brain as my thoughts shift down into depression. I can't be free, and that knowledge suffocates me. I let trivial things break me down. I cannot make it through this life another day. I do not want to. I am tired of a routine leading nowhere. I do not want to be inside my brain. I am trying to carry this burden with some form of dignity, but I am too weak. I am nothing. Oh Lord, if I must suffer like this, without a moment of waking peace, take me off the earth right now. End my mortal existence in a moment. A car accident, a brain aneurysm, a medical procedure gone terribly wrong, or a runaway semi-truck plowing me over on an afternoon run. I don't care which one. Just do it now so that all this can end.

Another Sunday

Another Sunday, another unpleasant social situation. I want to be part of one of the social crowds at church, but I take too much psychological space. People look like they want to be nice, but they don't quite know how to proceed. It's like my presence makes them want to cover their ears for all the blaring, hysterical static I unintentionally emit. The logical conclusion? My spirit must be bigger than my body. When God put my spirit into my body, He likely had to sit on my overstuffed 5'6 frame before He could zip me together.

When I want to leave Sacrament meeting or a social gathering, I remind myself of what Victor Frankl wrote in *Man's Search for Meaning*, ". . .in the final analysis it becomes clear that the sort of person the prisoner became was the result of an inner decision. . . any man can . . . decide what shall become of him - mentally and spiritually."

In my quest to become spiritually whole and emotionally resilient, I picked up the Book of Mormon to identify what doctrine led all three of my parental figures to be the antitheses of Christlike. In the first verse of the first chapter of the Book of Mormon, Nephi wrote: "... having had a great knowledge of the goodness and the mysteries of God."

What are the mysteries of God? And why is He a mystery? And how is He good? I want to become good. I don't want to be a victim, act like a victim, or survive a mental hand-to-mouth existence. And, I must know how an entire congregation of over one hundred people who claim to be in tune with the Spirit of God can see the constant pain of a child(ren) and do nothing. Molested, beaten, and emotionally manipulated, and no one says a word. Not one. Oh, wait, that's not true. They do talk when they compliment the parents, "What well-behaved children you have," as if silent, subservient children are the ultimate goal of parenting.

I guess I already know why people don't see the heartache they walk past every Sunday, though admitting the answer feels like someone dropped a boulder on my chest, and I'll never breathe the same again. No one looks past the expected performance of the obligatory holy habits. Churchgoers see other churchgoers through the lens of a checklist. Do they perform visible acts of service, come to church every week, know the stories of the scriptures, and can regurgitate fundamental doctrine? Are they willing to say prayers and hold callings? If the answer is yes, they're given the stamp of approval, welcomed into the fold, and enjoy the self-congratulating friendship of people who do the same. Surely, the people who know how to put on a good show must be disciples of Christ, worthy to act in His name and proclaim every thought and idea they have as something celestial. I think not.

Why don't more people in any Christian religion question their leaders when their leaders are teaching the gospel according to themselves? How about a "Can you show me where the practices of humiliation and shame are supported in the scriptures? How about violating children and watering down doctrine? Did God recently edit the Ten Commandments? Did He suddenly change His position based on popular opinion? Either live your religion or don't, but spare others the faith crisis of your hypocrisy. Oh, and Christ is only concerned with pleasing His Father, so maybe you should follow His example."

Silence is misinterpreted as agreement. Thus, allowing anyone, by the omission of verbalized dissent, to lead others away from God in the name of popularity, compassion, entertainment, or covering their sins is selfish. Thank goodness Sister Johnson spoke up when she saw that something was not right in my family. Her act of bravery stopped further, untold harm. Some people disregarded her and thought she was out of line. But she didn't care and said what needed to be said anyway. May God bless that woman's soul a million times over.

I must do the same, not that I am looking to accuse anyone of anything, but keeping watch for what doesn't seem right. For now, here I sit in Sacrament Meeting, again, with my opinions and feelings, soundlessly defying anyone to talk to me while simultaneously wanting a friend who won't slowly back away, ready to run, as soon as they see me, unfiltered. The bishop's talking about finding peace in the gospel, and everyone is nodding in agreement. Why are they nodding? What does 'peace in Christ' even mean?

A sentiment that I hate forces me from my existential questions "…families are meant to be united eternally and are a great source of joy." Nope. I'm done. Goodbye. No more church for me. It's a lie. Families are a source of unending despair and sorrow, and to be united eternally with any of my parents sounds like hell. No, thank you. I walk run towards the exit and sprint towards my Honda Civic as soon as I walk through the front doors of the church building.

After turning on my ignition, I turn it off again. Eternal families are intended to be happy and can only be happy if the members treat each other with respect, love, and compassion. Unfortunately, my parents chose to conduct themselves in such a way that prevented promises from being fulfilled because the promises are conditioned upon obedience to God's law. I know there are no perfect families, but I have seen good families. I have been in their homes and seen how their faces light up as they greet each other. When we lived in Coburg, there was a family in our ward who held a barn dance every year just for its fun. There would be food, dancing, music, and a general feeling of happiness. I could tell that the parents adored one another and their children. One of their daughters was my friend, and she exuded peace and goodness, even as a fourth grader. They returned to Canada before we started fifth grade, but their example has stuck with me. Oh, to enter a home like theirs every day. Not a home free from struggle, but a house full of love that made the struggle worth living.

I open the car door and head towards the church building, determined to find what my parents lost, joy in Jesus Christ, and faith in His promises.

Brother Adams is teaching Sunday School today. He's a jolly man, though he hardly looks old enough to be the recipient of such an adjective. Nor round enough. His copper brown hair and caramel-colored eyes seem rather unremarkable until he smiles. Brother Adams has a brilliant smile.

"Hi, Tessa! I'm glad to see you here."

"Yes, well, I'm here." I no longer feel the urge to make snarky comments, only understated observations.

"Take a seat, and we'll get started."

I sit in a seat against the wall, hoping I go unnoticed. Since the desks are connected to the chairs, I feel like I'm in elementary school whenever I sit in this room. Thankfully, I am in little danger of drawing attention to myself. Brother Adams is charismatic, relaxed, and easy to talk with. People cannot help but focus their eyes on him.

"Let's start by considering this truth: We choose who our masters are. Someone is always our master. We are free to choose whether we subject ourselves to God or Satan. The Lord wants us to be subject to Him. Before anyone gets riled up about the idea of masters, please remember that to be owned by God is to be owned by someone who has your eternal salvation in mind."

At the word 'subject,' my hand involuntarily shoots up, "When I put what you just said through the Tessa filter, I would phrase the same concept as the Lord wanting us to choose Him. The scriptures say that He invites us to come unto Him, but He will never force us. If we turn from His teachings, we turn from His safety. He also promises us peace, but I struggle to understand and accept that point of doctrine because I don't feel peace in my life. I would be interested in hearing others' perspectives." There I go again, as stealthy as a hippopotamus.

"Maybe you don't feel peace because you're still holding on to your favorite sins. I know that's what happens to me when I don't feel God's peace." A young woman with a high blonde ponytail offers her wisdom, and my eyes almost bulge out of my head. I wish I could go back a few moments and clarify that I am interested in everyone's perspective but hers.

After an awkward pause, an older woman who knows something of my family history raises her hand, "I think it's important to remember that there are chasms so wide and deep they take more time and attention to heal. But though they take longer to heal, and the process is much more exacting, in the end, those sorrows will be erased. And that's where peace comes in, knowing because of the Atonement of Jesus Christ all will eventually be made right, and not that everything will be made right this instant or even in this lifetime." She gives me a wink as she concludes her thought.

I give her an appreciative smile and mull over what she just said. Peace follows faith; faith is a synonym for trust. But why is God a mystery? How can I trust someone who remains a mystery?

"Not to make an abrupt turn, but I had the thought that I should read this quote by Joseph B. Wirthlin, one of our apostles, "To know God is to think what He thinks, to feel what He feels, to have the power He possesses, to comprehend the truths He understands, and to do what He does. Those who know God become like Him, and have His kind of life, which is eternal life[9]," Brother Adams looks up like he's waiting for someone to explain why that quote might have touched their hearts.

No one offers any information. I know precisely why he read that quote and what it means to me, but I can't articulate that to Brother Adams, especially in front of a Sunday School class. So, I'll write it down in my journal and keep it forever, as a reminder that God answered the question I asked only an hour and a half ago.

---

[9] Joseph B. Wirthlin, Our Lord and Savior, *Ensign*, Nov 1993

The Sixth Essay

I'm off to Dr. Meager's office again, with one last essay to read. I'm excited to read it to him because there is a miracle embedded in the end—a life-altering, life-saving miracle. I wrote my essay after church on the wings of a lesson about divine intervention.

"Hi, Tessa. Come on in," Dr. Meager got new shoes again. I've been seeing him for a few years, so I suppose it's been a while since his last new pair. This pair is a replica of the previous pair. I laugh inside because my uncle buys six pairs when he finds tennis shoes that he likes.

"Nice shoes,' I say, 'they remind me of my uncle. He's one of my favorite people. An earthly angel, but don't tell him that. He would roll his eyes, throw his hands in the air, mutter 'whatever,' and go outside to work on his yard. My uncle isn't one to receive compliments well, especially ones about angels."

"Tessa, I do believe you seem the brightest and happiest I have ever seen you."

"That's because I wrote my final essay, and it's all out. All the garbage is out," relief spreads across my face as I perch on the edge of the red chair like a fifth-grader about to spell out the final word of a spelling bee.

"Alright, well, let's hear it. Please, whenever you are ready."

***

Death and a Second Chance

Oscar Knurre died on June 24, 2004, during the hour of 5:00 pm. His third wife, of only eight months, died, too; she was only thirty-four years old. Their lives came to a screeching halt during a collision between their motorcycle and a proud, towering oak tree. The casualties were idiotically meaningless.

My oldest brother, Bruno, was at the scene. He and Dad had been enjoying their favorite pastime. According to Bruno's first-hand account, the accident scene was horrific, and how could it be anything else? Has anyone come upon a fatal accident that was not horrific? If so, I am very interested in talking with them. Dad's red crotch rocket had flown off the road while they were taking a curve. Distinct skid marks suggested that Dad was speeding when he tried to stop, an unsurprising discovery since Speed and Dad had been inseparable friends since childhood. The amount of force required to turn the bike's handlebars upside down and backward and send pieces of the frame splintering in every direction must have been substantial. The emergency personnel found his wife's helmet several feet away from her body; she died of head injuries.

Dad didn't die in an instant. Bruno, who had turned around when he realized Dad was not behind him, found him struggling for his last unconscious breath. Bruno took his shirt and tried to wrap it around Dad's chest just to do something besides stand helplessly. As Bruno recalls, Dad moaned and moved his head in his wife's direction and seemed to understand that her spirit was gone. He stopped moving and breathing as his spirit and body parted ways. The medical cause of death was blunt force trauma to the chest.

Bruno's dad, best friend, cheerleader, and confidant was gone. Bruno's loyalty to Dad was, in large part, because of Dad's loyalty to him. "He is the only person who never left me," he told me once. Now, he witnessed the one parent who loved him die. The death of Dad's wife caused Bruno another deep wound. She had opened her heart to Bruno by showing him love and respect, a courtesy he had never before experienced. I think the home Dad and his wife created had begun to heal the pains of that broken-hearted, dark-haired boy with big blue eyes and long black eyelashes—the boy who was abandoned and abused. But God took that away from him, too. God took everything Bruno loved, dangled it in front of his face, and lit it on fire as Bruno sat sobbing. But don't worry, God does these sorts of things because He loves us. God loved Bruno enough to ruin him. God should love less. I want less of God's love, not more of it. God's love is nothing but heartache, destruction, self-harm, suicidal ideation, depression, anxiety, fear, torment, abuse, and disease. God's love is fatal, and I want nothing to do with Him. He can keep His platitudes and manipulations. "Lovest thou me more than these?[10]" say the scriptures. I would like to ask Him the same question.

The aftermath of Dad's death burned bright and faded fast. Dad's extended family was notified, made travel arrangements, and all showed up with what felt like hypocritical "We love you guys." Shut up. Love is not showing up for marriages and funerals to ensure your face is seen, only to return home, rip off the hat of filial duty, throw it back behind the cobwebs in the attic, and return to your business as nothing happened. Souls are crying and barely hanging on for life while you sit in your life of comfort and ease, wondering when they'll get control of themselves, get over it, and learn to pretend like their clean homes and neat jobs are the makings of a life well-lived. We wouldn't want anything messy, uncomfortable, or inconvenient.

I learned of Dad's death during my evening shift at Dairy Queen. I started working there as soon as I moved in with Josephine after leaving Utah. I was at the register when the owner came up and relieved me of duties. She told me to head to the back, and she would take over. My heart sank because I thought I was getting fired. As I made my way out of the customer service area, I saw Josephine and her husband in the hallway. When I was hardly close enough to hear, Josephine announced, "Dad's dead." Immediately, I marched outside,

---

[10] John 21:15

screamed, threw my apron on the sidewalk, and made an embarrassing scene.

When I had calmed down sufficiently to drive, the three of us went to Dad's home in Eugene. A lot of people were there - relatives and friends. Sadie, who hadn't spoken with Dad in a couple of years, came, as did Dad's long-time friend Chad Jacobson. I liked Chad a lot. He was as faithful a friend as anyone could hope to find. What I don't like is trauma processing with an audience. I wanted to leave as soon as possible, but Josephine had to take on her motherly role of trying to console everyone with empty words. All words feel empty in trauma. So, I stood around awkwardly and do not recall talking to Bruno. Emerson was there, too. He was recovering after a point-blank encounter with a water balloon rocket launcher at scout camp, still healing from the surgery that saved his eyesight.

The house was dark and tired. I don't know why people stand around trying to say comforting words that offer no comfort. No, it's not alright. How do you know this is God's plan? How does anyone know anything? How about your mother abandons you, your stepmother rips apart your self-worth because it amuses her, and your father dies suddenly, and we'll talk about your God. Tell me, does He inflict so much pain upon you that death seems preferable? Does He tell you that families are forever and then send you to a family that has its own engraved door at the entrance to hell? Were you innocent of any malignant sin and suffered the pains and chains of hell anyway? Let me guess your solution; let's just take a wild guess. Does your answer have something to do with reading more scriptures? Saying more prayers? Partaking of the sacrament every week? I hate to dump mud all over your glitter-filled hopes, but those ritualistic habits don't do a thing. They don't make evil men good or good men better. They are no panacea for the ills of the world. But, please, go on, go on ahead and live your little life in your little world. It will come tumbling down someday, and you'll get to feel the betrayal of a God who said He loves you. If we could all be quiet during an unexpected death, that would be great.

Dad's mom, Grandma T, flew in from Florida, all business and panic, and was promptly dubbed 'The General.' Dad's other siblings flew in for the funeral, most notably his older brother and family. Dad had always admired my uncle until the year things fell apart in Junction City. Dad did not appreciate anyone who stepped in to help and acknowledged his wrongdoings for what they were, and hadn't talked to his brother since. His brother came anyway.

Funerals are expensive undertakings, which is why I don't want one. Who needs a costly casket that will be buried underground and hold the remains of a deteriorating corpse? Just take me out to sea and throw me overboard. Or burn me up. Either way, don't spend money, to quote the scriptures, "on that which is of no worth." Nonetheless, some people want to bury their dead in expensive caskets because that's the only kind of caskets there are, and procuring a casket is precisely what Bruno set out to do. An entire entourage entered the funeral home.

Once Grandma T saw the price tags, she started to estimate how to split the cost between the living adults. Seeing the eyes of the children who had just lost their mother and father, my uncle couldn't stand to listen to any more calculations. He turned to my aunt, exchanged looks, and paid for the entire funeral. My uncle gave thousands of dollars to a brother who refused to talk to him. Or, rather, he gave it to his children to alleviate whatever portion of pain he could. And isn't that the mark of greatness - someone who does the right thing regardless of extenuating circumstances because it's the right thing to do?

My aunt and uncle's kindness did not stop there. They found out I was living with Josephine. No element in heaven or hell could have forced me to live with Dolly ever again, and returning to Utah was out of the question. My aunt and uncle wanted to give me the best chance at life, which required time and space to heal. I couldn't do that if I were living with Josephine because she was trying to heal, too. Plus, she was studying to become a pharmacist while working part-time, and she hardly needed the added stress of watching after her mental illness riddled little sister.

I remember sitting in a bedroom at Bruno's house and going through pictures when my uncle tentatively came into the bedroom to ask me what I was doing. He does that, asks questions that have nothing to do with the reason he's there. But he always has a smile on his face and a twinkle in his blue eyes. He asked me if I wanted to live with them and said I was welcome in their home. Later, my aunt told me the same. They gave me time to think before giving them a definitive answer.

When I told Josephine of the offer, she told me to stay with her. She wanted me to live with her, and I wanted to live with her, too. Yet, for once, I had the gift of forethought, a glimpse at the consequences of either path. Moving to Alaska with my unknown aunt and uncle seemed like the choice with the best outcome. And by best, I mean one of safety, where stable adults could take on the stress of me. Josephine tried to convince herself that I was staying. I tried to take the coward's way out and tell her while she was sleeping. She woke up, held my hand, and asked, "You're going, aren't you?" her question felt like a repeated punch to my intestines. At once, I felt like throwing up, crying, and screaming. How could I betray my sister, who had given me so much?

But those feelings were not enough for me to change my mind. I packed my duffel bag, and Josephine drove me to her mother-in-law's house, where my aunt would come pick me up so I could fly home with her and her sons. My uncle had already gone home because he had to return to work. When my aunt came to pick me up, I was distraught because I had not given a full two weeks' notice at Dairy Queen. She told me that my job didn't matter, that they would be able to find someone else. And with her reassurance pushing me forward, I got into the car, and we drove to the airport.

I don't know what I was expecting, but I was surprised by the emptiness and the quiet when we landed in Fairbanks, Alaska. As we drove the twenty miles to their home, I noticed that the birch trees were thin, and the scrawny grasses were shades of brown and green. There was plenty of grass, but each blade looked scrawny. I suppose people and things that survive freezing temperatures tend to look a little haggard. I felt a little haggard, so I was surrounded by kindred spirits, even if the spirits were fictitious. As is my way, I talked nervously, a little too loud, and a little too fast.

Our year together was a rough one for all of us. I blew into their house like a storm and upended their lives. I was emotional, complex, broken, and predictably unpredictable. Every Saturday morning, I would make my way down the stairs where my aunt sat drinking her morning tea. I would talk, talk, and talk about the trauma that filled my body. She listened and asked questions. Occasionally, I could see a fire rise within her, and she tried to temper it. I thought she was mad at me and often got my feelings hurt. I learned a little too slowly that they were not used to communicating in the language of emotions.

Both of their sons played sports, and during the fall, the youngest was on a soccer team. After his game, we all climbed into the car, and I asked, "How did you feel about your game?" A long silence followed as they all looked at each other, confused. "Feel? What are you talking about?" They all laughed, and I didn't understand why they didn't understand my question. It seemed relatively simple to me. My feelings question became our shared joke, a memory of two worlds trying to understand each other. My aunt and uncle were so good to me, and I loved being there, but I didn't tell them. Around November, I started to feel better, happier. I lost the extra weight I had gained in Utah, and the world seemed brighter despite the ever-increasing hours of the night. And then, I went to visit Dolly, per her request, in December. Being near that woman triggered my normal trauma response, even though she was pleasant the entire time.

I gained a few pounds while I was there and a few more when I got home. I was angry and explosive. Thankfully, my aunt and uncle kept me around and didn't threaten to drop me off at the airport with a one-way ticket to anywhere but there. Instead, they kept loving me, as insistent as I was on being unlovable. We did have a lot of fun together, going to the movies, eating good food, and poking fun at each other.

One of my cousins loved to play practical jokes and once injected Tabasco sauce into my piece of my birthday cake while I was upstairs taking a phone call. Just my piece. When I came downstairs, I thought it was jam, gross jam, and kept eating to be polite. As usual, I took a little too long to catch on. We all laughed. Another time, that same cousin blew a foghorn in my ear while I was taking a nap. He was the only one who laughed that time.

While I lived with my aunt and uncle, Josephine and I spoke on the phone for an hour or more every Sunday. She would tell me about her week, and I would tell her about mine. Josephine wanted me to come back to Harrisburg to live with her. I wanted to as well, but I wanted to stay in Alaska more. I knew I was loved and taken care of; how I wanted to be loved and taken care of for as long as possible.

When the time came to choose which college I wanted to attend, I applied to Missoula, the University of Alaska - Fairbanks, and the University of Alaska - Anchorage. I chose the University of Alaska - Anchorage. My aunt and uncle were surprised but happy. I wanted to be emotionally stable enough to be part of their family and reasoned that Anchorage was close enough to be remembered and far enough to give them space. We scheduled a flight to Eugene the day after graduating from high school. I was supposed to visit Josephine for the summer, then fly into Anchorage, where someone from the university would meet me at the airport and bring me to the campus.

As soon as I landed in Eugene and got to Josephine's house, plans changed. I decided to stay with Josephine, go to school at the local community college, and resume my prior position as a Dairy Queen employee. Telling my aunt and uncle of my decision broke my heart.

***

"You love your aunt and uncle, don't you?" Dr. Meager asks.

"I really do. They saved my life. I don't know what trouble I would have found myself in had they not taken me into their home. I wish I could fly back and never come back to Eugene again."

"What's stopping you?"

"My pride."

"I can understand that. How is your relationship with Josephine now?"

"Good. We talk once a week. Thursdays at 9:00 am. Josephine keeps a tight schedule."

"Do you feel like you can talk to her about anything?"

"No. I don't feel like I can talk to anyone about anything, at least not in my normal life. I can talk to you about most stuff, but there are topics I don't bring up, things not worth trying to explain. Sometimes, when I explain a thought, it loses value because the person I am explaining it to either doesn't understand or doesn't think it's worth the same emotional investment."

Dr. Meager nods in agreement, "Do you tell God everything?"

"Why would I tell Him everything if He already knows?"

"Tessa, let me tell you something. I have three young daughters, ten and under. I know when they learn to ride a bike because I see them do it. But I still want them to come and tell me about their victory. I want to see their eyes light up. Similarly, when they fall, I want them to come to me with their tears because I am their father. If they were scared to come to me, I would be heartbroken."

"Do you believe in God, Dr. Meager?" Now I am asking the questions to which I already know the answer.

"Yes, I do."

The Space Between

I stopped visiting Dr. Meager in 2008 and continued fighting for my faith. Church was not pleasant; traumatic responses and unpleasant associations repeated themselves, though not in the same way, and I kept going. That's it - no magic wand, momentous occasions, or sharp turns where the clouds parted, and everything became easy. The trudge was a long, ugly uphill battle with enough rest periods to convince me to keep going. Jesus Christ carried me along, healing me from the wounds done in His name – though not as fast or in the way I wanted.

Additionally, Jesus Christ taught me about who He is – His mission, His character, and His promises.

"For this is my work and my glory, to bring to pass the immortality and eternal life of man.[11]"

". . . Jesus Christ . . . washed us from our sins in his own blood.[12]"

"But, God, who is rich in mercy, for his great love wherewith he loved us.[13]"

"And whatsoever thing persuadeth men to do good is of me; for good cometh of none save it be of me . . . For behold, I am the light, and the life, and the truth of the world.[14]

---

[11] Moses 1:39 (The Pearl of Great Price)

[12] Revelation 1:5

[13] Ephesians 2:4

[14] Ether 4:12

"To him that overcometh will I grant to sit with me in my throne, even as I also overcame, and am set down with my Father in His throne.[15]

As my relationship with Jesus Christ grew, so did my love for and trust in Him. I came to realize that the Lord only teaches His people to love and serve one another; abuse and manipulation are not included. Those who choose otherwise, and refuse to repent, are met with a heavy warning: "But whoso shall offend one of these little ones which believe in me, it were better for him that a millstone were hanged about his neck, and that he were drowned in the depth of the sea.[16]"

---

[15] Revelation 3:21

[16] Matthew 18:6

Falling in Love

Albert Einstein said, "Only a life lived for others is a life worthwhile." Jesus said, "Love your enemies, bless them that curse you, do good to them that hate you, and pray for them which despitefully use you and persecute you.[17]"

I'm trying to figure out the Lord's plan for me because I just turned twenty-three years old, and I'm ready to get out of Eugene as soon as I finish massage therapy school in a few months. I couldn't seem to pay attention long enough to complete a degree at the University of Oregon, so I chose massage therapy school because I get to move my body while I learn. I regret not earning a degree, but massage therapy isn't bad. I get to help people and learn a lot about the human body. Still, I feel like I gave up on myself by choosing massage over a bachelor's degree. However, the regular human touch helped me get through my breakup with Jared, so maybe massage therapy school is what God wanted me to do.

Most of my friends are moving away at the end of the school year, so I have little motivation to stay in Eugene. Bruno's married, his wife is expecting their second child, and he's on his way out of Eugene to pursue a different career path. Josephine is perpetually busy and is probably moving to Portland after graduating from pharmacy school in a couple of months. I feel like Eugene has nothing left for me. Massage therapy school ends in July, at which point I will have a marketable skill to open doors in new places. Working as a massage therapist on a cruise ship would be adventurous, except I don't like the

---

[17]Matthew 5:44

idea of being trapped on a boat. I like having my two feet on solid ground.

I could move to Utah like most people my age seem to do when they're unwed members of the Church. But I don't like the weather in Utah or the culture. Plus, Utah has its share of bad memories without the benefit of green in every direction. I don't know where to go, but I don't want to stay.

As I sit alone in the living room, I write in my journal, "*Please, Heavenly Father, help me be brave, honest, and good. I want to speak kind words first and last, to be a woman who is nicer than necessary in every situation.*"

I have moments like this where my desire to be Christlike runs through and around my soul, and then I am presented with a situation to prove myself. I usually fail. I know change takes time, but I'm as fast as a sloth. However, I find comfort in knowing that when I trust in the Lord and His timing, He always puts me in better situations than I would have seen for myself. For example, God led me to my roommates when I insisted I didn't want any. Surprisingly and thankfully, they don't take me too seriously and invite me into their social circle without reservations.

I know the Lord is more concerned with who I am than where I am, but where I live matters. I have an excellent job, but I want to pursue a different career path, such as developing a massage therapy practice. I want to get out of Eugene, get married someday, be a great massage therapist, stay home with my children when the time comes, see my family regularly, have a secure job, insurance, good friends, more patience, to laugh more than I cry, and to make a difference. I keep looking to other people to help me decide, but only I can make the final choice. Moving to Salem may be an option. I need to research their job market to check out what's available. I'll also consult the Lord through my scriptures. I find most of the answers to my life in the scriptures.

***

"Bruno! Come quickly," I'm at Bruno's house studying my scriptures because I wanted to spend some time with my one-year-old niece. She's blonde and blue-eyed, happy, and chubby.

"Yes, Tessa?"

"This is very exciting, so I need you to be excited."

"I'll try my best."

"You know how I've been praying about what to do with my life after I'm done with school in July, right? When my roommates ditch me for the dating pool in Utah? I think I got my answer. I just read in the scriptures, "It is necessary that ye should remain for the present time in your places of abode, as it shall be suitable to your circumstances.[18]" I guess that's the answer - to stay in Eugene?"

"I would say so," Bruno smiles at me like the watchful big brother that he is, "you'd better read a few verses down where it talks about saving all the money you can. You're not very good at saving money."

"Yeah, that's true. Let me read it aloud, "It must needs be necessary that ye save all the money that ye can." I look at Bruno; he's smiling.

I wonder why I must save all the money I can, other than that saving is wise financial management. Am I saving more because something horrible is about to happen? Whatever the case, I don't need to worry about it. I was answered and will follow through, regardless of whether I understand. Peace comes with knowing I am making the right choices and moving in the direction the Lord has chosen. When I'm not, I feel short-tempered and frustrated.

Elder Dallin H. Oaks taught this precise principle: "Remember that when your prayers do not seem to be answered in the way or at the

---

[18] Doctrine and Covenants 48:1, 4

time you desire; no matter how strong our faith is, it cannot produce a result contrary to the will of Him in who you have faith.[19]"

So much for trusting in the Lord, I've been a wreck for the past two weeks, during which time I have gained twelve pounds. Twelve pounds. I want to cut my fat off with a knife. But I don't need to dwell on my fatness because I get to go to the temple, the Lord's house, for the first time in a year. I feel a bit guilty going because I have not been very nice to my roommates lately - I've said unkind things and been cranky and impatient. I will be better this week. The Spirit in the temple replaces my greedy, self-absorbed nature with Heavenly Light. Someday, I will be self-disciplined enough to enjoy Heavenly Light all the time. Until then, I'll keep dumping out the filth with my still-on-the-same-lesson bucket.

When I walk into the Institute building where the young adults meet before carpooling up to the Portland, Oregon, Temple, I see someone new. A tall, slender, tan man with a big, happy smile, straight teeth, and curly hair is standing next to the bishop. I wonder what car he's riding in.

"Tessa, it's time to go,' one of my roommates grabs my arm and leads me towards the door, 'get in the car."

"Okay, okay,' I say as the four of us get into a blue sedan, "did you guys see the new guy?"

"No."

"Well, you should have. He's really cute. Also, I'm sorry for being unpleasant to live with during the last couple of weeks."

"We forgive you," they don't speak in unison, but I know they all forgive me. Bless them.

Our ward has a tradition of stopping at Fuddruckers for a pre-temple dinner. During our pre-temple dinner at Fuddruckers, the good-looking man I saw at the church building walks over and sits next to me, on purpose. There are plenty of other open seats, and I can't help

---

[19] Dallin H. Oaks, The Atonement and Faith, *Ensign*, April 2010, 30

but get giggly with excitement. He sets his order down on the table: three hamburgers, two servings of French fries, and a large soda. That's a lot of food. Maybe he's a poor college student who doesn't know when he'll eat again.

"Hi, I'm Tessa," I introduce myself, wishing I hadn't gained twelve pounds in the last two weeks. My roommate, who sits across the table, points to her shirt and then to me and mouths something I can't understand. When I look down, I see that I buttoned my emerald cardigan incorrectly. Perfect.

"Hi, I'm Eric," he smiles broadly with straight, white teeth. I do have a weakness for nice teeth.

"Where are you from? What brings you to Eugene? How long are you going to stay here?" I ask.

Wiping his mouth with a napkin and looking like he's trying not to laugh, he says, "I'm from Southern California. I just graduated from BYU, and I'm only in Eugene for a few months before starting my master's program.

"Why are you in Eugene for only a few months?"

"I am doing an internship with Oregon Ice Cream."

"What are you doing there?"

"I get to work in the research and development department making new ice cream flavors."

"That sounds like a great job. I love ice cream. My favorite flavor is chocolate, of course, because chocolate is one of my favorite food groups, but I like just about everything else. Well, almost everything else. I don't care for strawberry, or any berry flavor, any ice cream that's the color of playdough, orange sherbet, Neapolitan, or any other weird flavor. Oh, and cake batter ice cream is a little too sweet, don't you think?"

"So, you like chocolate and vanilla ice cream?"

"Yes. Oh, and pistachio. My grandfather used to keep pistachio ice cream around. I used to pour hot fudge on top and devour it like I'd never eat again," I can tell Eric thinks I am using sensory language to make a good story, which isn't wrong, but I'm also telling the truth.

"Ice cream is good," Eric says, before returning his attention to his hamburger.

"What did you earn a degree in?" I ask.

"Food science."

"I didn't know there was such a thing. How did you find out about food science?"

"My dad's a food scientist, plus the degree did not require anatomy and physiology, or biology."

"I love anatomy and physiology. I am in massage therapy school, where we learn a wide range of interesting topics. Listen to these fun words: xyphoid process, olecranon process, zygomatic arch, patella, cubiform, mandible, axon hillock, nodes of Ranvier, myelin sheath, supine, caudal, medial aspect, supraspinatus, anterior superior iliac spine, sartorius, quadratus lumborum, and, my personal favorite, fibularis tertius. Are you familiar with any of those words?"
"No, that's why I'm glad that I didn't take anatomy," Eric smiles and starts on his third hamburger.

"My roommates and I need to get going soon because they want to stop by Deseret Book before we go to the temple. Do you want to come over after we get back to Eugene? I don't know what we're doing, but I'm sure laughing will be involved."

Eric stares at me like I've just spoken Latin. After a painfully long pause, he says, "Yes."

"Great. See you at the temple."

***

"Did you see me talk to him? His name is Eric," I ask my roommate as we drive to the bookstore.

"Yes, I saw you. Also, you invited Eric over but didn't give him your phone number or our address."

"Dang it. I'll see him at the temple and give it to him then."

"Good luck. Remember how women and men sit on separate sides of the room in the baptistry?"

"You do have a point."

**

The Portland, Oregon Temple looks like a castle with its spires and smooth stone exterior - a castle from a fairy tale, not a medieval castle. Not all temples are equal in exterior beauty, but they all hold the same opportunities - to partake of sacred ordinances and make sacred covenants with God. I don't have many details of what goes on inside. Still, I know that the covenant of eternal marriage is the grandest blessing I can hope to receive – to live with Heavenly Father and Jesus Christ as an eternal and exalted woman, with my family by my side[20]. I used to think eternity sounded like a death sentence, and now I want nothing less. If my broken family can cause so much anguish, imagine the joy of an eternal family that loves God and each other without restraint.

While inside the baptistry, I try to focus on the spiritual and sacred nature of our visit, but find myself looking around for Eric with no luck. He must be in another room. By the time we left, I only saw him out of the corner of my eye once, smiling. He smiles a lot.

**

When I walk into church the next day, I see Eric sitting by himself and immediately take a seat next to him, as if he had saved it for me. He smiles and looks confused.

"I'm sorry about last night. I realized I invited you over without giving you my address. So, I've written it down for you. You can come over tonight if you want," I hand him the paper, hoping he'll look excited instead of confused.

---

[20] Doctrine and Covenants 14:7

He takes the paper and says, "Okay."

After church, I realized that I forgot to give him my phone number, again.

***

"Tessa! Eric's here," my roommate announces.

"He is? How do I look? Like I took an hour to get ready to look like I don't take that long?"

"You look great."

As I open the door, I almost trip over the pile of shoes that's collected at the front door, "Hi, come on in. I am making cookies. Do you like cookies?"

"Yes," he steps inside, wearing a cardinal red and yellow shirt with the initials USC on the front. His shorts are Stop sign red. What does USC stand for?

When I bring him a plate of cookies, he only takes a few. I guess he must not like them because I've seen how much he can eat. Note to self, don't make him cookies again, or at least not these cookies. A few other people from church come over, and our living room is full of people before too long. I don't want Eric to feel lost and awkward, but I don't want to glue myself to his side. When he leaves, he seems happy, so I must have struck the right balance.

As I close the door behind our last guest, I yell to my roommates, "Ladies, let's Facebook stalk Eric!"

"Oh, I love Facebook stalking people. Does he have a profile?' one of them picks up her laptop and starts click-clacking away, 'Hmmm...what's his last name? Jensen, right?

"Yes, Jensen." My insides twist in excitable knots.

"He's here. Eric Jensen, the tall one with curly hair. His profile picture is him standing with his family outside a house."

"Can you make him sound any less exciting? Let me see."
She's right; Eric is standing with his family in front of his house. Or at
least part of his family. He has at least one sister, parents, and an older
woman who looks like she could be his grandma. His dad looks really
tall, and his mom seems really short. After a few moments, I say, "I
think it's a sweet picture, and I am going to send him a message."

"You know you could have given him your phone number at
least fifteen different times, right?"

"Yes, but I didn't, and Facebook is the next best thing. I don't
want to wait to see him until next Sunday. And I doubt if he wants to
wait to see me. Clearly, Eric needs some excitement in his life."

Eric responds to my Facebook message quickly. A couple of
weeks later, we shared a magical, goofy, and romantic Memorial Day
weekend. Well, I'm not sure if romance is a word that can be applied
to the sparks that my relationship with Eric, but it's within the same
family.

The weekend started on the 29th when Eric, my roommate, and
I drove down to Wildlife Safari to see the animals, take pictures, and
enjoy the sunshine. My roommate's parents let us all stay the night at
their house. I'm pretty sure this weekend was the first time Eric has
spent more than a couple of hours around women he is not related to.
He looks slightly scared, and I'm unsure whether he likes listening or
doesn't like talking.

On the 31st, we all went running up Ridgeline Trail to the top
of Spencer's Butte. Eric and I ran while my roommate walked and
laughed at us. Eric beat me to the top, but I know he walked a few
times. I didn't. If my legs were as long as his, I would have beaten
him. By the time we got back to the car, we had mud up the back of
our legs and a few splashes on our shirts.

After our run, we took our sweaty, smelly selves to see *The
Prince of Persia* and bought lots of candy beforehand. I wanted to hold
Eric's hand, and I could tell he wanted to hold mine, but instead, we
ate candy and stole glances and bashful smiles. I want Eric to ask me

on a date instead of me asking him to go on adventures. I'm not sure what more I must do to convince him to take the risk.

***

"Tessa, Eric's here. Again." My roommate gives me a good-natured eye roll.

"Hi, Eric. I'm happy you're here. Do you want to go on a walk to celebrate the first day of summer?"

"Don't you two always go on walks?"

"Sure,' Eric says, ignoring my roommate, let's go on a walk."

Elated to be together after the painful fourteen hours apart, we walk past Hayward Field, over the Autzen Bridge, and towards the Prefontaine trails.

"I had fun at the beach yesterday." Eric seems quieter than usual, and now I am worried that I made our adventure at the beach more magical than it was.

"Me, too."

Now, I'm expecting him to drop my hand and explain how he likes me but doesn't think we should date anymore. I hang my head as tears well up behind my eyes. Thankfully, Eric seems lost in thought, so I can process the loss of what I thought existed before he notices. Or, at least put a temporary dam in place.

After fifteen minutes of silence, I started to let go of his hand. If he's done with me, then he's done holding my hand.

"What are you doing?" Eric looks sad when he feels our hands let go.

"Oh, um, nothing. I just needed to twist my ring around because it was jabbing my finger. See? All fixed." I put my hand back in his, waiting for him to make a joke or a goofy observation.

"I talked to my sister today."

"Oh? And how is she doing?"

"Good. She says she wants to meet you." *Regroup, Tessa. He still likes you if his sister wants to meet you. Chin up. All is well.*

"Is she going to come out to Eugene and visit you?" I ask.

"Probably not, but she still wants to meet the first girl I have ever dated."

"Are you serious? You've never dated anyone else?" I hope I didn't just embarrass him with my surprise.

"Well, I've gone on dates but never dated anyone. I had never held a girl's hand or kissed a girl until I met you."

I clap my hands on my cheeks to cover up the blush blooming on my face.

Eric gently pulls my hands away from my cheeks, puts them behind his neck, and hugs me for a long time.

Then, he whispers, "Tessa, I think I love you."

"I think I love you, too."

When he lets go, I allow him to see the joy on my face. No looking at the ground, using deflective humor, or running away. The mutual confession opens the floodgates and resumes our frolicking ways from before. By the time we get to my house, we must have walked five miles.

"Goodbye, Eric. I'll see you tomorrow."

"Bye, Tessa. I love you."

I'm smiling so big that I can't respond before he opens his car door. Now to resist the urge to travel via cartwheels. I think I could jump to the top of the house if I tried.

***

"I was thinking we could go on a walk tonight," Eric says, a few weeks after we told each other, 'I love you.'

"I would like that." I feel bad because I have been grumpy and moody all day. Not with Eric, just in general. I think my co-workers would have preferred it if I had called in sick. I hate days like this. I offer a silent prayer, *Oh Lord, please help me control myself so that I can show love to this wonderful man who loves me. He is a gift and an answer to my prayers. Please, help me treat him as such.*

Eric is wearing jeans, which is odd because he almost always wears basketball shorts, and it's a sunny July day. I wish I could be the wind swirling through the trees, the water molding to the shape of its boundaries only to defy their commands. What is a boulder to a river? Nothing but a rock that needs smoothing out.

"Tessa, are you okay?"

"Yes, I'm fine. Just moody for no reason; I am so sorry. I probably just need to eat something."

"Can we go on a walk first?"

"Sure, we can do that." Sometimes walks are outlets for trapped irritation, and I need to release the irritation, so I don't act crabby towards Eric.

"It's a pretty night. I like summer nights; it reminds me of growing up in southern California."

"I like summer nights, too, but I do not care for summer days."

"I know. You hate the heat." Eric laughs.

"Why are you laughing at me?"

"I'm not laughing at you, I'm happy, and sometimes I gig. . .why are you crying?"

"I feel like you're making fun of me." Now I'm sobbing.

"Wait, I don't understand why you're so upset. I wasn't making fun…" Eric starts rummaging around in his pocket, 'I am trying to find a way to ask you to marry me." In his hand is a timeless solitaire diamond on a silver ring. He kneels, like the gentleman he is, and officially asks, "Tessa, will you marry me?"

My grumpiness melts and gives way to elation, "Yes! Oh yes, yes, yes, I will!"

Both of our eyes are shining with tears. I can't stop myself from talking. All the plans I've made come spilling out, "I think we should get married in December because you leave for Fresno in a few weeks. I'll stay in Eugene and continue working at Oregon Medical Group while you complete your first semester. I finish massage school next week, so I could get a job as a massage therapist; however, I don't know how long the licensing process takes, and it's also expensive. Do we want to pay for me to get my license in two states? What do you think? After next week, I'll increase my hours to full-time. Do you care what the wedding colors are? My favorite color is green, and yours is red, so we can do red and green. Oh, wait, those are Christmas colors. But we're getting married during the Christmas season, so it makes sense and...."

"Tessa,' Eric interrupts, 'I prayed about us every night, Tessa. Every night when I got home from your house, I prayed to know if we were right for each other."

"I've been praying, too,' I admit, 'I don't think we've even known each other for two whole months so people will think we're crazy, but I don't care. Not a bit. I'll marry you, move with you to Fresno, live in a dumpy apartment to save money, and love you forever!"

When we tell our families, they laugh, question the wisdom of our choice, and declare their support. Dolly and her husband promise to pay for the wedding reception. I think she's changed. Josephine is the only person who gets mad, which I don't understand, because she is not foreign to swift-moving relationships. When I introduce her to Eric, she gives him a curt, 'Hello,' and walks past him like he's a sneeze.

***

It's a cold day in December, and Eric and I are getting married in the Portland Temple. My soul cannot hold the joy washing over me. Together we will have a home and a family. Soon, we'll add children, lots of children. When I imagined realities that felt impossible, I would think of a big, but not fancy house, full of kids running in and out with snacks, pails, and art supplies. A couple of dogs, too. A husband who adores me and still thinks I am pretty with unkempt hair, flour on my face, and tiny handprints on my once-fashionable wardrobe.

The Grace

The Past, Haunting

It's been over six years since I married Eric, and I don't know where the joy went. I feel like a shell of the woman he married. I was fun, energetic, outrageous, and, at times, full of mischief. I put jeans on, did my hair, and exercised. We hiked, drove to the beach, and kissed. We don't do any of those things anymore. We simply exist from one moment to the next. My days are measured from one nap to the next. I need more self-discipline, more faith. If I try harder, God will help me.

I tried to take our four kids to the library today: an eight-month-old, a two-year-old, and a four and a five-year-old. After getting them out of the car, I tried to hold back a full-on panic attack as I looked for dangers to which they were blissfully unaware, and we barely made it to the front door. One of the library security personnel was standing just inside the entrance, an older gentleman. Three of my kids ran past him, and I looked haggard and worn, trying to keep up so I could keep them quiet. That man looked me straight in the eye and said, "Geez, Mom, don't you know when to stop?"

Like I do, I give him a polite smile and fake laugh. Then, with my heart beating in my head and tunnel vision closing in, I stormed into the library, snapped at the kids to grab a book, marched them out to the van, and sped away. My body was shaking with rage by the time we got home, and I continued to snap at them until we were all safely inside, the front door locked. I sat down on the couch and put my head in my hands, trying to find my breath.

"Mom?" Bruce, my oldest son, asked.

"What?" I said, with unrestrained anger in my voice as I lifted my head, though I was not mad at him. Bruce didn't respond. He just looked at me with fear in his eyes, waiting. My heart broke at that moment. I was making him scared, as my dad had done to me. I apologized to him, but I knew he wanted to get away from me as quickly as possible. Whatever he was going to ask me was no longer worth his time. I don't deserve to be his mother. Or anyone's mother. I'm fat, gross, ugly, and mean. I stay awake only as long as necessary.

Once Eric gets home from work, I usually drag myself to my room and gorge on Trader Joe's chocolate-covered marshmallows and peanut butter cups. Then, I vacillate between sleep and consciousness until a little person comes in and tells me it's time for dinner. I heave my fat, disgusting body out of bed and sit down at the table like a storm, making the entire experience miserable for everyone.

I feel as hopeless and depressed as when I went to see Dr. Meager ten years ago, but this time it's a different brand of darkness. It's as if every morning, the devil whispers in my ear, *Don't ask stupid questions, Tessa. You're a slave to your body, your broken brain, and your incessant recall of memories. Forget them, and your problems are solved. Ta da! Die, and your children can be free from your curse. You're doing to them what Dolly and Sarah did to you. You're a monster. There's no magic, no spiritual cleansing, and no healing that can fix your problems. No medication, either. You're a disappointment to God. He doesn't love you, and He doesn't want to hear from you. He gave you your husband and your children, and you're not even grateful. Just put yourself to sleep. That's right. Eat and sleep. Eat and sleep. Or you could just try harder to be less stupid. Or can you? You can't do much, can you? You're worthless, unwanted, and remember, God told your mother to leave you. You remember that any time you think He's good. He promised you everything, but He took everything. Remember His pattern. Do you believe that He's given you your husband and children without strings attached? He'll rip them away from you, too. You'll come home, and they'll be gone. You'll drive in your car looking for them, tears falling faster than the rain can fall.*

And then God will send a storm you can't escape. That's exactly what
your God's love looks like, and you know it.

When I have the strength, usually on a day that one of my kids
tells me that they love me, I fight back, *"Oh, shut up, Satan. Do you*
ever shut up? You never stop talking. Someday I will slam the door
when I hear you approach. Someday. When that day comes, I will have
the strength to share my triumph with someone who has the same
despairing eyes I see in the mirror. They won't believe me because I'll
be unrecognizable from the person I am today. I'll be a woman as wise
as a serpent and as gentle as a dove. Unapologetic in her discipleship.
Compassionate. A woman who cares for the poor - the unnoticed,
ignored, and marginalized. Someday."

Satan always responds, *"That day is not today. I'm still here."*

He's right. Why don't I wake up with God whispering in my
ear? I have felt suicidal, apathetic, and everything in between. I had
tubal ligation on my birthday to prevent any further pregnancies. I
wish I hadn't. The surgery is done, and there is no use in marinating in
resentment and sorrow. I am angry at myself for not losing the baby
weight, binge eating, for giving up on exercise. I may look human, but
I'm just a trash can. A physical, spiritual, and emotional trash can. I
am not the woman my children need me to be. I am not strong, and I
quit everything I start. The thought of how much work it will take to
drag myself out of this pit is staggering. It's too hard. But what's the
alternative? Do I want the consequences of the road I'm on? Even
now, my mind feels clouded. I keep thinking of what a disappointing,
revolting, and failure of a human I am. I expect to feel immediate
relief when I pray, but I don't. When I try to move forward, I usually
find myself waking up in my own drool on the couch. My life is
moving from the couch to my bed, to the floor - wherever I can sleep.
I've let my testimony of Jesus Christ burn out and nearly die, but a
couple of embers remain.

I want my children to be better than I am and find happiness
living the gospel with so many beautiful promises. Trying to maintain
a relationship with Jesus Christ requires a lot of effort. Prayer,

scriptures, and especially going to church. I don't need any of those things to find God, and I'm also lying to myself. Elder Richard G. Scott said that scripture study is more important than anything else I could be doing instead, even more important than sleep. So, I will try again, even if my efforts are not what they used to be. I used to be determined and immovable, fun, vibrant. I didn't realize it at the time, but a few things are realized in real-time.

Most of my six years with Eric have been happy, with the usual ups and downs of battling mental illness and the desire to run out of church. But, ever since Vivian, our youngest, was born, I can't shake this eternal midnight. I want to tell you the happy parts of our life, so you know that none of my current internal wars has to do with my husband or children. It's all me, me, and my problems.

Eric and I were married for ten months before Bruce was born. I did not know the luxury of clean air until we moved from Eugene to Fresno, California, with its terrible inversion, otherwise identified as trapped air pollution and concrete landscape. My first attempt at going on a run left me feeling like someone was administering a slow poison into my muscles. Six weeks later, the slow poison feeling combined with morning sickness left me bedridden for the duration of my pregnancy. Morning sickness is an inadequate term to convey the magnitude of depleted vitality. In any case, neither my baby nor I had any physical health complications requiring medical attention.

However, our get-out-of-medical-scares coupons were used up when Bruce was born. He nearly choked to death a few hours after his birth. Eric had gone home to take a shower and a nap after Bruce had fallen asleep, exhausted after being thrust into the world. I was about to take a nap myself, but decided to admire my little boy one more time. When I walked over to his bassinet, Bruce's face was purple, and his eyes were terrified as he tried to move his head from one side to the other. Fluid was bubbling out of his mouth. Instinctively, I swooped him up and hit his back as hard as necessary.

Copious amounts of amniotic fluid flew out of his mouth like projectile vomit. I never thought I would be happy about getting covered in bodily fluids, but, at that moment, I was elated. Two nurses rushed in after the worst was over. They helped me change and checked on Bruce, who was, gratefully, relatively unscathed. Later, when we were leaving, one of the nurses said, "You'll have to tell Bruce when he's sixteen and refusing to listen to you that you saved his life once." Maybe I saved it twice: once on the day of his birth and once the day we drove out of Fresno for the last time. We were moving near Seattle, Washington, to Eric's new job.

As we made our way through Oregon and Washington, in a U-Haul with our faithful Mitsubishi Outlander attached to the back, I explained to Bruce what a tree looks like and that green is a color found in nature. Bruce, who had no idea what I was talking about, laughed and sucked on his toes. Bruce's eyes crinkle on the outer edges when he laughs, like my uncle's and Emerson's. Eric smiled at me, also laughing. We were driving into an unknown adventure, made more adventurous with the knowledge that I was eight weeks pregnant. We were so happy.

Once we made it to our Washington destination, we pulled up to our two-bedroom, third-story apartment. The apartment looked modern and clean, complete with a washer and dryer. I set to work making it look as cozy as I could and watched myself perform a natural human phenomenon - the re-creation of our home from one location to the other. The floor plan changed, but our home did not. We had the same furniture and decorations, and we were still us, with the same habits, preferences, and idiosyncrasies. I lashed out in an angry panic several times during the move, which I apologized for and attributed to past unpleasant experiences.

That June was likely the rainiest June I had seen, and I loved it. Pouring rain means it's time to bake chocolate chip cookies and banana bread. I imagine heaven smells like a mixture of Pacific Northwest rain mixed with fresh-baked chocolate chip cookies. The rest of the summer, we were not so blessed. The sun shone brightly. We spent our time going on walks, hikes, and guessing if our new baby was a boy or a girl. When the ultrasound tech said, "You're having a girl," Bruce started crying, not about the announcement but about dropping his toy car. Nonetheless, the timing was priceless, and he was unimpressed when we told him that his little sister would be named Fiona.

In September, when I was six months pregnant with Fiona, Granny and Pa drove up from Eugene to pay me a visit. My heart nearly burst with joy when I walked down the stairs to meet them. Pa wore his usual plaid shirt, red this time, and Granny looked fancy in her small high heels and gold necklace. But the visit was not happy. Not at all. I assumed they were visiting to see Bruce and to tell me they love me, that I'm doing a good job, and to spend time with me. I was wrong. Instead, they scolded me as I sat on the floor, six months pregnant, with Bruce running all over like a wild man. When the scolding was done, they left.

My crime? Avoiding Dolly. On our way to Seattle, we stayed the night at Granny and Pa's house, and Dolly had been there. Our visit was pleasant enough. Before going to bed, Granny and I had a conversation that stirred up the pain and heartache from years gone by as if I were watching the scenes in real time. Dolly's past treatments entered my memory, along with the free fall into self-destruction that inevitably followed. As a child, Dolly chipped away at my soul with small comments and passive-aggressive slights, but, as an adult, so long as I am in her good graces, we can get along. Until she reminds me that she was still, her, especially when her comments remind me that she still dislikes Bruno, still declares herself innocent of all wrongdoing, and still practices the art of victim-blaming Josephine. My words are stuck inside of me when these reminders flare; I am physically unable to have a straightforward conversation with her because I would end up apologizing for my perceptions, emotions, and experiences as if I made it all up.

So, after the predictable pain resurfaced, I stopped talking to Dolly. I ignored her phone calls, texts, and letters. I wanted her to leave me alone, and could not give her the courtesy of telling her so. I felt weak and pathetic around her, and my mind would rip itself apart for days afterward. Binging, sobbing, and lashing out would play on repeat for days. To prevent putting my husband and son through that cycle, I avoided Dolly. Now, Dolly's parents brought the torment into my home under the guise of concern.

Pa asked me to make up with 'my mother' because I know better than to harbor ill feelings since I had been through the temple. He explained how Dolly did not have an easy time being married to Dad and how he, Pa, was so mad at me that he wasn't going to give me any green beans. Pa knew how I loved his green beans, so his comment was calculated to hurt. I was also advised to tell Dolly that I am learning to be motherly through this pregnancy as a way of making amends, as well as some other suggestions on how to blame, shame, and berate myself to give Dolly the praise and respect she is due.

Worse than Pa's demands, Granny said that she wanted me and Dolly to dress her in her temple clothes when she passes away. For that to happen, I need to "get over whatever I think happened." I sat politely, smiling and apologizing, until they hugged me, told me that they loved me, and left. When I closed the door, I went to the kitchen and binged. I snapped at Eric when he got home and lost my patience with Bruce. After registering the hurt on their faces, I apologized and ate more.

I cried all night as powerful contractions seized my womb, contractions that were too early. Fear for Fiona overtook me, and I lay on my bed feeling helpless as violent sobs racked my body, one right hook after the other. Eric slept soundly next to me. I knew I could have woken him up, but what was the point? He had to go to work in the morning.

By the morning, the contractions had stopped. I determined never to give Granny, Pa, or Dolly that kind of influence over me again. But by the afternoon, I convinced myself that I was wrong for my actions and perspectives and was responsible for causing more pain. Soon after, I apologized to everyone, including Dolly. I thought, *Pour the blame on me one more time, cite my mental illness, moods, and sensitivities. I am the cause. I am responsible.*

Afterward, I pled with the Lord to remove my anger and fill my heart with forgiveness and love. I prayed to see the error of my ways to be who He wants me to be. I went to the temple and tried to scrape all hints of negative feelings out of my heart and mind. A recurring thought came to me; *their feelings are not worth your self-destruction. You are not responsible for their decisions, and you are allowed to hurt. You cannot sacrifice yourself for their gain. Jesus Christ has already sacrificed Himself for all of them, including Dolly. He can heal them. Forgiveness does not mean allowing yourself to be repeatedly bludgeoned.*

I interpreted this thought to mean that I should keep trying by doing as Granny advised - to just get over it and put a smile on my face. Why, when I receive impressions from the Lord, do I automatically filter them through my damaged perspective? What I see is rarely what is. Or is it? Do I think my view is damaged because it goes against what other people tell me I should see? Why are they, meaning Dolly, Granny, and Pa, so bothered by my pain that they go out of their way to tell me how I'm wrong? And why, why, why, must they drag religion into this?

Let me tell you what I wish I had said, *"Don't you dare drag the temple, my motherhood, my pregnancy, or your beans into this conversation as tools of manipulation. You should have told me the truth about why you wanted to visit, so I could prepare myself for the blast on my character and the twisting of beliefs. Do you know who else has been through the temple? Dolly. Did you have a similar conversation with her when she was dating while still married? How about when she got married right after her divorce? When she chose to stay married to a man whom she knew had violated her daughters? How about when Bruno hid behind the trees lining your fence line and cried because all three of you treated him like a pariah instead of comforting and nurturing him for the heartbroken boy he was? Do they teach cruelty in the temple? Do they teach shaming in the temple? If I must forget about whatever I think happened, then So. Do. You.*

Look in the mirror instead of using your microscope of spiritual superiority to burn the ants of your disgust.

And my pregnancy? My son? I considered those off-limits in the world of gaslighting, but here we are. To start, let's let go of the notion that children of trauma and divorce are supposed to form parental attachments to whoever their parent decides to marry. Did you know that when Sarah took us into hiding, Josephine wasn't allowed to play outside or look out the window? When Dad found us, we were handed over to him after not seeing him for six months. I didn't even know who he was and was forcibly taken, per court order, from my mother. MY MOTHER. As a baby. Do you suppose I was cognitively able to understand and process what was going on? Hmm? And all this nonsense happened before I could talk and before I understood words like 'fear, panic, or trauma.' So, no, my motherhood has not conjured up an acceptance or tolerance of Dolly's decisions any more than Sarah's."

Of course, I would never speak those words. I felt terrible and un-Christian thinking them. I prayed for forgiveness and tried again to be quiet; I stuffed all of that noise down with some brownies and made myself sick on peanut butter cups, marshmallows, and popcorn. I tried to be everything they wanted me to be. Later, Dolly told me that she asked Granny and Pa not to say anything to me, and Pa apologized for "opening a can of worms." He asked me to keep calling Granny every Friday so we can have our weekly chat, like we've been doing for years.

If I want God to forgive me, I must forgive them[21]. However, while I am guilty of holding a grudge and clinging to past hurts like they are the air I breathe, God did not leave me alone to flounder after my grandparents' horrible visit. His tender mercies poured down in greater helpings than my circumstances and selfishness. Eric held me and kept me going when I wanted to marinate in self-pity. My aunt and

---

[21] Doctrine and Covenants 64:10

uncle came to visit separately, one on either side of my grandparents' visit. I don't know where I would be without them. I hope I am as generous with my love as they are; they love me even when I'm a monstrous snapping turtle. Why do I reserve the worst parts of myself for the people who love me the most?

Bruce and his mischievous grin and boundless energy were another tender mercy. We went on several walks a day. He walked at eight months old, and by eleven months old, we walked the ¾ of a mile to and from the local grocery store together. On days when the rain poured down, I took Bruce to the bottom of the stairwell, where he would crawl up the three flights of stairs. We did that repeatedly until he lay his sweet head on his arm, the sign that he was tired and ready for a snack and a nap. Snacks and naps dominated our schedule.

We lived in that third-story apartment for eighteen months before moving into our modest home, where we now reside. I found the listing for this house while looking for housing on Zillow and couldn't believe that it hadn't been snatched up right away; three bedrooms, one bath, a garage, and a sprawling lawn with plenty of fertile ground for growing imaginations and housing the shrieks of children. As soon as we stepped out of the car, I knew it was meant to be. To clarify, I generally don't agree with the sentiment, "it will be if it's meant to be," especially as it applies to personal choice. I especially don't agree when people claim their suffering caused by another person's selfish choices was 'God's plan.' No, it was not God's plan that your marriage failed because your spouse wouldn't get help for their addiction, or your parents were abusive, that you became paralyzed in a drunk driving accident, or that your identity was stolen, and you lost everything.

God's plan does not include His children harming one another. His plan atones for that harm through the sacrifice of His Only Begotten Son, who will work all things together for our good. Also, we are to act for ourselves, not to sit idly by reacting to our circumstances. Think of the difference between action and reaction, offensive and defensive. I don't want to live my life thinking of all the things that have happened to me as if I were a celestial experiment. Throw me down and I will get back up, though my legs may shake. Maybe all I can do is put one foot in front of the other, only to have that foot land in a pile of mud and my legs fly out from under me as I whack my chin on the sharp edge of a table, but I will stand. Someday, I will even stand with a straight back, squared shoulders, and my head held high.

Before we moved, I started looking for higher education options. Everything cost more than we could afford. Still, Eric was supportive and encouraged me to keep looking. Soon, I learned of the Pathways program through the Church Education System. If I fulfilled the prerequisite education and religion courses for the first year, I could enroll in one of BYU-Idaho's bachelor's degree programs. The cost? Only $69 per credit. My heart soared when I realized the treasure I was handed as if it were made for me alone, gift-wrapped in green and tied with a silver bow.

I signed up for two classes. One was entirely online, while the other was held once a week at the Institute building on the University of Washington's campus. Every Thursday, I drove to class in bumper-to-bumper traffic; it took over an hour to get there and thirty minutes to drive home. I did that from September 2013 to June 2014. I've taken one or two classes every semester since, plugging along until I finish in five or six years. I wish I could take more classes, but I have other priorities. Times and Seasons, I suppose.

After we moved into our house, Emerson lived with us while he found work and decided what he wanted to do with his life. I loved having Emerson in our home, though I knew it wouldn't last long. He was in his early twenties, with many opportunities stretched before him. The day he moved out was a hard day, even though he only moved a few miles away. I simply enjoyed having him around. I cherish any time I get to spend with my siblings.

We knew we would need to live on a strict, if not impossible, budget when we went from renting an apartment to renting a home. Our financial reality put a strain on Eric, even though he claimed it didn't. Not long before our move, I had submitted the paperwork for a massage therapy license in Washington upon the urging of my friend. I wasn't going to do it, but she encouraged me relentlessly. I thought of finding a massage therapy job during evenings and weekends but had done minimal exploring. While we were out running errands one afternoon, I noticed a Massage Envy a few miles from our home. I promptly disregarded employment as an option on account of advice I had received in massage therapy school: "Never get a job with Massage Envy. They are a terrible franchise."

A week later, after continued prayers for direction, I received what I asked for in the middle of sweeping evidence of the outdoors off the floor. Our house smelled of freshly mowed grass and the threat of rain.

The thought entered my mind, "Apply to Massage Envy."

I was surprised by the sudden prompt because I was thinking of what to make for dinner and whether I should do my homework or watch mindless television. I followed through with the impression and soon started working at Massage Envy. When I brought home my first cash tips and saw the relief on Eric's face, I knew I had done the right thing, despite my preference to stay at home. How was I going to work fifteen hours a week, take two classes, and raise two kids? My answer came on the wings of a beloved hymn as if the Lord sang the song Himself.

> *Fear not, I am with thee; oh, be not dismayed,*
> *For I am thy God and will still give thee aid.*
> *I'll strengthen thee, help thee, and cause thee to stand*

God, Prayers, and Babies

Within two weeks of starting work at Massage Envy, we found out I was pregnant with our third baby. Eric and I smiled as broadly as we did when we saw the test results for Bruce and Fiona. When we told Bruce and Fiona, they asked for more crackers and went about their business, screaming and jumping off the couch onto the mountain of pillows and blankets they'd dragged out of their room.

Oliver was born at thirty-six weeks and two days. I started crying when my water broke in the middle of the night because he wasn't considered full-term yet. We were five days shy of thirty-seven weeks. Would his lungs be fully developed? Would he need to stay in the NICU? Eric told me everything was going to be okay. He was worried, too, but didn't tell me until after Oliver was born.

When we got to the hospital, my amniotic fluid was running down my leg and onto the floor. A nurse instructed me to wait, unfazed. She might have been unfazed, but I was phased. I can't think of anyone who enjoys the feeling of sitting in their own mess as it continues to seep through their pants. I think when people do the same job over and over again, they forget that they are helping a fellow human being and how much their attitude and level of care matter. The nurse made it abundantly clear that I was nothing more than another pregnant woman, insisting I was in labor.

To verify that I genuinely was leaking amniotic fluid and not purposefully urinating on myself, the nurse went through the effort of doing a fern test, where amniotic fluid is placed on a slide. If it looks like a fern branch under the microscope, it's the real thing, not a yellow imposter. During this time, I was in active labor, but I assume, because I did not appear in great distress, she took her time getting me into a room. I informed her that Oliver was my third baby and that my labor went quickly.

"Okay, we'll see how this labor goes. They are not all the same," the nurse said.

I wanted to say, "Don't patronize me about labor. I know my body, and I know my baby is coming." Instead, I said nothing until I took off my soaking pants, "He's coming," I said in what was apparently too calm a voice.

"Okay, just a minute. Let me get things ready." She kept clickety clacking away on the keyboard, not bothering to look me in the eye.

Without a single push, Oliver fell out of my body. I know that's not a poetic way of describing how he came into this world, but it's nonetheless accurate.

"He's out. My baby is on the bed," I said.

"Oh my! Umm, here, let me get him." As she picked Oliver up and put him on my chest, I felt terrible for her. She looked frazzled and slightly panicked. When she paged the doctor, I thought she was going to cry. And then I remembered my days at Oregon Medical Group. Doctors were not always kind to the nurses if a baby was born before they arrived, as if the nurse had any control over another woman's body. So when I heard the doctor's steps, I got nervous as if I were the nurse.

Thankfully, when the doctor rounded the corner, he had a big smile on his face, "I missed the first birth on my first day as a doctor, so it seems fitting that I miss the last birth on my last day." A relieved smile crossed the nurse's face, and I was glad.

Oliver was a smaller baby than our other two, but in no danger of being too small. He was covered in vernix, a waxy coating that preterm babies have an abundance of, making him look more vulnerable. We did end up staying in the NICU for a couple of nights - it was such a sterile, mechanical-looking place. Babies were in incubators and connected to machines through tiny wires and hoses;

they reminded me of a diesel truck engine at the mechanic's. I scolded myself for crying so hard after being told that Oliver needed to stay in the hospital for a couple of days. I knew he was going to be okay. Some of the other babies, though, the nurses didn't know how long they would be in the hospital or if they would live.

Bruce and Fiona loved their new brother as soon as they saw him. Bruce was content to watch Oliver from a distance, while Fiona insisted on putting her face in Oliver's face. She alternated which toy she set on him as he lay swaddled, suggested outfits, and brought me clean diapers. Eric hovered his USC football helmet over Oliver's head, making everyone laugh. So naturally, we all took turns wearing the helmet. I've never felt so well-rested when having a newborn as I did with Oliver. He slept swaddled on my chest when we were in the NICU because I refused to leave him in the cold, unwelcoming bassinet. When we got home, we continued the pattern, and we both slept a lot. Oliver was a happy and content baby with fuzzy white hair. We've called him 'little fuzz head' ever since.

Emotionally, I felt pretty stable after Oliver was born. I started doing CrossFit with Emerson when Oliver was nine weeks old. Much of the baby weight came off quickly, but a few weeks went by and the scale did not move. My old nemesis lit up like a neon sign, "Tessa's Fat, She'll Always Be Fat, She's Worthless and Fat." Que binge eating, body comparison, and diet obsessions. At least I didn't gain more weight. One hundred sixty-five pounds became less disgusting to me the longer the scale stayed there. I resumed my normal cycle of exercising to stay chubby. After all, I weighed 160 pounds when I met Eric and got married, so five extra pounds was, I told myself, not terrible.

Nine months after Oliver was born, I took another pregnancy test. Positive.

***

Vivian was born seven months ago on Father's Day, and that's where we are now. Four babies in four and a half years, and yes, we wanted all of them. Yes, I know what birth control is, and yes, my hands are full. Why do people say, "Looks like your hands are full," as if I am unaware that I have one toddler clinging to my leg while screaming as if he's been forcefully relieved of an appendage, while trying to comfort a tired infant, and keep two other toddlers from running off after whatever looks adventurous or sparkly? And why is my intelligence constantly in question? I didn't have children because I'm not smart enough to do something else or feel like it's my religious or social obligation. I have children because I want them.

Have you ever held a newborn baby? I once read that babies prove that God wants the world to continue. I would add that babies prove that God is a God of miracles. Tiny, perfect miracles that look like little balls when they curl their knees to their chest. I find joy in watching their stretches and yawns, their tiny hands, and the way their round cheeks rest so trustingly against my chest, usually with a closed fist resting in front of their mouth. When I hold my children, I want to be a more Christlike person so they can live their lives free from the pain of my failings. Who knows what the sum of their psychiatry bill will be after they're done repairing what I've broken? When I held our oldest son in my arms for the first time, I wanted to capture the moment in a snow globe and put it on my nightstand.

I didn't realize the transcendent emotions that come with motherhood. I knew my God-given calling would bring me joy, but I believed that happiness and love had limitations. I would give up my life for my children, and I'm not only referring to taking a bullet or pushing them out of the way of an oncoming car so that it hits me instead. No, when I am my best self, I would give up my sleep, food, convenience, plans, and selfishness. Elder Jeffrey R. Holland said it better than I.

". . . no love in mortality comes closer to approximating the pure love of Jesus Christ than the selfless love a devoted mother has for her child. When Isaiah, speaking messianically, wanted to convey Jehovah's love, he invoked the image of a mother's devotion. "Can a woman forget her sucking child?" he asks. How absurd, he implies, though not as absurd as thinking Christ will ever forget us.[22]"

A mother can forget her sucking child, but I will not forget mine. Each time Eric and I found out we were pregnant, we started a list of names. Generating a list of girl names was easy because our tastes aligned. Boy names, however, were hard because our tastes were on the opposite end of the spectrum. Eric regularly repeated, "Tessa, you can't just think of a cute name for a three-year-old. A baby boy eventually grows into a man." Despite our disagreements, we had a boy, and a girl's names picked out by the time we went in for each anatomical ultrasound. We had one ultrasound technician who was so underwhelmed with her job that when she said, "It's a boy," I thought she was about to fall asleep.

We also enjoyed many hours guessing who our kids would look like and what personality they would have. Would they inherit the intense and expressive brow lines of the Knerre line or the prominent, sharp chins on the Jensen side? The angular chins are a dominant trait on Eric's mother's side, so they are really an Anderson trait. I'm clarifying this for genealogy purposes. Since Eric and I both have blue eyes, we liked to guess the shade our kids would have. Would they be bright, gray, or deep, compared to the sky or the ocean? Unrelated, a boy at church once told me that my eyes were as blue as toilet water. Anyway, I hoped for a baby with black hair because Bruno has black hair and eyes the color of a stormy ocean, and I find the combination striking. We assumed there would not be many color variations since Eric and I have similar European ancestry - lots of Scandinavian and a hearty mix of other northern countries. We were mostly right.

---

[22] Jeffrey R. Holland, Behold Thy Mother, *Ensign* or *Liahona*, October 2015

Bruce was born with copper-red hair and eyes the same color as Bruno's. Fiona came out bald with Eric's aquamarine eyes, while Oliver and I share the same blue-gray eyes. Oliver is the toddler version of Eric. Eric 2.0. Vivian was born with brown hair, and lots of it, according to the Jensen standard of lots. Her eyes won't decide their permanent color for several more months. For anyone hanging on the edge of their seat about the brow lines, all but Oliver are clearly Knerre descendants. We'll know more about the jawlines as their faces mature.

Emerson, with his penchant for generous compliments, told me, "Oliver's face needs something to hold his cheeks up." He also asked me, at eight months pregnant, "Do your shoes have the structural integrity to hold you up?" Emerson makes me laugh.

As I watch my kids, I pray for their health and safety and for eyes to see them as individuals so that I can love them in the way they need. One-size-fits-all does not work for parenting. I wish I didn't need sleep. That way, I could give them all the attention and energy they want. When one of them looks up at me, believing that I can make everything better, I don't want to let them down. I guess I would need four sets of arms to accomplish that goal. I hope they grow up knowing I love them and learning to love each other. Oliver is not impressed with his new baby sister, probably because he's still a baby himself; he didn't walk until the week before she was born.

Vivian came into the world after two hours and ten minutes of labor, punctuated by the involuntary noises coming out of my mouth due to the severe pressure. The contractions were bearable, but the pressure was torture. For a few minutes, I was convinced that my tailbone would snap off. No bone snapping occurred, a loud cry rang out, and the birth of our baby was complete.

Eric wrapped his long arm around my shoulder and brought me to his chest while I held our newborn daughter on my chest. The rhythmic sound of Eric's beating heart was a welcome calm after the violent birth. Steady, unfaltering, predictable. When I looked up at him, assuming he was admiring Vivian, I found him admiring me, his eyes full of selfless, unconditional love. I don't think many people get to experience pure love from another human. But I do. What did he do to become so good? Good, wholesome, kind, selfless. While we waited our required 24 hours at the hospital, he helped with everything he could. "It's my privilege, not a chore," he said.

Blissful moments don't last long, which is why they are moments and not periods. Due to my mental health medication, my milk did not come in, which means I did not experience the expected twenty-pound weight loss as I did with my other children. Why am I fretting over the number on the scale when I have more important things that need my energy?

I am thankful for my eternal family. I adore them, but I spend more time worrying about horrific circumstances than enjoying their company. I worry that a horrible tragedy will strike, and I will be left alone with nothing but memories and longing. I am afraid Vivian will die in her sleep, that my other kids will get run over, strangled by a cord, fall off of a play structure and split their heads open, get kidnapped at the grocery store in broad daylight, that our house will burn down while everyone but me is inside, carbon monoxide poisoning, a robber breaking in and stabbing Eric to death, high-speed vehicular accidents that end in death, suffocating, and cancer. I refuse to go out in the living room at night or sit in front of a window because I'm convinced that someone will drive by and shoot me in the back of the head.

I know God will comfort me and give me strength if I put my faith in Him. He's done it before. I try to summon my faith by silently singing hymns and primary songs, but this fear follows me like a shadow. Prayers chase away nothing. They don't bring light, not even a ray of sunshine breaks through. I keep writing my prayers in my journal,

Please, Lord, please, please, please reassure me that my family will be okay. I'm sorry for my doubts, and I know I am fat. I weighed in at 180 lbs. yesterday. I want to cry. I took pictures of my appalling

condition as motivation to change. I don't know how much or how long I cried in complete and utter despair. Losing forty pounds is too big and too hard of an obstacle. I should resign myself to being fat and disgusting so that I stop failing. I hate, hate, hate this battle with my weight. I know I cannot escape this. The only way out is through hell. Again. I don't have any fight left in me. How did I let myself get to this place? I lack faith.

Eric is the greatest blessing I have aside from the Atonement of Jesus Christ, who makes all things possible. I know that I could live my mortal life without Eric if I had to, but I could not live it without you. I know I need to spend time with you, but sometimes I don't want to. I want to sleep or watch TV or eat until I'm sick. I am often angry with you because I don't feel loved or cared for in any way - or not in the ways I want. Please, let me see your hand in my life so that the feelings of abandonment will subside. I know my perception is a lie, but it feels like the truth. Satan seems to want me more than you do. I can feel him waging war every day. But I cannot hear you. I'm scared, and I cannot hear you. So much for the promise of peace. What peace? I'm doing everything I can, and you decided to take a leave of absence.

I read a quote the other day, and I don't know who said it.

> ". . . qualities we can command - such qualities as thoughtfulness, patience, a kind word, and true delight in the accomplishment of another. These cost us nothing, and they can mean everything to the one who receives it. [23] "

Sounds neat. I'm tired and can't control anything. Sugar literally controls my life and I hate to use the word 'literally' because it's popular vernacular, which I try to avoid on principle. *Oh Lord, why have you left me?*

---

[23] Jeffrey R. Holland, "How Do I Love Thee?," *New Era*, Oct. 2003

Worsening Symptoms

I hate when people cite my mental diagnosis as the reason for all my struggles. I don't believe it's that simple. I also hate when people try to give me coping advice, like I haven't thought of every alternative to dealing with mania and depression. I especially hate it when it comes from people who come from happy homes where they are loved. What do they know of heartache? I feel like I'm spinning my tires in the mud and getting nowhere, big surprise.

I have so much anger in my heart. I don't know why; I've been given everything I ever wanted. I started crying in the parking lot before work the other day because I was so frustrated with the all-consuming, borderline rage that multiplied in my heart without notice until it was a full-fledged fire. Oh, I stopped taking my medication in January. My doctor put me on Abilify, which costs over $300, with insurance. It did nothing but give me uncomfortable side effects, like brain zings and restless legs. I told the doctor that my other medications work just fine, but he convinced me to switch, probably because I'm tired, which translated into less mood control. I think there should be an understanding that we cannot medicate away the human experience. Sometimes I tell myself that if I learn whatever I need to learn due to this illness that it will go away. I know such an idea is a complete lie. I will only be free from this cage after I am dead. Even then, I am sure my self-discipline will be insufficient.

I can, and do, find fault with nearly everyone as a self-protective mechanism when I'm like this. At church, as usual, I feel on the outside of the female social circle. It's the same in every ward, so the problem lies with me since I am the common denominator. I want to change; I want to love the gospel, and that cannot happen if I let doubt and fear rule my life. Right now, I couldn't escape Church if I wanted to because Eric has visible responsibilities.

I try to support him as he goes to meetings and visits the new people who move in, but I get mad when he's away because my anxiety catapults to new levels if he's not home when I expect him to be. If he's ten minutes late coming back from work, I start looking for accident reports, convinced that a police officer is about to knock on the door and ask me to identify Eric's mangled body. I repeatedly pray for the Lord to lend me the courage to support Eric. When we got married, we made a covenant to do what He asked us to do, and I intend to keep my promise, no matter the cost.

My good intentions last until Sunday mornings when I am left to get three small children and an infant ready for church while Eric's attending meetings. Vivian's easy to get ready. I put her in clothes, whether a dress or a cozy sleeper, buckle her in her car seat, give her a bottle, and she's a happy baby, content to eat while playing with her feet and making cooing sounds. Oliver is content to be dressed and go about his business of people watching and carrying around small stuffed animals. Fiona wears a fancy dress. That girl loves tulle and sparkles, like me. And then there is Bruce. Bruce hates wearing clothes and despises anything with long sleeves, buttons, and zippers. He flails and screams, throwing his head back and forward, usually hitting me in the face in the process. If I put Bruce's shoes on, he throws them off. I consider myself a quick learner, so now I put a pair of shoes in the diaper bag and let him walk out in his socks. If Eric wants him to wear shoes at church, he can fight the battle.

Despite the predictable morning battles, we always make it to church on time. Arriving late to anything gives me heart palpitations. If I need more time, I simply start getting ready earlier. To Eric's credit, he usually bathes the kids before he leaves, so I cannot genuinely claim that I do everything myself. But it feels that way. Why does my reality have to swing around with my emotions? The same situation can arise three weeks in a row, and, depending on my mood, it can be the best experience in the world or a debilitating curse that God knowingly thrust upon my innocent soul.

I hate going to church for my usual reasons of distrust and PTSD, but now it's worse because I serve in the primary. Who asks a mother with four small children to teach primary? I don't have the emotional capital to entertain or teach my own children, much less someone else's, no matter how sweet, precious, and wonderful they are. I want to be in adult classes and engage in spiritual and intellectual discussions. Instead, I have unspoken thoughts and questions screaming inside of me.

Today, the usual people are talking to their usual friends. Someone will feel sorry for me, say hello, and ask, "How are you doing?" Of course, they don't want to know how I'm doing, so I say 'fine' and make my best attempt at an artificial smile. Emerson says it's easy to tell whether my smile is genuine or forced. My canine teeth don't touch my lips when my smile is genuine. He's right, not that it's a conscious decision on my part. He reads people's body language as if he had studied it as a second language. I guess he did, given his military training and experience as a Marine.

I like being early, but I don't want people to talk to me. I don't want their pity, their obligatory friendship, the "her name got brought up in a meeting, so let's make sure she feels loved." I don't want to pretend friendships at church when there's no real friendship during the week. It's not accurate to say I have no friends at church or have never had friends at church. But I usually don't feel safe being myself and expressing my opinion. Me, me, me. That's the only person I seem concerned about. What if I thought kind and generous things about others?

As it stands, I'm fat and gross. But I'm here. I keep coming, week after week and year after year, hoping that someday I won't need to go home and practice slow breathing and work through a racing heartbeat, tunnel vision, and pressure on my head that feels as if someone is tightening a vice with all their might. The flood of rage follows - I make biting comments, start a one-sided fight with Eric, cry, apologize, and binge eat on homemade pie and cookies until I feel nothing but food-induced sickness. I hate Sundays.

The opening hymn starts, and I can see Eric out of the corner of my eye. He wants to put his arm around me or comfort me in some way. I turn my head towards him and cut his attempts down with a glare. He looks down at the floor. I hate myself. I reach my hand out and whisper, "I'm sorry." Eric smiles and says, "I love you." I can see the hurt hanging in his eyes. Hurt that I caused, that I put there. Why do I take his unconditional love and shred it to pieces? Because I'm a one-half monster. Dr. Jekyll and Mr. Hyde. Eric's angel and his adversary. Coming to church unlocks the beast in me, and we switch places. The real me is behind bars, scared, silent, and protected. No one gets past the rage monster.

I don't deserve to take the Sacrament. I make my kids cry, and I just hurt my husband. I write in my journal, *Oh Lord, what do you want from me? Take it. Whatever you want, I'll give it to you. You don't need to punish me anymore. I am sorry for everything, for being me. I am sorry for my sensitivities, for caring, for failing, for hurting my family. I'm sorry for complaining, for my ingratitude, my stupidity, my loneliness. I'm sorry for letting you down, for living below my potential, for abandoning opportunities, for judging others, for getting hurt, for getting fat, for wasting my time, for losing my patience. I'm sorry that I can't forgive my parents, that I can't say, "It's okay." I'm sorry I was vulnerable and hurtable. I'm sorry I was a child. I'm sorry I was born. What more can I say? What more can I do?*

The deacons, the ones who pass the Sacrament, are making their awkward way up and down the rows. Bruce and Oliver will be deacons one day. What are they going to do when they see their mother seething with rage in the name of self-preservation? Let me play out the scenario: they will think they are responsible for, and for managing, my problems. They'll dance around my feelings, trying to be loyal to both their mother and the Church I can't stand. Finally, they'll make a choice because my moods will force their hand, and whatever they choose, my heart will break. My hand shakes as I write,

Oh Lord, I cannot cause my children more pain. I cannot be the source of confusion and become guilty of the same sin as my parents. I cannot tell my children that I love the gospel, that I love you, and hate your church. I don't hate your church. I hate the symbol of sorrow I associate with your church, burned into my soul by people who never knew you. I know fear and pain are not the symbols of your church, that coercion and abuse are malignant sins. I cognitively understand I'm wrong, but I can't change it. I can't change my feelings.

I stop writing for a moment and glance over at Oliver, cuddled in a ball on Eric's lap. He's a gentle soul, meant to nurture and care for creatures much smaller than him. Or plants. Meanwhile, Bruce's feet are wildly flailing in the air. He's stuck upside down, again. He is afflicted with an underdeveloped sense of caution but a healthy appreciation for adventure. Bruce wants to be good, not because he's scared of punishment but because he genuinely wants to do what is right. Whatever he does, he'll do it while wearing as few clothes as possible.

Vivian's asleep in her car seat with her pacifier falling out of her mouth. She's wearing her lavender sleeper with the white polka dots that says, 'Little Sister' across the top in pink. She's only ten months old, so we're still waiting for characteristics to present themselves. So far, she's loud, happy, and loves to eat. Not too long ago, Emerson observed, "I've never seen her without food in her mouth." He's right. Vivian's favorite food is freeze-dried frozen yogurt bites.

Fiona keeps making vain attempts to put a bow in Vivian's hair. She haphazardly stuck five in her own hair before we came to church, so she has a few to spare. Fiona was born with the gift of knowing her mind. Her confidence seems unbreakable. But anything can be broken, and I can't let that happen to her. I can't let her end up like me; fat, depressed, paranoid, broken, making poor self-sabotaging decisions, with potential flaming into smoke in front of her eyes.

Oh Lord, I can't get in the way of my children. They need a different mother who can infuse their lives with love, laughter, and ambition. Someone with enough energy to keep up, someone unselfish, and someone who treats their father with more respect. I am not that person. I have nothing to give them.

A rare and clear thought comes to my mind as if spoken from heaven, so I write it down, "*Tessa, you were meant to be stronger than you are. I need you to be stronger than you are.*"

I furiously continue writing; r*eally? That's your response? A kick in the back while I'm already lying on the floor in the fetal position?*

Tears flood my eyes and weave down my face, a few pooling on top of my lips before falling onto my lap. Why didn't God tell me something else, like 'I love you, you're doing great? How can I get stronger when I have nothing left?

Sacrament meeting continues to trudge by, a couple of talks, a few head nods, kids crying, wrappers crinkling, and at least four people hacking through coughing fits. Finally, our bishop stands up to close the meeting. He received the calling to his lofty position about several months ago. He's well educated, with a stunning wife and four sons. He seems nice, but anyone can seem nice. And, nice is different than good.

"Before I announce the closing hymn, I want to extend an invitation . . . '

Oh, boy, here we go with the invitations and the claims on promptings and revelation. What will it be today? Will we get an invitation to live on our food storage for the next three weeks to verify its efficacy? Do we get to do an extensive service project? Run ourselves ragged? Spend our time teaching other people how important families are while spending hours away from our children and spouse?

". . .please consider reading the Book of Mormon this year. It will change your life."

Read the Book of Mormon? That's it? Reading every page of the Book of Mormon is hardly an insurmountable challenge; it's just over 500 pages. I've heard this promise almost as many times as I have listened to the word, 'Amen.' I know studying the scriptures changed my life; I have found comfort and answers within the pages many times. Most significantly, I stayed in Eugene when I wanted to leave. Then, Eric came. Through the scriptures, Jesus Christ has taught me to change and taught me gospel principles, most especially the eternal nature of the family. The Book of Mormon doesn't offend me, but I was hoping for a more complex answer. A simple answer makes my problem seem simple, and if it's simple, why is it a problem?

Accepting the Invitation to Change

I've started reading one chapter of the Book of Mormon per day because it's a manageable goal. I have tried reading a few verses at a time in the past, but the effect is like when I try to run 4.9 or 5.4 miles; it doesn't work. Halves or wholes. Those are the options. This time, I hold the book further from my face than I would otherwise, as if I might get splattered or burned. I'm afraid God's going to give me a long list of everything I am doing wrong, and, as a result, my head will hang lower as my self-hatred increases. Oh well. Fear and faith cannot coexist, and I'm tired of giving fear center stage. Tired. Exhausted. Tired. Exhausted. Can I please find another adjective?

In the months since starting the Book of Mormon, I started exercising regularly again and binge-eating less. My weight has dropped from 183 to 163. I haven't been this small in at least two years. I feel better. I don't spend as much time lying on the couch, crying in despair. I am still outside the social circle at church, but that's not going to change any time soon. But I no longer feel hopeless.

Plus, I will resume the slow process of chipping my way through my college classes. I originally planned to be done by now. I'm not. No surprise that I didn't meet my deadline. But, I was an excellent little workhorse, making my way through one or two classes each semester up until this past January, when I decided to take a break. I thought I was giving myself a break from the stress of school, but I needed the focus because it propelled me forward—eustress instead of distress. I am learning that I find no joy when I try to remove all sources of discomfort. Growth requires pain, and so does running uphill.

The new fall semester starts in September. The class load may seem like one more thing on my overflowing plate, but I need to finish my degree. I want to accomplish what I've told myself is too hard. The anticipation of starting over for the last time spills over into my day. I feel lighter, more capable. I constantly remember the time my dad told his friend I was smart. I am smart. I may have taken leave of my senses a few times over, but I'm still intelligent.

I record in my journal, *Oh Lord, I know you can help me. I understand that the impossible is made possible through you. I know it, but I don't know if I believe it applies to me. It must. My marriage to Eric has been one life-changing event after another. These last few peaceful months are a welcome reprieve. Oliver just climbed into the chair with me to cuddle. He is such a sweet boy and now refuses to wear pants. Endless terrible possibilities could befall him or us. Here I go, back to my morbid thoughts like they're a security blanket. Please, help me learn to trust you and remember the principles you have taught me. I am thankful for your gospel of peace and love. I don't understand everything, but I know your ways are right and good. All goodness comes from you, even if the person doing good does not know of, or believe in, you. I saw a quote from Oscar Wilde on Facebook yesterday that gives me hope to learn to control my thoughts and moods.*

"A man who is master of himself can end a sorrow as easily as he can invent a pleasure. I don't want to be at the mercy of my emotions. I want to use them, to enjoy them, and to dominate them." What laws of heaven govern such a magnificent blessing? What can I do to draw closer to you and become your friend?

As my request formed in my mind, I knew the answer: spend more time in the scriptures.

"How?" I ask out loud as if the Savior is sitting across from me.

"Wake up earlier," comes the straightforward reply.

I write, *"Your solution seems unreasonable because, as of today, I can hardly pry myself out of bed at 7:30. Bruce and Fiona entertain themselves until I get out of bed. If I wake up earlier, they will want my attention, as they should, and no studying will take place. I'll reread the same verse three times due to the scheduled interruptions at thirty-second intervals. I'm doing better than I was. In January, I was napping or lying down for at least half of the day."*

Again, I feel the Lord's response in my mind, *"Tessa, you asked me what you can do to receive the magnificent, your words, blessings you desire. I told you the remedy in three words. The solution will not change, but you can choose to heed my wisdom or ignore it."*

I nod my head in acknowledgment, knowing how arrogant I sound in my claims as if I know more than Christ. Nevertheless, I'll forever be impressed with my efforts to avoid what I think too hard. Rather than making excuses, I would save hundreds of hours and thousands of words if I just did what I knew I was supposed to do.

One more thought, *"You cannot understand all things now. Stop thinking of why it's difficult and start thinking of why it's worth the sacrifice."*

Vivian's cry signals the end of my prayer. When I walk into the girls' room to fetch her from her crib, her chubby hands are wrapped around the edge of the crib as she bounces up and down with a huge, drooly smile. Babies find endless entertainment and excitement in discovering their bodies' new abilities. Their reaction is as if they didn't know their strength. "My legs can stand? Can I make this new sound? I wonder how loud I can get. Look! I can put my toes in my mouth and feel my new teeth. I bet you didn't know I could climb on precarious surfaces because I can. I can even smear spaghetti sauce all over my face and wipe it on anything except a towel. How can life get any better?!"

As I pick Vivian up, her legs keep kicking. I try to hug her, but she pulls her head away and points at the door. Excitement is afoot, and she must see what it is. Based on the squealing and exclamations going on in the living room, I already know. Bruce and Fiona have removed every couch cushion and pillow and used them as a jumping pit. Oliver's watching from his perch on the arm of the couch. He seems to absorb their physical experience as if it's his own, so he has no reason to join. However, Vivian wants her chance, and Fiona is giddy to accommodate.

The sunlight dances through the blinds, making our house and spirits lighter. Whoever designed our brown couch was likely unaware that its broken condition - the peeling, the sunken cushions, the holes – would give it a new life. Bruce's beaming smile melts my mother's heart. He'll go to kindergarten in the fall. I'll be at work by the time he gets home from school on Monday, Tuesday, and Friday, which means I'll see him for only an hour in the morning. My stomach drops at the realization. But if waking up at 6:00 am means I get more time with my son, I'll do it without protest. I'll study my scriptures while he plays with his dinosaurs, and, if I'm lucky, he'll smile at me and scoot closer.

More Rejection

Just when I think I've escaped the chains of abandonment, Josephine blocked my phone number. We have spoken once a week for most of our adult lives, on Thursdays at 9:00 am. I schedule appointments and outings around that time because I know Josephine is a woman of order by nature, and on account of her busy schedule. So, if I miss my time slot, I must wait until the following week. She's my sister and my friend. I have no idea what happened. We talk about my school, her work, our kids, and everyday things.

I didn't think she would ever block my phone number. At first, I assumed her phone went straight to voicemail because she had lost it. Then, after a couple of weeks, I started checking accident reports.

While I was recounting my worries to a friend, she said, "Sounds like your sister blocked your phone number."

I laughed. "Josephine would never block my phone number. When Josephine gets mad at me, she ignores my calls until she feels better and we resume our conversations. That's been our communication style for over a decade."

After my friend left, I used Eric's phone to call Josephine, honestly expecting her phone to go to voicemail. It rang instead. "Hello, this is Josephine."

"Hi, Josephine. This is Tessa. What's going on?"

There is a long pause.

"I can't talk to you anymore. I'm sorry." Her voice quivered like she was trying not to cry.

"Why can't you talk to me?"

"I need to go now; I need to save my marriage. Goodbye, Tessa." Before she hung up, there was a pause, as if she was waiting for me to say something more. I kept my mouth shut and let the inevitable pain rush in, like a river full of white rapids, pushing me under and slamming me against the rocks, blow after blow. Josephine just threw me away without warning or explanation. Just like Sarah, almost.

I cried, sobbed, and berated myself for asking or expecting anything from Josephine. I reviewed our recent conversation, checking that I didn't say anything unkind about her husband. We're not each other's biggest fans, her husband and I, but I haven't talked to him since Josephine graduated from pharmacy school, and even then, it was only for a few minutes. I don't know what I did wrong, and I doubt I'll know for many years to come. When Josephine makes up her mind, she blazes her trail without apology, like a tiger in the jungle, answering no one. I was a branch in her way, an annoying monkey whose noise became too loud, a bird with a broken wing, too weak to fly. Where is my journal?

"Why, Heavenly Father? Why must living be so painful, so disappointing? I want to believe Josephine still loves me. Please, let Josephine feel the love you have for her. I could use a manifestation of your love as well. "

A phrase from the scriptures comes to my mind, "wounded in the house of my friends.[24]" Jesus, like me, was wounded in the house of His friends, forsaken, forgotten, abandoned.

Half of me wants my emotions to take control. I want to be mad at Josephine, so her decision hurts less. I keep writing, *please, lend me your strength to make the right choice, the one that you would make in this situation.*

My scriptures are sitting in their usual place, on top of my other journals filled with prayers, scriptures, and quotes about Jesus

---

[24] Doctrine and Covenants 45:52

Christ. Scriptures that, when I'm not reeling from a proverbial punch in the gut, sound excellent. If a speaker were to reference them in Sacrament meetings, I would nod and smile, glad that my life is part of the gospel. But now, with an opportunity that sits before me to practice my Christian virtues like forgiveness and long-suffering, I instinctively recoil.

Still, I have sustained enough muscular injuries to know the consequences of refusing to move after injury; the muscles stiffen, weaken, and, if too much time passes, atrophy. I've come too far to turn around, and I can't stay where I am. The only way out is through, so here I go through the pain. Instead of picking up my scriptures, I go to the Church website, churchofjesuschrist.org, to look through talks that our leaders have given.

After a series of searches, I arrive at a talk given by Jeffrey R. Holland. I like Elder Holland because he has a lot of big emotions that he wears on the outside, like me. He said,

> ". . .cease withholding our means because we see the poor as having brought their own misery upon themselves. Perhaps some have created their own difficulties, but don't the rest of us do exactly the same thing.. . Don't we all cry out for help and hope and answers to prayers? Don't we all beg for forgiveness for mistakes we have made and troubles we have caused? Don't we all implore that grace will compensate for our weakness, that mercy will triumph over justice, at least in our case?.... I know that God knows, and He will help you and guide you in compassionate acts of discipleship if you are conscientiously wanting and praying and looking for

ways to keep a commandment He has given us again and again.[25]"

I usually equate 'means' with money and 'poor' with those who lack money. But, what if 'means' includes much more than the money in my bank account, like my forgiveness? And what if 'poor' includes the people who hurt me? What happens if I replace some words?

For example, "Cease withholding *your forgiveness* because *you* see the *people who hurt you* as having brought their own misery upon themselves."

Alright, okay. I am commanded to forgive, I get it. That's what I have been trying to do! Maybe when I ask for the Lord's help, I should be more specific about what I mean by the word, 'help,' I want Him to take all the pain away in a gust of divine wind as if it weighs nothing more than autumn leaves. But the weight is now so heavy that my footsteps leave deep tracks everywhere I go.

My family history is one of the first things I tell people, out of habit, because I need to explain the burden that I think they can see. I have woven the trauma into my identity. "Hi, I'm Tessa. My family imploded, I'm mentally ill, and here is a detailed recounting of every shocking or amusing anecdote. What's it like to have parents that love you?"

People. Conversations. That's where I'll start. I'll practice asking people about themselves. I'll step away from the practice of making extreme declarations like, "I'll never talk about family trauma again!" because it's an unreasonable expectation to place on myself, and I will fail, then I'll get discouraged and give up.

---

[25] Jeffrey R. Holland, "Are We Not All Beggars?," *Ensign*, Nov. 2014

Making Progress

Great news! I have reason to celebrate and praise the Lord! I have a multitude of reasons every moment, but today I have a little extra, a gift meant just for me, packaged so flawlessly that only God himself could be the giver, more green wrapping, and another silver ribbon. Based on what I thought I needed, I initially anticipated finishing my degree by the spring of 2021. However, upon utilizing the course planning tool available on BYU- Idaho's I-learn, I can complete it by July of 2019 if I work harder than I have ever worked before. I won't have time to do much outside of school and work, but the sacrifice won't be forever.

If I am to finish my degree by July of 2019, I must take 3-5 classes per semester. I can do it. We can do it. There are three people on my team: Jesus Christ, Eric, and me. I look at it this way: Jesus is the investor who's done this a million times before, Eric is the unfailingly loyal supporter, and I'm the worker. Thank the Lord my father taught me to work hard. As I've mentioned, when I asked him what our last name, Knerre, meant, he said, "Hard worker," and walked away as if the answer was obvious.

Can you feel the joy shunting my blood from my head to my feet and back again? I, Tessa Jensen, get to earn a Bachelor of Science in Public Health Education and Promotion. Isn't the thought delicious? I can almost see my name on my degree. Should I have a party when I'm done? Who would I invite? Everyone, I suppose. The cashier, the librarian, the sanitation worker, my OB/GYN. I'm practically levitating. When I told Eric, he looked happy for me but failed to summon the reaction I was hoping for. I told him to keep confetti in his desk drawer so that he could throw it in the air on demand.

***

"Eric, I cannot take on one more responsibility," I say as Eric folds laundry, and I work on homework.

"I don't think anyone is asking you to." He cannot keep from smiling like my frantic energy amuses him.

My words pour out in a torrent, "I know. I just needed you to know that I can't do any more than I am doing. I am sorry I leave you to pick up my slack. I'll try to cook a good meal this week, and I'll mop the floors and deep clean the kitchen. There have been several weeks when we have spent less than two hours of quality time together outside of me asking you for help with my homework. It's a good thing you come from a family that appreciates music because I got 100% on my music analysis assignment. If you had not been there to explain the questions and walk me through the material, I would have struggled a lot more than I did. I don't speak music, and I don't appreciate the classical variety. It reminds me of long nights at the concert hall when I was a kid. When Josephine and Bruno went to Cal Young Middle School, Dad traded nights at the ticket counter at the concert hall for instrument rentals and flute lessons. Bruno had, and still has, a musical talent. He played the flute beautifully and quickly picked up other woodwind instruments. Anyway, the concerts were torture because I got so tired, my legs ached, and we, without fail, had a most unpleasant drive home. We also had to dress up in the embarrassing hand-me-downs we wore to church.

Oh, and, most importantly, my professor told me that my writing was impeccable. I am inspired to press forward when I do well on assignments because it's proof that I'm not terrible at everything. I know God is sustaining me and lending me His strength, but I am stretched as thin as I can be," I pause for a breath.

"You don't need to worry about the housework. The kids and I can do the chores. You focus on school, and we'll take care of the rest." He's still smiling. Why is he smiling? I haven't heard Eric complain about my all-consuming schedule even once. I'm sure he has complaints. Everyone has complaints.

"I'm so sorry. I am making you do too much. You already work and . . ."

"And so do you. Tessa, you work twenty hours a week, take four classes, and, most importantly, make each of our kids feel like they are the most special child in the world. Give yourself a break and let me do my part." Eric starts rubbing my back like he does every time I get worked up, like he's soothing a toddler who walked into the corner of a table.

"Okay, but the girls' room is a mess, and the floors need vacuuming, sweeping, and mopping, and I don't feel like the cleaning gets done unless I do it. Messes stress me out. I can't focus on my work when my surroundings are chaos, and that's what they are." I try to keep my voice steady, but I can feel the monster trying to free herself.

"Just ignore it," Eric says

"Do you suppose we would be having this conversation if I could simply ignore the mess and the undone tasks?"

"No, I don't suppose. But I don't notice or care about messes as you do; I'm not leaving it undone so that you feel inadequate. I need you to tell me exactly what you want. Make me a list and I'll do it."

"I shouldn't need to make you a list. You should see that something needs doing and do it."

"Your definition of what needs doing, and my definition are different. If you want a job done, you need to tell me. Tell me when and tell me how. I cannot guess what you're thinking." His face looks bewildered, as if he doesn't know what further explanation to offer, but knows I will require more. This time, I request nothing.

When Eric reasons with me, I feel like he's taking sandpaper and rubbing it across my face to sand off my stupidity. I'm ashamed of my mood swings again. Tears burst out of my eyes, "Why not? Why can't you guess what I'm thinking?" He's quiet and calm as he continues to console me with his touch as he waits for my storm to pass, my congested, tear-stained, gulping storm. Ten silent minutes pass by. Silent but not strained.

"I'm sorry, Eric. I said you were doing too much, and then I accused you of doing too little. I want everything I do to be done well, if not perfectly. I got 92% on an Environmental Health assignment. My mistakes could have been easily avoided if I had paid closer attention and tried harder. I'm sorry I took my stress out on you. I love you."

"I love you, too, and 92% is something to be proud of, not cry over. You're doing so well. Let's go to sleep. We're both tired, and morning comes early."

"I'll help put away the laundry. I could have got 100% if I had studied harder."

"Let it go, Tessa. Let it go."

I wonder how many people get to fall asleep knowing they are loved unconditionally and without restraint? If the pain encompassing the world is any indication, I say very few indeed. When I am not crying over failed perfection, I marinate in the joy of a dream in reach. Joy makes room for admission. And I have something to confess. I'm starting to forgive myself for my mistake, my most profound regret. As I mentioned, I chose to get a tubal ligation, and that's when the thickest darkness came. I didn't want to do it, but I convinced myself I had no other birth control options. When I went in for the consultation, the doctor asked me if I wanted the surgery. I answered in the affirmative. When I checked in at the hospital, they asked me the same question, and as they rolled me through the operating room doors, they asked one more time. Every time I wanted to say no, but ultimately went against my heart. I made a permanent decision in an emotionally compromised state. Lesson learned.

You may wonder how sad I could be about sterilization when I have four children. I don't know if I can articulate feelings in a way that makes sense. But my emotions don't need to make sense to you because they are fundamental to me. I had the God-given ability to be part of creating life and purposefully destroyed it. Eric didn't want me to do it, but I did it anyway and made his decision for him. He may have wanted more kids. I didn't ask because I was offended by my assumptions; Eric wished to maintain his fertility to have more kids if I die, and he marries someone else. Do you see what he has to live with? Accused and declared guilty before he could speak.

When Eric picked me up from the hospital, a heaviness wedged between us. I went to bed for three days, where I read book after book on the stories and horrors of war. Eric came in to check on me every so often. I glanced at him, told him I was fine, pulled our light blue bedspread over my head, rolled onto my side, and closed my eyes until he walked out. I had nothing to say, and I didn't want him to look at me. I didn't want God to look at me either, so I stopped praying and studying my scriptures, with a few exceptions. And, when I did pray, I made sure that God knew that I knew how worthless I was. "Less than the dust of the earth." I felt like the little girl standing in her mess all over again, every available option leading to punishment.

I wrote in my journal: *I could do nothing to please my parents except punish myself before they could, and nothing I do pleases God. So, before He chastises me for my stupidity and rashness, I'll punish myself in the most brutal ways I can think of. I'll cut myself down with a word, break my dreams with a condescending side-eye, and weave a thread made of shard glass through my brain until I question every thought and forget who I am. I'll make myself disappear. I'll be quiet. If His forgiveness means my destruction, I'll carve my heart out with a dull, rusted, serrated knife and smile with every drop of blood.*

I'll be less than human. I'll eat the scraps that fall off the celestial table like the dog I am. But, at least I'll be a well-fed dog. And, I will avoid the perpetual whiplash of being yanked between happiness and torment. I won't have to worry about falling short because Jesus will only ever need to look down in pity on my undeveloped potential. If only I were more self-disciplined and less like me.

Not long ago, I lamented to Emerson that I should stop caring because I end up crying and getting hurt. He said, "If you didn't care, you wouldn't be Tessa." And that's the most sincere compliment he's ever given me.

As a side note, Emerson and I don't appreciate encouraging comments like, "Good job! You're doing awesome. You got this." We need stats that support and preferably replace meaningless platitudes. What's my split pace in this race? Am I on target? What is good about this essay? In other words, what on earth does good mean? We don't know because 'good' is subjective and can hold so many metrics that it ceases to be a trustworthy complement.

The physical recovery from the surgery was inconsequential, but the spiritual and emotional repairs only began when God told me that I am not meant for smallness.

More Progress

One school year down, and one week until my final year of college starts. Thus far, my favorite class has been Humanities, not surprisingly. Think of all the human sacrifices required to get us where we are today and the range and depth of emotions that have accompanied the wars, famines, and plagues. Think of the authors with a vision of the future, what we can gain and lose, the painters who captured human form and emotion, and the physicians who identified the causes and cures of diseases and vitamin deficiencies. When humans cause each other significant harm, God's right there, ready to make something magnificent after the destruction.

Some people have an aversion to humanities, anthropology, and sociology - the soft sciences – because such studies lack equations and the guarantees of the Law of Gravity and that nine added to nine makes eighteen. On the other hand, my soul gets fed in the humanities for precisely the same reasons. If someone says, "Take out the garbage," my natural response is, "What kind of garbage are we talking about? Generational garbage of harmful traditions, like the banana peel of my mother's lies, or the garbage in the kitchen? I'm just curious because both are rather pungent."

Unfortunately, I don't have any more humanity-esque classes left, which means plenty of growth and learning lies ahead. While I was reviewing degree requirements, I realized I had made a mistake on my course schedule. My degree requires an in-person internship. Before I can file an internship request, I must be enrolled in, or have taken, specific classes, including epidemiology. Epidemiology is a 300-level class, and those are generally full by now. But I may be in luck.

Within a few clicks, I've found the openings I need to change my schedule around to fulfill all the prerequisites for my internship, which means I am taking epidemiology, anatomy and physiology, program planning and implementation, and environmental health. I am going to throw up. I don't even know what epidemiology means. The study of epidemics? More statistics? Probably. I know from experience how much time anatomy and physiology can take, but it shouldn't require as much study as it did in massage therapy school. Anatomical language is not foreign to me, but I must find more study time in my already packed schedule. I know God will help me, and I know He has prepared a path I cannot see. He keeps His promises. *Where do I find more time?*

I could wake up earlier, at 5:00 am instead of 6:00 am. Last year, I adjusted my sleeping schedule, and I can do it again this year. If I don't wake up at 5:00, I'll either forfeit the hour I spend with the Lord every morning because I will have more homework than I can handle or fall behind in class. Those are the options. Not to be extreme, but this semester is a scheduled-to-the-minute situation. It's alright. I can do it, with God. We've done it before. I may not have the strength or wisdom, but He does. Now I need to find an internship for the winter semester.

Bruce and Fiona started school a couple of weeks ago. Bruce is in first grade, and Fiona begins kindergarten. Since Bruce began kindergarten, we have walked to school every day, rain or shine, except during a week last winter when I fell victim to the flu. Now, Fiona gets to go to school, too. She nearly exploded with joy on her first day. She posed for a picture with Bruce, who looked underwhelmed, and ran-walked for the doors without looking back. Her excitement has yet to wane. You'd think Fiona was going to Disneyland every morning for all the squeals and giggles that erupt from her five-year-old body, unless you're like me and don't like Disneyland.

To make the one-mile journey from our house to the elementary school practical, I put Oliver in the stroller and Vivian in the baby hiking backpack. Vivian's almost too heavy to carry, but I consider her weight a back-strengthening exercise. On the way to school, we pass a community of manufactured homes, foundational construction for a new apartment complex, and a small group of businesses before arriving at the crosswalk. We navigate overgrown foliage, cracked and uneven sidewalks, and puddles. Bruce weaves in and out of bushes, climbs on rocks, and runs up and down, back and forth. He makes me nervous, and I am guilty of scolding him sharply.

Bruce looks crestfallen when I scold him because he's never trying to scare me, and he wants nothing but to have fun and be good. Today, he is wildly energetic because the sun is shining. Along with new imaginings of dinosaurs, the sun inspires a collective willingness of the community to acknowledge each other. Because of such sunny days, we've made friends on our walks, friends we've never spoken to, like the bus driver of bus number seventy-three, the man in the white car that turns onto Scriber Lake Road at precisely 8:21, and a woman who works at the school who drives a little red car. I feel like we're being watched over with our group of community friends.

Before we pass the group of buildings, I look up at the board that lists each business name and stop when I read, 'Girls on the Run' written in pink, purple, and green. I've heard of this organization. From what I can discern, their mission has something to do with girls and running. I've never noticed the sign, which I find interesting because it's a pretty noticeable sign amidst its dull neighbors. I should send them an inquiry about an internship when I get home.

Excited at the prospect of finding an internship so quickly, I make a beeline for home as soon as I see Bruce and Fiona enter the school building. After I unload Oliver and Vivian from the backpack and stroller, I give them three bags of gummy snacks to occupy them while I email Girls on the Run. Then, I quickly draft an email explaining that I need an internship to fulfill my degree requirements and am willing to work for free. Offering to work for free is probably not the best practice when requesting an internship, but I am desperate. After sending the email, I expect to hear crickets. But, happily, I'm wrong. By 3:00 pm, I have an interview scheduled in two days. But first, I must apprise Eric of my progress.

"Eric! How's your walk going? Guess what? I have an interview with Girls on the Run for a possible internship. It's in two days. What should I wear? Should I wear my hair up or down? We will need to find childcare for Oliver and Vivian while I do my internship. I don't know how much it will cost, but I assume it will be a lot. I know people at church have said they would be willing to help with the kids if needed, but this kind of commitment is too much to ask—two kids for twenty hours a week for ten weeks. We could offer to pay a fair price, but anyone who can do it has kids. Hey, do you think the internship will work out? Maybe they will like me so much that they'll want to hire me, and I can quit my job as a massage therapist. I am super excited. Are you excited?"

"Yes."

"You don't sound excited. You sound bored. Are you laughing at me?"

"No, I'm not laughing at you. I just like that you're so happy. Everything will work out as it should, and we should probably wait to find out what the internship entails before making big plans."

"Why do you stab my party balloons with needles as fast as you can? I was so excited, and now you've come and dumped your reasonableness all over my party."

"I'm not trying to; I just think we should find out what we're doing before we get too far ahead in the planning process."

"Fine. Let's be boring." I know Eric is not trying to hurt my feelings, but sometimes I want him to come along when I'm swept up in excitement.

"I love you."

"I love you, too." I sound like a pouty preschooler. I'm an expert imitator because I've been one, and I have several.

***

My interview is at 9:30 on Thursday, which means I must ask for help because I cannot take Oliver and Vivian. I'm afraid to ask for help because I think people don't like me. Overwhelmed and nervous, I write in my journal, Heavenly *Father, please help me see the way people express their love and concern. I tell myself that no one likes me and then compile distorted evidence to confirm my belief. I don't have time to waste on that nonsense right now.*

I can see the finish line in my mind's eye, the day I will hit the final submit button to finish my degree. Tessa Jensen, Bachelor of Science in Public Health Education and Promotion. With the end in mind, I know the sacrifice I must make—goodbye pride, and hello asking for help. I send out a group text to some of the ladies from church to save time. The responses don't take long to come in. Different variations of "I would love to help, but . . ." I burst into tears, embarrassed for the asking. I rest my forehead on my arm and sob.

"Mom? Mom? I hungy. Get food, peez." Oliver tugs on my sleeve, his blue eyes looking up underneath an impressive set of lashes as if he believes I can do anything.

I quickly wipe my tears with the back of my hand, wondering why I avoid letting my children see me cry.

"Okay, show me what you want." I smile as I place my finger in his outstretched hand, and as I do, Oliver notices my tear-stained face.

"Sad, Mom? Oh no." His eyebrows wrinkle in concern, and his raspy voice quivers. Oliver was born with a raspy voice that makes him sound as empathic as he is. I don't want him to worry on my account, so I swoop him up and kiss his porcelain face all over. He giggles and twists in the Chewbacca pajamas he's been wearing for a year. Admittedly they look a might uncomfortable, but he doesn't seem to think so.

He points at several snacks all at once, "Ah! That!"

I pick up the animal crackers, "You want these?"

"No! No cackers. That!"

"Cereal?"

"No! That!"

My tears threaten to pour down my face again. Apparently, trying to find a snack for a three-year-old who just ate three bags of gummy snacks is my tipping point. I've been told that I shouldn't figure out what my kids mean when they use generic grunts and words. Instead, I should help them practice saying the word they can't say. Unfortunately, I don't have the emotional capital to do that today, so I lift him to the snack shelf, "Pick up the snack that you want to eat, please pick it up."

"Got it!" Oliver triumphantly waves more bags of gummy snacks above his head.

"Good job, Oliver. I should have guessed that you wanted more gummy snacks this whole time. You love gummy snacks, huh?" When I set him down, he nods vigorously as he scuffles his feet around in a circle, swinging his arms around in celebration.

As I open one bag, Vivian comes thundering around the corner, lifting her hands in expectation. Nothing brings my kids running to me like the crinkling of a wrapper. They can be outside at the furthest corner of the yard, jumping through the sprinkler and yelling, and still hear the crinkle of my chocolate chip bag or my Trader Joe's peanut butter cup. I can count down the seconds until eight little legs gallop like a herd of elephants, dripping water all over the floor, and come upon me with red faces, eager smiles, and outstretched hands.

Speaking of wrappers, taking a turn around the soothing yet destructive cycle of a sugar binge tempts me. When I ask for help, I want to run, hide, binge, and cry. I'm embarrassed and scared. In the middle of my thought, I hear a text message alert from one of the ladies at church. "I can do it!" Those words, 'I can do it,' bring relief rushing through my veins, washing away the self-imposed shame. Finally, I have help. I want to collapse on my knees and praise God. Instead, I say a prayer of gratitude in my heart.

The Internship

Miraculously, I got the internship. To clarify, I say miraculously because of the details orchestrated on my behalf, not because I think I'm incompetent. I started in January and work for free in exchange for experience and internship credits. When the ladies of GOTR interviewed me, they told me I could bring my kids with me because they believe in a supportive work environment. I thought they were giving courteous lip service until I drove up and saw a four-year-old Harry Potter traipsing in behind his mother with a wand and a mischievous grin.

So, I bring Oliver and Vivian with me most days. Two friends offered to alternate watching the kids once a week. I didn't think they considered me a friend, but rather an obligatory service project due to church assignments to check in on me. I am grateful for whatever the motion, be it desire or obligation. I don't like to be indebted to anyone, and they won't accept payment, so I will find another way to return their kindness. When they offered me their time, I felt like an artery to my heart had been cleared of plaque, letting my circulatory system operate at optimum output.

In my own words, GOTR is a non-profit organization designed to infuse girls between 3rd and 8th grade with confidence, life skills, and what it means to be a good friend, culminating in an end-of-season 5k. Staggering numbers of supporters and contributors are required to keep the program running. The four women who run the show work relentlessly between community outreach, grant applications, managing schools, supplies, volunteer coaches, and teams.

I primarily help with collating paper and supplies in preparation for the spring season, but the real work lies in observations: what they do, how they handle predictable and unpredictable problems, and the quality of their relationships with each other. Today, a couple of board members are stopping by to talk with Tanya, the executive director. As they come in, she introduces me,

"This is Tessa, our intern. She does a great job, and we appreciate her help."

I feel like I'm twelve rather than thirty-two. "You're helping me in return. Without you guys, I don't know how I would have fulfilled my education requirements." We have a moment of appreciation, and I'm immediately uncomfortable.

"Remind us again how you found Girls on the Run?" the board member asks me.

"Oh yes, I walk my older two kids to school, and we pass this office complex. On a lovely September morning, I looked to my right and saw the Girls on the Run sign. I'm surprised I hadn't noticed it before."

"You didn't notice it because we were not here last year. 2019 will be our first season in this office, and it seems we are already rapidly outgrowing it."

"Really?" I don't know how long I stood with my mouth open as the pieces of a glorious, stained window of realization came together. When I took a break from school, I thought I had missed opportunities, thrown them away with the other collateral damage of mental illness. Yet, God was preparing miracles during the very moments I felt I was failing. If I were home, I would fall to my knees and weep tears of humble gratitude. Such a generous gift for me, more than I expected or hoped for. Who am I that Jesus Christ would arrange lives and circumstances to make my education possible?

For the next few weeks, our focused mission at GOTR revolves around program promotion at the local elementary and middle schools. The season officially starts in March, but we have a lot of prep work to do. During our most recent visit, I overheard a comment lamenting that underprivileged girls are not picking up the flyers, which means they are not signing up.

When I looked at the flyer, I instantly knew why: a lot of text and the cost of $185 in bold lettering. I learned about reaching target populations in my program planning and implementation class. Text-heavy marketing does not do well, nor do most things that show a high price tag. Girls and parents living in underprivileged circumstances will not look further at something they can't afford. Yes, underneath the cost, there is an asterisk stating that no girl will be turned away based on the ability to pay, but the information is as good as absent for how well it's camouflaged. Maybe I can help them. But, how do I help without sounding rude, like, "Hey, everything you've done isn't working, and, because I took a class, I know everything?"

I may not know everything or much at all, but I know that the heavy text and price tag must go. Risking the possibility of looking like an arrogant fool, I walk into Tanya's office. My hands are shaking, and my voice trembles. I feel like a shy elementary school girl asking the substitute teacher to use the restroom. Courage doesn't always look bold or sound confident; sometimes, courage is a woman in her thirties, shaking from the fatigue of going against her nature.

After talking with Tanya, she asked me to present the information to the board of directors, so I prepared a PowerPoint presentation, complete with the whys, hows, and practical application of reaching target populations. I was so happy and immediately started imagining a job at the completion of my degree. I could quit my job at Massage Envy and do something that makes a difference. I thought I could help further the cause of GOTR and help girls find their potential. I love running, have been running for twenty years, and GOTR uses running as a means to accomplish its mission; I couldn't think of a better fit. While writing my prayer down in my journal, I felt like I should look at a quote I wrote down a few months ago.

"As the heavens are higher than the earth, God's work in your life is bigger than the story you'd like that life to tell. His life is bigger than your plans, goals, or fears. To save your life, you'll have to lay down your stories, and minute by minute day by day, give your life back to Him." - Adam S. Miller.

I need to think about this for a minute.

***

"Hi, Eric. I don't think Girls on the Run is going to work out. I really wanted it to, but I don't think that's what God has in store for us. I lifted my hopes so high on what seemed like a sure thing. But, oh, the stories I tell myself and the infantile wisdom I apply to God's understanding. Such a waste of time. I am tempted to think that GOTR doesn't want me because I made some mistakes with the schedule and coach boxes. One of the coaches was particularly vocal about her missing name tags. But I know Tanya and the other ladies. They would not let a few errors stop them from hiring me if they thought I was a good fit. I think they want to hire me but can't. In any case, I know it's not what God wants, and the rest doesn't matter."

"I know how much you wanted it to work out, Tessa. I support whatever you want to do."

"Like I said, I don't think they could hire me if they wanted to; I'm just letting you know that I am not hanging my hopes on that dream hook anymore. I am not upset about continuing to work as a massage therapist, either. I think I need a few days to process the change in my plans, and I'll be fine.

Eric reaches his arms out and brings me to him, comforting me in his wordless way. I curl my knees to my chin and rest against his chest.

"Do you want to know what I read in the scriptures this morning?' I ask, 'I read a few verses from the Doctrine and Covenants, chapter eleven." I pull up my phone and read, ". . . wait a little longer. . .and, then, behold, according to your desires, yea, even according to your faith shall it be done unto you. Keep my commandments; hold your peace; appeal unto my Spirit. . . cleave unto me with all your heart. . .be patient until you shall accomplish it. Behold, this is your work, to keep my commandments, yea, with all your might, mind, and strength.[26]"

"I know God is on our side even though it seems like He's taking apart what I thought He had put together," I say, trying to hold my tears back.

"He is on our side, but it's still okay to be sad."

"I love you, Eric."

"I love you, too."

Now that I've accepted that Girls on the Run is not in my future, I am grateful the hours are coming to an end. My family needs them to come to an end. We are spread too thin. The last couple of months, we've gone beyond burning the candle at both ends; we've thrown the candle in the fire and become a waxy gas waiting to become tangible once more. God gave us the strength to do what was expedient or practical to Him. I repeat to myself, "GOTR was part of the journey, not the destination."

One more scripture passage comes to mind, a comfort in the final attempt to master my feelings.

"Murmur not because of the things which thou hast not seen, for they are withheld from thee and from the world, which is wisdom in me in a time to come . . . thy time shall be given to writing and learning much. And thou needest not fear, for thy husband shall support thee. . .thou shalt lay aside the things of this world and seek for the things of a better."

---

[26] Doctrine and Covenants 25:4-10

Wounds Closing

I'm happy to report that I finished my degree last month. I thought I would feel a great sense of accomplishment when it ended, but I didn't. I was definitely happy, but not elated. Maybe I should have planned a party. We did, however, go out to dinner, and the kids jumped up and down and gave me chocolate. I immediately started looking for other projects to start. Eric asked me to stop, rest, and relax. I don't know how to do that.

I went to the temple last night and, upon my return, ate a bunch of garbage food that I knew would make me sick. To mitigate the symptoms of my early morning sugar hangover, I exercised, drank a fruit smoothie, and found my bearings in the scriptures. Right now, I am studying for a General Conference talk for a lesson I am teaching on Sunday. I readily accepted the assignment to teach twice a month, but I feel exposed and stupid every time I do. However, I learn priceless gospel truths and principles in the process, so sounding like an out-of-tune foghorn seems an insignificant investment.

Perhaps I would be at ease if I didn't spend my energy assuming the ladies don't like me. Assigning my discomfort at church to an unfounded assumption seems preferable to addressing, again, the reasons I leave with a pounding headache, shortness of breath, and uncontrollable sobbing. Most Sundays, I can make it to the car without breaking down. I hate when people see me cry. Their expressions of concern embarrass me.

I want a complete desire to attend church, not half or three-quarters of a desire, so I keep going. I know Jesus Christ lives, loves me, and has provided a way for me to return to Him, which includes partaking of the Sacrament and devoting my time to His mission – "to bring to pass the immortality and eternal life of man, "(Moses 1:39). I must learn to love others when I feel unlovable and unlikeable and not assume that they have the same feelings towards me as I have towards myself. Some may think, "If Jesus loves you, why does He require your effort? You believe in Him; isn't that enough?" No. Belief is not enough, not if I want the promised blessing of all that God has. I must become like Him, and God is more than belief. He is charity, power, intelligence, wisdom, and mercy—love, compassion, determination, perseverance, forgiveness, and grace.

When I say 'all that God has,' I am not referring to jewels, money, fame, artifacts, or any other lifeless thing that we give value. I refer to joy - Christlike love, eternal families and friendships, never-ending opportunities to learn and grow, responsibilities, and duties. An Olympian cannot become an Olympian simply because they believe they can, any more than I can become a physician because I think the profession aligns with my desire to care for humanity. Belief is part of the equation of eternal life, but by itself, it's only a variable.

Knowing what I know, why would I forfeit eternal life with Jesus Christ over offenses, actual or imagined, and trust issues? I don't go to church to fulfill social needs or because I want people to think I am good. Unfortunately, church attendance is not a reliable indicator of character. My sacred relationship with my Savior does not hinge on what others do or say. Listing off identifiable accomplishments like titles of service positions or the status of mission service mean little to me. If local leadership teaches or endorses anything contrary to the doctrine found in the scriptures and the messages of God's prophet and apostles, I refuse to support them. I balk at the idea of, "Well, he's the Stake President, so what he says must come from the Spirit." That lovely, idealistic sentiment only holds water if said individual lives the gospel according to Christ, not himself. Otherwise, they base their decisions on the fallible opinions of a man. The distinction is vital. Without it, nearly irreparable consequences follow, and the repairs can take generations.

God, the unchangeable God, is who He says and always has been. Thus, I will do what He commands me to do. Still, I use my anger as protection as if it's on autopilot, and I don't know how to switch it to manual. I know I sound like a child in doing so, but I tell myself lots of stories. "If no one comes in, no one can hurt me. I'm broken, and my sharp edges hurt people. I'm awkward with too many opinions, and I roll around laughing when I hear amusing new words - like 'cattywampus.'" The first time I heard the word 'cattywampus,' I laughed for a solid thirty minutes.

I struggled in class the last time I taught because I felt misunderstood. The details are unimportant, but I walked out feeling like I never wanted to teach another Sunday lesson. I thought about handing my notes to someone else and telling them to teach since they found my approach bothersome. But, again, stories I tell myself. I'm sure the woman was only sharing her opinion, and I took it as a personal attack. The lack of sleep from the night before may have had something to do with it. The lens I use to see social interaction relies excessively on my physical state. I'll work on that, too.

Before my most recent experience, a man in our ward offered wisdom that scooped some of the hurt out of my heart and replaced it with healing truth. He spoke of Alma, a prophet in the Book of Mormon, teaching his people to remember the captivity of their fathers so that they could remember their divine deliverance, not to recall and refuel injustices. His people could have focused on the cruelty their forefathers endured, but focused on the miracles Christ performed. When I heard the word 'cruelty,' I felt like God acknowledged that my parents' choices were, at times, cruel. Yet, Jesus sees me and I. Am. Not. Crazy.

How can I hope to be Christlike when I still have animosity in my heart towards Dolly and Dad? Sometimes I want to love Dolly. I've tried to develop a relationship with Dolly. Then she sends a passive-aggressive text and claims that she's learning to stand up for herself, which sounds ridiculous because Dolly is the only person Dolly has ever stood up for. See? I have lots of repenting to do. Upon reading the text, I feel like a little girl again, in trouble, unlovable, and in charge of making her happy. But I cannot give her happiness. However, if I could just change my reaction, I would be fine. If only I could reprogram my limbic system, perhaps I could gain a firmer hold on my emotional behaviors.

Then what? I adjust my emotions to give her what she wants? I say, "It's okay, don't worry about me. I'll pretend like everything is fine and forget whatever I think happened." And that's been the strategy all along: get me to question my competence; if I deem myself incompetent and her competent, I will ignore my feelings every time. I'll berate myself for being too sensitive and apologize for thinking I was hurt.

Hold on, revelatory moment, gaslighting is not just her preferred form of emotional abuse. That's Satan's strategy: convince Tessa, from birth, to doubt herself, and she will hand over the labeling of her emotions to someone else. She will hand over her worth, her ambitions, and her opinions. She'll let people who claim to love her repeatedly harm her in the name of forgiveness, and she will become destructible. Convince her that love means keeping the waters from rippling when someone else does a cannonball. Find people to accuse her of selfishness, call into question her compassion and values, until she's so scared of being seen as capable of causing the same harm she experienced that she forfeits everything - her dreams, her identity, and her God.

I don't know if Dolly can cognitively identify her behavior because evidence suggests that emotional manipulation is a multi-generational trend, so cleverly embedded that it's practically DNA. It's a way to win arguments (if one defines winning by silencing the other party), to control, and absolve oneself from the pricks of conscience. Control can be overt - loud, physical, easily observed - it can also be covert - silent treatments, facial expressions, withholding affections.

The second is significantly less noticeable and easily denied. No wonder the devil laughs when we deny his existence.

Adherence to his half-truths and no-big-deals lays families to waste and people to an existence less than human. So, we frantically search for a numbing agent, unable to love, perpetually entertained, searching for worth at the bottom of a tube of lipstick or the applause of unknown and unnamed people. Social media has turned us into one big social experiment, using praise as the placebo that never has, and will never, have the power to heal our pain. But let's lay that topic down for another time.

Right now, I feel like the Count of Monte Cristo when he finally puts the pieces of his betrayal together, except my prison is not made of stone, and I am far from starving to death. The enemy was never my dad, Dolly, or Sarah. They are, and were, fighting their own private battles. They were not trying to destroy me or hate me. I have to believe that they all, for a small period of time, had the best of intentions. Especially Dolly. Otherwise, why did she marry Dad when she was not attracted to him and when she could have kept living comfortably with her parents?

The Sun Shines

I don't want to hang onto anger anymore, not even a sliver. I've said and written the word so many times as if it's an unconquerable vice. Instead, I want to be full of joy and love for others and develop fulfilling relationships. However painful the path to complete forgiveness, I'm reasonably confident that I don't yet understand what that path entails. Christ leads the way. The trail looks suspiciously like a dark and murky forest full of thorns and poisonous serpents, but I need not worry. I'm with an expert guide who has traveled this same road before.

God does not expect me to forgive in an instant. I've made vain attempts to cover the symptoms without addressing the cause. Acknowledging the reason and managing it are as far apart as observing noxious weeds and pulling them. Indeed, I can give myself some grace because the desire to be like Christ burns within me. I am not all bad.

A brief scene danced across my eyes last night as I said my prayers. I tentatively took a step. I could not see through the thick fog and chill that surrounded me. The air smelled clean, like fall rain washing away the summer smog. As soon as I put my foot down, a step appeared, bright as polished gold and solid as stone. I cautiously took a few more steps with the same result. When I looked over my shoulder, I realized that every step was luminous and immovable, and the longer I hesitated, the flatter the incline became. No cracks, no deviations. When I turned around, faith replaced fear, and I began to run as fast as I had strength. The gradient nearly became as steep as a ninety-degree angle. Lesson learned? Faith is not clear knowledge. Faith requires action.

Perhaps my next step of faith requires developing friendships with women in my ward. Some of the ladies hold a monthly book club. One woman invited me several years ago when we moved into our home, but the timing wasn't right due to a perpetual lack of sleep. Now that my youngest is a toddler and I have earned my college degree, I don't have a reason not to go, other than a natural aversion to such social gatherings.

My last book club experience in a different ward went terribly. I sat silent, wishing I could run out the door without drawing attention to myself. I tried talking to the host, but she was not interested. I had tried talking to this particular woman before with the same results. So, I felt silly and stupid. Many of the women there were good friends. Not the kind of friends who have known each other for fifteen years, who have an abundance of inside jokes, but friends who had recently met and gave each other smirks when someone was different. I almost cried, and my friend, who had convinced me to go, who had never seen me in such a social situation, wondered where I'd gone and who had taken over my body.

I arrive at the host's house on time, which is not a time most people prefer. Before knocking, I consider running back to my car and driving home. Then, with anxiety-ridden reluctance, I knock. The host opens the door, and I quickly ascertain that I'm the first to arrive.

"Oh, hey, come in. We have book club down here."

We take the stairs down to her basement. Split-level homes have an endearing quality because the aesthetic reminds me of my grandparents. Thankfully, this home smells of apple crisp baking in the oven and not musk and mildew. Not that my grandparents' house smells of musk and mildew, just old homes. Anyway.

"Did you read the book?" the host asks.

"I did not, but I thought I would come anyway. What book are we discussing tonight?"

"Educated, by Tara Westover. She was raised a member of our church, attended BYU, and her parents were crazy. It might be hard for you to read because of trauma in your life."

I wince, regretting that I share my experiences so openly. As a result, people know more about my life than they do about me. I want to change that.

"I like reading books about the trauma others experience. I mean, that came out wrong. When I read sad stories, I know that I am not alone. Sorry. I say dumb things when I mean to say something else."

She laughs, "I do the same thing."

"Umm, I decided to come to book club because I feel uncomfortable around people at church. I feel more welcome at work than at church. Of course, I want to feel welcome at work, but I want to feel welcome at church, too. Not that you asked. Sorry. Excuse my nervous verbal vomit." My cheeks feel hot, and I wish I could shove all my words back in my mouth.

Before she can respond, someone opens the door, "I'm here!"

One after another, ladies come in at five to ten-minute intervals. To keep myself from running out, my phone becomes the most fascinating thing I've ever seen, and I pretend like I'm expecting a message. *Stay for 45 minutes, Tessa. Just stay.*

An animated conversation begins. Plenty of "Can you imagine? How could they? She's amazing," go around. Some of the events they relate sound horrid; others sound familiar, normal. Here's the thing about average: it's all relative. My dogs getting shot in the head was unsurprising behavior. Dolly refusing to give me a ride to school when I didn't have a coat and the rain was pouring down was expected. My father performed crude surgery on Bruno's toenail, also normal.
I did not process how abnormal my life was until I shared memories and experiences and saw people's reactions. I knew people had parents who loved them and treated them kindly, but they were the exception to me. Otherwise, I operated under the assumption that other kids' parents only seemed nice, like mine. Once, when the time came for a

new bishop, I was told by several people that the next person would be my dad. See what I mean? No one has any idea what goes on behind closed doors.

Be quiet, Tessa. No one needs to know your business or your opinions. Just listen. Someone's talking. They sound like me. Am I talking? Yes, yes, I am. I am talking without reservation, oversharing.

"We had to kneel, lift our hands over our heads, and bend over to make sure our clothes were modest in front of my dad. We weren't allowed to eat snacks without asking. Otherwise, we got accused of "stealing from the family." CPS got involved and did nothing because my parental units tried to rewrite history for self-preservation purposes. My brain broke when I was thirteen and again at sixteen, and I've been binge-eating ever since to cope. What's your favorite kind of chocolate?"

The ladies listen, then I talk some more. I can't stop myself from talking. Thoughts and memories come pouring out. I hate that I came.

By the time I leave, it's after midnight. Eric called three times to check on me. I should read Tara's book while I work on writing my book.

When morning comes, I have an overshare hangover. I shouldn't have said anything. I made book club about me, and now I am more hesitant to go to church than before. Why must I insist on embarrassing myself like it's a hobby? Do I hold myself to a higher standard than God does? Am I unforgiving? Am I not feeling what I should feel? Am I supposed to have familial love for my parents before claiming forgiveness? Because I do not. Anger no longer consumes me when I talk about them, but it's still there. May God forgive me. I will try to be more like Jesus Christ.

I stare at cracks in the wall on mornings when my brain has been overloaded with an emotional dump. I don't know much; I don't know how or when the healing process for early trauma will be complete. But, I do know that I am in the process of deliverance. Christ has compensated for every hurt and injustice. The incessant recounting of my past means God blessed me with discerning eyes - I could tell that something was wrong, even if it seemed normal. Imagine if I thought my home was typical and perpetuated the cycle.

"Mama!" Fiona is awake and ready to get fancy. She started first grade a couple of weeks ago and has lost none of her enthusiasm from last year.

"Hi, Fiona. Are you excited for school today?"

"Yes. Do you like my outfit?" She cocks her head to the side, sticks out her arms, and slowly turns around so I can adequately admire her pony leggings, rainbow tutu, and cat shirt. She's clipped five big bows in her hair again and stuck her ponytail on the side of her head.

"You look lovely, and you're lovely. What do you think you'll do at school today?

"Talk, read, eat, maybe do a craft and talk and talk and chat."

"Sounds like you're going to have a great day."

"I will, but I will miss you and Vivian."

While Fiona talks, Oliver comes in and stands behind her. His eyebrows wrinkle into a grumpy expression, "You won't miss me?"

"Oh, Oliver. Of course, I will miss you; I was just talking about the girls," she hugs Oliver. Fiona's becoming an expert at smoothing things over. Oliver requires lots of hugs, kisses, and praise.

I try to help. "You get to be with Vivian and me, Oliver. We can make cookies and watch a show. Does that sound fun?" He sticks out his tongue as his eyes smile.

"But I want to make cookies and watch a movie." Fiona begins her protest, talking loud enough for Bruce to hear her.
"I want to make cookies and watch a movie, too. That's not fair."
Bruce heard Fiona.

"You two get to go to school and do all sorts of fun things, like recess, crafts, and talking with your friends," I say.

"I don't like talking to my friends. I only talk dinosaur," Bruce says.

"True, true. And you get to run around on recess pretending to be a dinosaur with your friends." Bruce's teacher told me that Bruce leads a pack of five or six little boys pretending to be velociraptors around the playground, each with their arms in the proper dinosaur position while making screeching dinosaur noises.

"I still want to make cookies and watch a movie," says Bruce.

"Me, too!" adds Fiona.

"We will on another day, but today I am baking and watching a movie with Oliver and Vivian while you're at school."

Bruce and Fiona slump their shoulders forward and drag their feet to the bathroom to brush their teeth.

They've forgotten about the movie and cookies by the time we get to school. Every morning, we walk to school, they work on memorizing the Articles of Faith, while I work on committing The Living Christ to memory. I want to fill their minds with the words of God before it's filled with something else. Some call it indoctrination. I call it spiritual fortification. I know that nothing good comes from a dance in the darkness. There's no enlightenment, only the realization that no one should have gone there in the first place.

When we get home, I see a text alert on my phone from the woman who hosted the book club last night. "Thank you for coming last night, for talking with us, and for being you." Tears spring to my eyes, and I silently thank God for her kindness.

Liberation

I woke up to a letter from Eric on my pillow;

Hi Tessa,
I love you so much! You are so beautiful and wonderful. I'm
so lucky to have you in my life. You are so smart and are doing
amazing in your pursuits and writing. I don't think I could ever
do what you are doing. You are also a wonderful mom. Our
kids are lucky that they have you. I hope you don't get
discouraged as you continue to do all that you do. I'm sorry
that I don't tell you how much I love you and how beautiful
you are. I will try to do better because you are my life and
mean more than anything to me. I hope you never doubt that, I
know that I am not so easy because I'm quiet and am a weird
sports nerd. I just want you to be happy. You are the best. I'm a
very lucky man. - Your husband forever, Eric.

Eric also bought me flowers and my favorite box of chocolates
from See's Candy - the nuts and chews variety. We don't do too much
in celebration other than spending time together, which I think is the
point. I often feel sorry for Eric because he deals with me - my moods,
though they don't swing as wide as before, are still difficult to live
with from day to day. Occasionally, I see him tiptoeing around like
he's walking on my eggshells, and I want to punish myself for creating
such an atmosphere in our household. Eric embodies the notion a man
recently repeated at church, "frequent love notes do more to facilitate
good behavior than harsh corrections." Not that he treats me like a
precocious child, though I do act like one sometimes.

Eric wants me to be happy and, sadly, puts the responsibility for my happiness on his shoulders. He, therefore, feels like a failure when I inevitably have an emotional come apart. When I take complete leave of my senses, it's terrible. I'm, well, I'm mean. Even though I apologize minutes later, the words escape like knives and cut his heart, the heart that I hold in my hands. I hate and disgust myself on those days.

Mental limitations. I don't like to think of myself as having mental limitations. Doesn't that sound awful, like I'm inept and stupid? But if people have bodily limitations, like blindness, they are physically incapable of seeing. Or, more accurately, I imagine they learn to see differently and have an expanded understanding of what it means to see. Maybe my mental limitations have expanded my knowledge of what it means to feel.

How can I see my struggle with bipolar disorder as a power and not an eternal handicap? I wonder if Jesus will heal my brain as soon as I am resurrected, or if there are more lessons I need to learn that can be learned in no other way? Perhaps with each mastered lesson, my brain heals relative to the intensity of the coursework.

I'm not mad about the illness anymore, but I'm still embarrassed. Can everyone see the brokenness? Are people my friends because they feel sorry for me? I bet they are. "Poor Tessa can't keep it together. Let's be her friend so she doesn't hurt herself."

Oh, Tessa, shut up. Don't do this to yourself. Stop right now. Eric's coming back from letting the dog out.

"Good morning, Tessa. Happy Anniversary. I love you."

"Hi, Eric. Did you have a good sleep?" Inquiring about the quality of my family's sleep is a preoccupation since I relate low emotional function to poor sleep. For me, lousy sleep = a lousy day.

"I slept alright. What do you want to do today?"

Waking up is a long, slow-motion process. Eric rubs my back and waits for me to remember my love of productivity to propel me out of bed. That, or one of the kids, usually Fiona or Vivian, sometimes both, runs in and jumps on me.

"Just be with you," I say as I snuggle deeper in my warm covers.

I can hear little feet thundering towards our door, "Mama Mia! It's time to wake up!" Fiona loves calling me Mama Mia. I used to think that Mom was the only acceptable maternal title for me. But I changed my mind while I listened to the sweet voices of my children. Now, I like whatever they call me. After the girls come the boys, and soon we are cuddling on the bed like a litter of kittens.

Eric, who does not enjoy cuddling as I do, tolerates the display of affection for a few minutes, "Alright, I'm done. There are too many people on this bed."

The precious moment leaves as quickly as it came. I wish I had a butterfly net to capture it and put it in a snow globe to keep it forever.

"Eric,' I call out as I hear him get out the waffle iron, 'I want to go to the temple tonight. Does that sound good? I can find a babysitter."

"Yes. Whatever you want to do sounds good to me."

After returning from the temple, I write in my journal a question that keeps coming to mind, *"What does it mean to be a righteous, noble, and brave mother? The righteous element seems self-evident, but what is noble and brave in the sight of the Lord? All I can think of is the word 'certain.' Synonyms for the word 'certain,' include, as connected to faithful, convinced, positive, confident, firm, definite, assured, dependable. Motherhood.*

What happens when mothers are closer to the antonyms of certain - confused, negative, fearful, weak, doubtful, undecided, and untrustworthy? I've lived that answer. Can you think of anything easier to manipulate and control than someone confused, pessimistic, fearful, and weak? That's exactly what I was."

When I look up from my writing, I see my family's picture on the wall. Vivian is wearing two different shoes, and Oliver holds a tiny leaf that he found that day. I laugh with joy and knock over the cup of water sitting in front of me. I swiftly moved my journal because my journals are the one tangible thing that I would mourn if they got ruined. The books and pages are filled with my prayers to Heavenly Father in the name of Jesus Christ. They are the proof that as soon as I turned to Him, He answered. My parents' poor decisions could not stop Him, my mental illness could not stay His hand. Not even my poor choices and sins could diminish His relentless and unwavering love for me.

Jesus Christ was never silent; He was teaching me to speak, "Lift up thy voice, O daughter . . . cause it to be heard.[27]"

---

[27] 2 Nephi 20:30

Acknowledgements

Though an incomplete list, the earthly angels who made the completion of my book possible are;

My husband, Eric. He encouraged me, held me, and gave his quiet, immovable, unfailing support.

My precious children, Bruce, Fiona, Oliver, and Vivian, who encouraged me with their sweet words and said, "I know you can do it, Mom."

Natalie Jackson, who repeatedly told me to write my book over the last nine years in her aggressively helpful way. Love ya, girlfriend.

Alison Pope, who listened to me for two years, over endless hours and countless miles, talking about my goal and celebrating every step. Oh, bless us.

Lainey Nielson, who edited my first draft with professional grace and an analytic eye. Without her, the book would have been much less than what it has become.

Carly Bagley, who proofread my book and saved me significant professional embarrassment. She discovered that I once wrote 'your' instead of 'you're,' and 'stocking' instead of 'stalking.'

Monica Puffpaff, who let me use her sound equipment to record my audiobook, and left Marco Polos regularly telling me that my book was worth writing.

Elliott Lauritzen, who told me to flex my literary muscles and get over trying to please people because, "It's your book and who cares what anyone else thinks. If they don't like it, they can go pound sand."

Follow me on Instagram
@tessasjensen

Did you enjoy my memoir?

If so, I would be honored to write yours.

As a ghostwriter, I'll help bring your story to life in your voice so that you can share it with the world. Your life matters, and your influence reaches far more people than you realize.

When we take time to understand each other's experiences and perspectives, we grow in compassion. And compassion leads to improved relationships, which leads to unity. Sharing our stories has the power to make the world a kinder, better place.

Visit my website at tessa-jensen.com to learn more!

www.ingramcontent.com/pod-product-compliance
Lightning Source LLC
Chambersburg PA
CBHW071141130626
46553CB00004B/1473